ON THE MYSTERIES
OF THE WORD

MICHAEL SERVETUS
ON THE MYSTERIES OF THE WORD

AN ANNOTATED TRANSLATION OF
The Restoration of Christianity
BOOKS 3 AND 4 ON THE DIVINE TRINITY

translated by
Peter Zerner and Peter Hughes

edited with an introduction by
Peter Hughes and Lynn Gordon Hughes

Blackstone Editions

Blackstone Editions
Toronto, Ontario, Canada
www.BlackstoneEditions.com

© 2024 by Lynn Gordon Hughes
All rights reserved
Published 2024

978-1-7386994-0-7

Front cover image: *St. Michael and the Dragon*
Walters Art Museum, Baltimore, MD
Creative Commons W.26.131R

In Memoriam
Peter Hughes

Arbores serit diligens agricola,
quarum aspiciet baccam ipse nunquam

Books in This Series

Volume 1: *On the Trinity and the Bible*
    The Restoration of Christianity:
      On the Divine Trinity, books 1 and 2
      Translated by Peter Zerner and Peter Hughes

Volume 2: *On the Mysteries of the Word*
    The Restoration of Christianity:
      On the Divine Trinity, books 3 and 4
      Translated by Peter Zerner and Peter Hughes

Volume 3: *On the Holy Spirit*
    The Restoration of Christianity:
      On the Divine Trinity, book 5
      Translated by Peter Zerner, Peter Hughes, and
      Lynn Gordon Hughes

Contents

Preface *by Lynn Gordon Hughes*	ix
Key to Annotations, Symbols, and Abbreviations	xiii
A Note on the Text	xx
Introduction	1
The Restoration of Christianity	
On the Divine Trinity, book 3	29
On the Divine Trinity, book 4	75
Appendixes	133
The Paris Manuscript, book 3	139
The Paris Manuscript, book 4	169
Annotations	207
Bibliography	248
Index of Biblical References	261
Index of Authorities Cited	270

Preface
by Lynn Gordon Hughes

This is the preface I never wanted to write — the one in which I must announce the death of my husband, Peter Hughes, and introduce myself as the newest member of the translation team.

Peter Hughes and Peter Zerner started translating Servetus's *Christianismi restitutio* (*The Restoration of Christianity*) in 2005. Their goal was to produce an annotated translation of the first part of *Restoration*: the five books and two dialogues on the Trinity. They worked on it together until Peter Zerner's sudden death in 2019.

At that time the project consisted of draft translations, in various states of completion, of books 1 through 5 and dialogue 1. Nothing had as yet been done to turn the translations into published books. But after the loss of his co-translator and friend, Peter Hughes turned his attention to the work of preserving Peter Zerner's legacy. He began editing the translation and writing annotations. He composed a "Translator's Preface" introducing the project and explaining the team's approach to translation, and he wrote an introduction for volume 1.

The work proceeded at a leisurely pace, however, for Peter could not resist the temptation to start other Servetus-related projects at the same time. An article on the portrait of Servetus. An article, co-written with a colleague in Spain, on Servetus's role as a medical

Preface

pioneer. Most ambitious of all, he proposed to write an intellectual biography, to be called something like *A Life of Servetus in 10 Books* (the number of books was still to be determined).

As Peter's spouse, I have been an interested bystander, cheerleader, and informal editor throughout the project, but Peter and I planned that I would take on a more active role after I retired from my day job. In preparation for this, I started studying Latin in 2020. I retired in July 2022 and immediately started preparing volume 1 for publication.

Peter and I looked forward to a long and fruitful collaboration, but this was not to be. He was diagnosed with cancer less than four months after I retired. The completion of volume 1 was delayed by his illness and treatment, but it was finally published in the spring of 2023.

Despite his illness, Peter hoped and believed that he would be able to see volumes 2 and 3 through to completion. In the year following his diagnosis, he did manage to complete volume 2, except for the introduction, and he started work on volume 3. He also wrote the article on the portrait of Servetus, completing it from his hospital bed while recovering from surgery.[†] Toward the end of 2023, however, his health began to decline rapidly, and he died in April 2024. The biography, alas, will never be written. But the article on Servetus as a medical pioneer may yet see the light of day—it is currently being adapted as an appendix for volume 3.

Before Peter died, I promised him that I would—*Deo volente*—bring the translation project to a graceful conclusion by completing and publishing the remainder of the five books on the Trinity, though perhaps not the dialogues. This volume, containing books 3 and 4, is a partial fulfillment of that promise.

At the time of Peter's death, the only substantial work left to do on volume 2 was to complete the introduction. This I have done to the best of my ability, based on a draft that Peter left behind, other published and unpublished writings of his, and many long discus-

---

[†] Peter Hughes, "Portrait of Servetus," *Journal of Unitarian Universalist Studies* 46 (2023), 1-17.

sions about what he wanted to include. I am sure that it would have been much longer if Peter had finished it—his introductions tended to run to 50 pages or more — but I hope that nothing essential has been omitted.

A surprisingly difficult task was to select a title for this book. For a long time the working title was *On the Mystery of the Word*. This is a good title for book 3, but what about book 4? Peter and I discussed various possibilities but never settled on one. In the end I decided to go back to our original idea, but with one important change: *On the Mysteries of the Word*, plural. For book 4, it turns out, is filled with mysteries of the Word. In book 4 we read that the Word contains life, light, and the forms of all things; it is the archetypal world, the archetypal light, God's wisdom, the primal element, and the primal seed. It is, in short, a deeply mysterious entity.

I am honoured to have been entrusted with this mystery. I dedicate this book to the memory of Peter Zerner and Peter Hughes, who brought to this project all of their resources of creativity, dedication, curiosity, courage, and love.

Acknowledgements

This book has benefited from the resources of the University of Toronto libraries and the support of the Centre for Renaissance and Reformation Studies at the University of Toronto, where Peter held a fellowship. Parts of the introduction were adapted from articles previously published in the *Journal of Unitarian Universalist History*. Our friend Paul Howard did the text matching to identify the parallel passages in *On the Errors of the Trinity*, and kept up Peter's spirits with weekly video chats.

During the eighteen months of Peter's illness, we were sustained by an incredible support team, which allowed Peter to continue doing the work he loved, almost to the end of his life. Our family and friends were always there for us, even when they had to travel to Toronto from New York, Massachusetts, Rhode Island, Illinois, and British Columbia. We owe a special debt of gratitude to Peter's wonderful Personal Support Worker, Hena Salam, and his palliative care physician, Dr. Breffni Hannon.

Key to Annotations, Symbols, and Abbreviations

Bible Books, Chapters, and Verses

In referring to the books of the Bible we have adopted the names commonly used in English Protestant Bibles. In particular, the four books called 1-4 Kings in the Vulgate we call 1-2 Samuel and 1-2 Kings.

For the convenience of modern readers who would like to track down Servetus's biblical citations and allusions, we have provided verse numbers, to the extent that they can be ascertained. Since Servetus wrote before versification had become established, he did not have the same sense of pinpoint location that later writers would develop. Some of his references are to a whole chapter, or to several verses scattered throughout. In quotations he occasionally stitched together several disjoint phrases from different verses in a particular chapter, adding connecting words of his own.

Sometimes chapters within books of the Bible are divided in different places in various versions of the Bible. In particular, there are two ways of numbering the Psalms: Roman Catholic Bibles use the Septuagint numbering, while Protestant Bibles follow the Masoretic Hebrew numbering. In most cases the Protestant psalm numbers can be obtained by adding one to the number that

Key to Annotations, Symbols, and Abbreviations

Servetus cited. In the translation, we have retained the numbers that Servetus used, but in our footnotes we refer the reader to the English Protestant chapters and verses.

> shape, likeness, and image of Jesus Christ that Moses saw. This is borne out by David's use of this word in Psalm 16, which is Psalm 17 in the Hebrew numbering: *I shall see your face, and I shall be satisfied when your image appears.*[a] Balaam saw this image from afar (Numbers 24). *I shall see him*, he says, *but I shall not look at him now, nor from*
>
> ---
>
> [a] Ps 17:15. [b] Num 24:17. [c] Ps 80:1 (Ps 79:3 in Vulgate). [d] Ps 80:3, 7, 19. [e] Ps 4:6, 44:3. [f] Ps 89:15. [g] Isa 6:1-2. [h] Ezek 1 and 10 (entire chapter); Dan 10:4-20; Ex 24:9-11. See especially Ezek 1:4; 10:4; Dan 10:6. [i] Rev 1:12-20; 4:1-8.

Servetus cited Psalm 16 (Vulgate numbering), but the footnote is to Psalm 17. (Here Servetus himself mentioned that that Psalm 16 is called Psalm 17 "in the Hebrew numbering," but he did not do this consistently.)

Abbreviations

The following abbreviations are used when referring to frequently-cited works and collections of works.

Calvini opera	*Ioannis Calvini opera quae supersunt omnia* (vol. 29-87 of *Corpus Reformatorum*, 1863-1900)
Errors	Servetus, *De Trinitatis erroribus*
Institutes	Calvin, *Institutio Christianae religionis*
PG	*Patrologia Graeca*, ed. J.-P. Migne (1857-1866)
PL	*Patrologia Latina*, ed. J.-P. Migne (1841-1855)
Restoration	Servetus, *Christianismi restitutio*
TDOT	*Theological Dictionary of the Old Testament* (Grand Rapids, MI: Eerdmans, 1974-2021)

Key to Annotations, Symbols, and Abbreviations

Typographical Conventions and Punctuation

The following conventions are used in all translated text.

Page Numbers

Page numbers in the translated text show the location of page breaks in the original sixteenth-century publication. Page numbers are printed in boldface and enclosed in square brackets, e.g. **[10]**.

Note that **all** references to page numbers in *Restoration* (in annotations, cross references, index, etc.) use these standard page numbers.

Headings and Other Text Supplied by the Editors

Square brackets are used to identify text added to the translation to improve clarity. This includes section headings and subheadings that have been added in order to bring out the structure of the text.

> [*Patterns and Reflections in the Light of God*]
>
> The way to think about a pattern in God can be demonstrated by thinking about [patterns in] other things. For if God made a microcosm [for example, a human being]

In this passage, square brackets designate a subheading and some additional text added by the editors.

Headings Supplied by the Author

In a few places, the original printing included marginal notes that indicate divisions of the text. In such cases we have formatted them as headings or subheadings, enclosed in curly brackets.

> {*Elohim*}
>
> [*What Exists from Eternity*]
>
> In order to be able to give a more reliable account of the name Elohim, we must look into what has appeared [in

This passage has a heading supplied by Servetus (curly brackets) and a subheading added by the editors (square brackets).

Key to Annotations, Symbols, and Abbreviations

Quotations

Quotations from the Bible are printed in italics. Quotation marks are used for non-biblical quotations.

> the teachings of the Torah, Philo proves the existence of ideal forms, explaining the words of Moses, *Blot me out of your book.*[e] Here Philo says, "Moses calls the word of God a book, in which the existences of all things are written down and engraved."[f] Psalm 138 (in the Hebrew Bible, Psalm 139) renders this beautifully. The prophet David

In this passage, the quotation from the Bible is shown in italics. The quotation from Philo is in quotation marks.

Cross References

Marginal notes are used to cross-reference passages from *Restoration* to parallel passages in *Errors*.

> but not his face (Exodus 33).[d] To see him from behind is like seeing him with his face covered. Terror overwhelmed them when they turned their eyes to this face, and they *feared* that they *were going to die* (Exodus 3 and 20 and Judges 13).[e] Because of Adam's sin the face of God was hidden, and before it stood *a flaming sword* (Genesis 3).[f]

Err, 88v

This passage is related to one on page 88v in Errors.

Annotations and Footnotes

Annotations are explanatory notes, varying in length from a few sentences to multi-paragraph mini-essays. They are located at the end of the volume, after the appendix. Annotations are numbered sequentially within each book. They are identified by superscript numbers in the translated text.

Footnotes are found in translated text and also in editorial content, such as the introduction and annotations. In translated text, footnotes are identified by superscript letters, starting over with "a" on every page. In editorial content, footnotes are

Key to Annotations, Symbols, and Abbreviations

numbered sequentially within each document and identified by superscript numbers.

> and that all things are contained and held together in the One.⁽¹⁸⁾ Only the One is beautiful and good in itself. Other things are not called beautiful and good, except by participation in the One.ᵃ And they are more beautiful the closer they come to it. The One is **[131]** the sole ψύχωσιν

In translated text, superscript numbers indicate annotations and letters indicate footnotes.

When annotations are referenced (in other annotations or in footnotes) they are identified as follows:

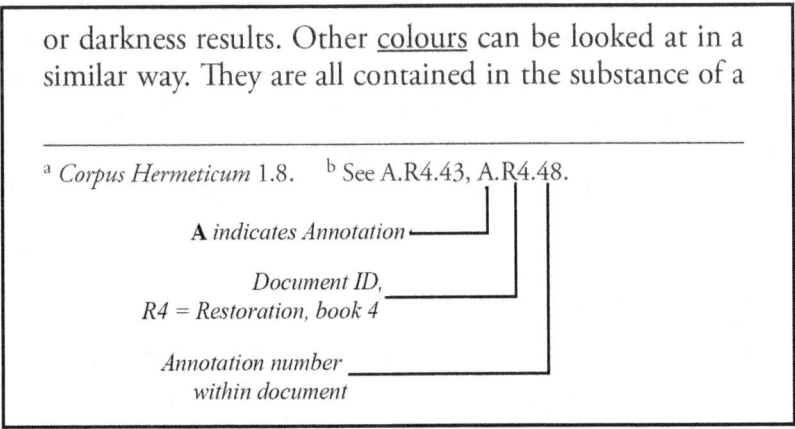

In this example, A.R4.48 indicates annotation 48 for Restoration book 4.

Identification of Works Cited

Works cited in footnotes may be identified in several different ways.

1. The most frequently cited sources are identified by abbreviations, e.g. *Errors* or *Restoration*. See the list of abbreviations above.

2. Works that are listed in the bibliography are identified by author and title, sometimes in shortened forms. Full publication details are found in the bibliography.

3. For works not in the bibliography, full publication details are supplied in the footnote.

Key to Annotations, Symbols, and Abbreviations

Titles of works written in Latin (or in other languages using the Latin alphabet) are given in the original language in the footnotes, even though they are referred to in the main text by their English translations. For works written in languages using other character sets, such as Greek and Hebrew, English titles are used in footnotes.

The use of square brackets around the name of an author indicates that the work is no longer believed to have been written by the supposed author. Context should be sufficient to distinguish between the use of square brackets to indicate pseudepigrapha vs. the use of square brackets to indicate text supplied by the editors.

Use of Page Numbers and Section Numbers

Most of the primary sources cited in this book use some type of section numbers, so that they can be identified without having to specify a particular edition. Where this is not possible, page numbers are used; the edition is specified in the Bibliography. For works that are in the standard collections *Patrologia Latina* (PL) or *Patrologia Graeca* (PG), the location information is included in the footnote.

The Paris Manuscript

There is a manuscript, located in the Bibliothèque Nationale in Paris, which contains a draft of part of the "On the Trinity" section of *The Restoration of Christianity*. The manuscript has been transcribed and translated by Peter Hughes. The translation of books 3 and 4 from the manuscript is included in this volume as an appendix. The Paris manuscript is described in more detail in the introduction to the appendix.

Most of the typographical conventions used elsewhere are also applicable to the appendix. However, in the appendix, two sets of page numbers are shown. Page numbers in the manuscript are printed in boldface and enclosed in triangular brackets, e.g. **<10>**. To aid in matching the manuscript text with the corresponding text in the printed version, page numbers from the printed edition are also shown. Where the text of the manuscript is different

Key to Annotations, Symbols, and Abbreviations

from the final version, the variant text is underlined in both the appendix and the main text.

Although most of the footnotes and annotations found in the main text are also applicable to the manuscript, they are not repeated in the appendix. Any footnotes in the appendix point to references or features that are specific to the manuscript.

> **(A)** [122] We shall say more later about spirit and light. For now it will suffice to say that the true substance in the Word was <u>the visible hypostasis that brought to life that ideal form, the human being [Christ], as the next book will explain.</u>[a] <u>In the Word was the ideal form of the human Christ, and also the substantial seed of his begetting.</u>[b] This man could not have been said to be *truly the Son of God*,[c]

> **(B)** [122] We shall say more later about spirit and light. For now, let it suffice to say that the true substance in the Word was <u>made visible and tangible in Mary: just as a thick cloud can be touched, especially when **<141>** it condenses into water. Later you will easily understand that these are modes of the substance of God. For now, understand that the action of the seed and the begetting drove [the process] by which the body was begotten by God — truly and naturally begotten.</u> This man could not have been said to be *truly the Son of God*, if God

This is the same passage, as it appears in the printed version of Restoration (A) and in the Paris manuscript (B).

- *The variant text is underlined in both places.*
- *(A) shows the page number from the printed version* **[122]**. *(B) shows both the page number from the printed version* **[122]** *and the page number from the manuscript* **<141>**.
- *Note that footnote superscripts a, b, and c are shown in (A) but not in (B), although footnote c (at least) is relevant to the manuscript.*

A Note on the Text

The Restoration of Christianity

Only three copies of the original printing of *Christianismi restitutio* are known to remain in existence. They reside at the Bibliothèque Nationale in Paris, the Österreichische Nationalbibliothek in Vienna, and the University of Edinburgh. In 1790 a transcription based on the Vienna copy, made to match the original pagination, was published in Nuremberg by Christoph Gottlieb von Murr. This was reprinted by Minerva of Frankfurt in 1966.

Until recently most scholars who have consulted *Restoration* have used the Murr transcription, which contains a number of copying mistakes, a few of which are significant. Fortunately, the Paris copy is available online on BnF Gallica, the web site of the Bibliothèque Nationale. The first 576 pages of the Vienna copy are reprinted in *Miguel Servet: Obras Completas*, vols. 5 and 6 (ed. Ángel Alcalá). As these two copies of *Restoration* are defaced or damaged in different ways, it is helpful to be able to inspect both.

The Paris Manuscript

The Paris manuscript is also available online on BnF Gallica, as Latin manuscript 18212.

Introduction

This is the second volume of the annotated translation of Michael Servetus's major work, *The Restoration of Christianity*. Volume 1 contained books 1 and 2; this volume consists of books 3 and 4. All of these books form part of the first section of *Restoration*, "Five Books on the Trinity."

In volume 1, we saw Servetus in his analytical mode: deconstructing what he believed to be a false and pernicious version of Christianity. In particular, he took issue with the doctrine of the Trinity, as it was understood by both the Catholic church and the new Protestant movements. In book 1, drawing heavily on his earlier work, *On the Errors of the Trinity* (1531), he laid out his arguments against the accepted doctrine of the Trinity. In book 2 he analyzed twenty specific passages from the Bible, introducing the reader to his theory and practice of biblical criticism. These two books clear the way for what is to come. Beginning with book 3, Servetus turns from analysis to synthesis. In the remaining three books of "On the Trinity," he will begin to reveal his vision of a new and improved version of the Christian faith.

Introduction

Overview of Books 3 and 4: The Hedgehog and the Fox

"A fox knows many things, but a hedgehog knows one big thing," runs the ancient proverb.[1] Among the five books on the Trinity in *The Restoration of Christianity*, book 3 is the hedgehog: an extended, and at times lyrical, meditation on a single big idea. Book 4, which ranges restlessly over a wide variety of topics, is the fox.

Book 3 is the placed at the centre of the five books on the Trinity, and it contains Servetus's central message: *Christ is the face of God; to see Christ is to see God, and to see God is to see Christ*. Much of this book is a development of ideas that Servetus had been working out for many years. There are numerous parallels, especially in the early part of the book, with books 4 and 6 of *On the Errors of the Trinity*.

No such simple summary can do justice to book 4. Because book 4 contains so many different ideas, and such intricate interconnections between ideas, the editors of this volume have found it necessary to provide three different levels of headings and subheadings to guide the reader through the text — thirty headings in all. (Book 3, in contrast, has no subdivisions at all.) Whereas each of the other four books on the Trinity has a clearly defined central topic — the Trinity, the Bible, the Word, the Holy Spirit — book 4 defies simple categorization.

To understand what unites the various topics covered by book 4, it is necessary to look back at book 3. In book 3, Servetus argued that God can be known through Christ and only through Christ. But this cannot be the whole story, because there were and are wisdom traditions that do not involve Christ at all. Servetus had long been interested in Jewish writings, both ancient and modern. And in book 4 he demonstrates that he is familiar with, and appreciative of, wisdom drawn from pagan sources. He did not believe that outside of Christ there is no truth; rather, he thought that outside

---

[1] The ancient Greek poet Archilochus recorded the maxim, though he may not have originated it. Erasmus included it in his *Adages*. It was popularized in the twentieth century by the philosopher Isaiah Berlin, who wrote a famous essay in which he categorized various historical figures as either hedgehogs or foxes. (According to Berlin, Plato is a hedgehog, and Aristotle is a fox.)

of Christ there are only partial truths. Book 4, in all of its variety, is a kaleidoscope of those partial truths.

Key Concepts in Book 3

The Face of God

Servetus's version of Christianity is notoriously hard to describe. One could pile up names that have been applied to his philosophy, theology, and heresies, and still not have an adequate or complete description of his system of belief.[2]

In his magisterial survey, *The Radical Reformation*, George Huntston Williams admitted that Servetus's theology is "hard to classify."[3] But in his translation of Stanislas Lubieniecki's *History of the Polish Reformation*, Williams offered an intriguing suggestion. In a caption to an illustration, he wrote, "An image of the Trinity, close to the Christology of Servetus, but scorned by [Giorgio] Biandrata."[4] Is it possible that a picture could encapsulate a complicated and mysterious theology better than the thousands, and tens of thousands, of words penned by theological critics and analysts down through the centuries?

The picture is one of several woodcuts reprinted in a sixteenth-century Unitarian work, *False and True Knowledge of the One God*, edited by Giorgio Biandrata.[5] It shows God the Father hidden in a

---

[2] In the introduction to the first volume in this series, Peter Hughes considered and rejected various labels that have been applied to Servetus's theology — heretical trinitarian, unitarian, Arian, modalist — before concluding that Irenaeus's concept of "the economy of God" comes closest. Jerome Friedman, in his systematic analysis of Servetus's theology, called him a "modalistic trinitarian," a "Neoplatonic and Gnostic emanationist," and a "Pelagian millenarian," and described his belief system as "variously a messianic form of Neoplatonic Judaism, a free will oriented Gnosticism, or a generally Hellenistic Christianity permeated with heresy." Hughes, introduction to *On the Trinity and the Bible*, 36-45. Friedman, *Michael Servetus*, 134-135.

[3] Williams, *The Radical Reformation*, 1297.

[4] Stanislas Lubieniecki, *History of the Polish Reformation*, trans. George Huntston Williams (Minneapolis: Fortress Press, 1995), 926.

[5] Biandrata, *De falsa et vera*, 51. Note: page numbers refer to the 1988 edition. The original edition is unpaginated.

An image of the Trinity, which George Huntston Williams described as "close to the Christology of Servetus"

cloud, presenting the crucified Christ, who is visible down on earth. Sent forth from Christ is a dove, the Holy Spirit, winging its way below. Looked at in one way, it seems like quite an orthodox Roman Catholic illustration, as it was certainly meant to be. There are three parts to God — the Father, the Son, and the Holy Spirit — a very identifiable Trinity. In *False and True Knowledge,* this picture is presented as one of "the dreadful images of the three-in-one God."[6] The derogatory Unitarian caption reads, "This is a portent of the Antichrist, showing that nothing of the flesh of Christ comes from the Virgin, but that it all actually descends directly from heaven."[7]

Now let us look at the same picture from Servetus's radical point of view. Note that, along the sight-line from earth, the three figures merge into one. The image of God the Father, represented as an old man dressed up in papal garb, would not have appealed to Servetus, who wrote that the Pope in his finery was "the most shameless of harlots."[8] But let us put that to one side. Up there in the cloud, beyond human sight and ken, is God the Father. "God in himself, infinitely surpassing everything, is to us incomprehensible, unimaginable, and incommunicable," wrote Servetus. "None of us can see him, unless he accommodates himself to us and appears in a form that is within our ability to perceive."[9] The old man in the tiara is just a symbolic representation, standing in for what we cannot begin to comprehend.

On the surface of the cloud, which we can see, is Jesus Christ, who appears to us as a man, something that we can comprehend. He is shown carrying a cross, indicating that this is not just the image of a generic human being, but an individual with a story, a story that includes suffering and sacrifice. We cannot see into the entire Godhead, but we can see Jesus Christ and, since his attachment to the cloud indicates that he is part of the Godhead, through him we can, to some extent, see God himself. We don't see anything but Christ,

---

[6] Biandrata, *De falsa et vera,* 45.
[7] Biandrata, *De falsa et vera,* 51.
[8] *Restoration,* 462.
[9] *Restoration,* 136.

but in him we somehow also see the Father — or at least what the Father means us to see. As far as we humans are concerned, the face of Christ is the face of God.

Using this model, we can now understand how Christ can be, as Servetus argued in book 1, both the Son of God and God himself.[10] The Father and the Son are not, as in trinitarian theology, two separate persons within the Godhead. Christ *is* God — God as seen by human beings. Servetus speaks of the Father, the Son, and the Holy Spirit, but, he reminds us, "there is only one person, and only one face."[11]

Original Sin

If Christ is the face of God, this means that, before the Incarnation, human beings were not able to see the face of God. They could catch glimpses of it, but the face itself was veiled in darkness and cloud. This was the consequence of the primal sin in the Garden of Eden. "Because of Adam's sin the face of God was hidden, and before it stood a flaming sword. He who had previously been visible to Adam afterward became invisible. Sin caused the face of God to be hidden, the cloud of his anger having been thrown over it."[12]

Servetus did not deny that the disobedience of Adam and Eve had altered the relationship between God and humankind. The darkness and clouds that veiled the face of God were the product of human sinfulness. Yet, even during the time of darkness, God continued to show mercy to human beings. "He entered into the spirits of human beings in various ways, without being seen ... In various modes, God rallied unhappy [human] nature, held captive by Satan, to his side."[13]

More than most other Christians, Servetus believed that Christ, the second Adam, had effectively healed the damage done by the first Adam. In the incarnated and risen Christ, the veil that hid the

---

[10] *Restoration*, 5.
[11] *Restoration*, 109.
[12] *Restoration*, 96.
[13] *Restoration*, 123-124.

face of God has been torn away, and we can once more see the face of God, as we were meant to see it.

> At last [God] was revealed to us, shining in spite of the darkness, and seen with his face unveiled. The Word was made flesh and we saw his glory. We saw the glory of God in the face of Jesus Christ. We saw Christ, and in him we saw the Father. In him we saw the light, God himself shining.[14]

This is very Good News indeed. It lays the groundwork for Servetus's optimistic view of human nature, a theme that will be further developed in later parts of *Restoration*.[15]

The Word

The Bible contains hundreds of references to "the word of God" or "the word of the Lord." In the generic sense, the word of God is any message from God that is revealed to a human being. "The word of the Lord came to Abram in a vision." "Moses commanded the children of Israel according to the word of the Lord." "The word of God came to John the son of Zacharias in the wilderness." "Faith comes by hearing by the word of God."[16] But the specifically Christian concept of the Word rests on just two verses, both from the Gospel of John.

> In the beginning was the Word, and the Word was with God, and the Word was God. (John 1:1)

> And the Word became flesh and dwelt among us, and we beheld his glory, the glory as of the only begotten of the Father, full of grace and truth. (John 1:14)

John 1:1 lets us know that we are in the realm of mystery, for by ordinary logic it is impossible for something to be with God and, at the same time, actually to be God. John 1:14 asserts that Christ is somehow both the only begotten Son of God, and the incarnate

---

[14] *Restoration*, 124.

[15] Servetus's views on original sin are discussed in "On the Destruction of the World, and its Restoration by Christ" (*Restoration*, 357-409).

[16] Gen 15:1; Num 36:5; Luke 3:2; Rom 10:17.

Introduction

Word of God. On these two verses is built a vast superstructure of theology. In Peter Lombard's *Sentences,* the most important theological text of the Middle Ages, one of the four books is entirely devoted to "The Incarnation of the Word." In book 3 of *The Restoration of Christianity,* Servetus presents his own theology of the Word. As with the Trinity and other aspects of Christian theology, Servetus had his own idiosyncratic understanding of the Word.

According to John 1:14, the Word became flesh. The verb "became" was highly significant in Servetus's concept of the Word. It meant that the Word was not an eternal, unchanging aspect of God, existing outside of time. Instead, the Word exists in time; it undergoes change; it has a history. The Word that was with God in the beginning, the word of the Lord that came to the prophets and patriarchs, and the Word that become flesh, are one and the same Word, appearing in different forms at different times.

The Word was the creative force that brought the universe into being: God *said,* let there be light. When the patriarchs and prophets of the Old Testament saw God or heard God's voice, they were seeing and hearing the Word that was going to become Christ in the future; hence these revelations could be called prefigurations of Christ. Servetus believed that references in the Old Testament to Wisdom, angels, cherubim, Elohim, or gods can all be understood as foreshadowings or prefigurations of Christ — revelations of the Word. So can the insights of pagan philosophers regarding the Prime Mover, and the intimations of divinity that are available to the unaided reason of any human being who observes nature.[17]

At the time of the Incarnation, the Word became Christ, and no longer existed in any other form. "The Word, which was the λογος (*logos*) or ideal reason, now refers to a human being." "What was once the Word is now the Son. And the person of the Son was once in the Word."[18] After the resurrection, the Word was God again. "Just as, in the beginning, Elohim and Jehovah were the same — because

---

[17] *Restoration,* 112.
[18] *Restoration,* 92, 108.

God was the Word — so too are they now, since Christ has been raised to his original glory."[19]

Person, Face, Image, Likeness, Appearance, Form, etc.

In book 3, Servetus frequently refers to "the person of Christ" or "the person of the Word."[20] The word "person" was clearly important and meaningful to him. It is equally clear that it did not have the same meaning for him that it did for trinitarians. He categorically rejected the trinitarian formula that God is three persons in one essence, or that the Father, Son, and Holy Spirit are persons. "The sophists," he railed, "have made up metaphysical, incorporeal, and invisible persons — or what are foolishly called persons."[21]

For Servetus, "person" means "outward appearance, face, and presentation." When the Bible says that "God is no respecter of persons," it means that God "has no regard for outward differences, such as whether someone is male or female, slave or free, Jew or Greek, rich or poor."[22]

Servetus coupled the words "person" and "face" in the theologically significant statement quoted above: "Christ is the person of the Word and the Word is the person of Christ, but there is only one person and only one face."[23] Throughout book 3, Servetus uses a cluster of words that are all related to the idea of visual representation or appearance. "Person" is one of these words. "This πρόσωπον (*prosopon*, person) — this person, this countenance, this face, this representation of humanity in God — lies mystically hidden in all the passages of scripture that speak of image, face, and person."[24] In the course of translating book 3, the translation team compiled a list of fifteen of these terms, and made a "cheat sheet" to make sure

---

[19] *Restoration*, 136.

[20] *Restoration*, 92, 101-110 (many times), 117, 120, 123.

[21] *Restoration*, 108.

[22] *Restoration*, 108, quoting Gal 3:28.

[23] *Restoration*, 109.

[24] *Restoration*, 92-93.

that these words were translated in a consistent way.[25] None of these words are exact synonyms. They all have their own shades of meaning. What they have in common is that they all refer to something seen by an external observer, and not to any inner reality or essence. By grouping the theologically loaded word "person" with other words having to do with external appearance, Servetus was emphasizing that he did not intend to speculate about "persons" within God. When we see Christ, we see the face of God; we see the person of God. We cannot get any closer to God than this. As in the illustration in *False and True Knowledge*, God is hidden in the cloud, inaccessible to the finite minds of finite creatures.

Key Concepts in Book 4

The Omniform Essence and the Names of God

Throughout book 4, Servetus refers to the concept of the omniform essence of God — that is, the idea that God "has within himself the essences of infinite thousands and the natures of infinite thousands."[26] For Servetus, God is radically One — "only one person and only one face," as he said in book 3 — but also radically Many. He contrasts this idea with the trinitarian formula, which he deplores, that God consists of three persons within one essence.

Servetus associates the complementary ideas of God as One and God as Many with the most well-known names of God in the Hebrew scriptures, יהוה (*Yahweh* or *Jehovah*) and אלהים (*Elohim*). Since the word *Elohim* is grammatically plural, it represents the multiplicity of things that exist within God, and also the multiplicity of ways that

---

[25] The fifteen terms are:

Aspectus – face	*Instar* – image, "is like"
Character – likeness	*Persona* – person
Effigies – likeness	*Phantasma* – mental image
Exemplar – model	*Similitudo* – likeness
Facies – face, appearance	*Species* – appearance, visible form
Figura – shape, figure, prefiguration	*Visio* – vision
Forma – form, shape	*Vultus* – countenance
Imago – image, likeness	

[26] *Restoration*, 128-129.

Introduction

God that can appear to human beings; hence, for Servetus, "Elohim is [God's] visible appearance."[27] The name Jehovah, on the other hand, represents God's ineffable essence. It is the mysterious name, unknown to the Patriarchs, that God reveals to Moses when he charges him to lead the people of Israel — the name that observant Jews consider too sacred to pronounce aloud.

The discussion of the names of God, which occurs at the very beginning of book 4, incorporates some previously written material that sits somewhat awkwardly in its new setting. The first part of the section on the name Jehovah, which closely follows a parallel section in *On the Errors of the Trinity*, dives deeply into technicalities of the Hebrew language that will not turn out to be particularly relevant to what follows. And the first part of the section that Servetus himself labelled "Elohim" is a comparison of Jewish and Christian ideas about the things that exist in eternity, in which the name "Elohim" is not even mentioned. These digressions get book 4 off to something of a shaky start. The key ideas to take away from the "Names of God" section are that God contains multitudes and that the name "Elohim" in the Bible signals some sort of manifestation or revelation of God.

Ideal and Substantial Forms

The "theory of Forms" or "theory of Ideas" is a philosophical theory associated with Plato — "associated with," rather than "taught by," because Plato's relationship to the theory is somewhat ambiguous. Forms are associated with Plato because they are discussed by characters in some of his dialogues. The dialogue form, however, is better suited for proposing intriguing suggestions than for elaborating theories. To the extent that there is a "theory" of Forms, it is the work of later philosophers picking up on Plato's suggestions.

The theory holds that there is a realm of pure archetypes or essences called Forms or Ideas (by convention, these terms are capitalized in English, to distinguish them from ordinary mundane forms and ideas). All real physical objects are merely imperfect copies based on these prototypes — imperfect, because real objects

---

[27] *Restoration*, 125.

are changeable and perishable, whereas Forms are eternal. This may be contrasted with Aristotle's view that objects are composed of matter and form, but that matter and form are inseparable and have no independent existence.

Servetus makes use of the concept of Forms throughout book 4, but especially in the section that he called "The Ideas or Forms of All Things are in God" (*Ideae seu formae omnium in Deo*). The word he usually used for Ideas or Forms was *idea*, a direct transliteration of the Greek ἰδέα. Since the words "idea" and "form" have other meanings in this text, and the use of capital letters for "Idea" and "Form" (a usage that gained currency in the mid-twentieth century) seems anachronistic, we have translated *idea* as "ideal form."

Servetus incorporated his understanding of ideal forms into his Christian theology by locating the realm of ideal forms within the mind of God. In a few places he goes further, identifying ideal forms specifically with the Word of God. This appears to be an idea that he encountered at a late stage in the composition of *The Restoration of Christianity*, for it was not included in the draft of book 4 found in the Paris manuscript.[28] Moreover, he explicitly attributes the idea to specific Church Fathers, which suggests that he had not fully integrated it into his own belief system.[29]

From the consideration of ideal forms, which exist in the mind of God, Servetus passes to a discussion of substantial forms, which are embodied in corporeal objects. He explains that there is a natural kinship between the upper world of ideal forms and the lower world of corporeal things. He suggests that the forms of all created things may contain a spark of the divine. "Because [God] contains in his essence the ideal forms of all things, he may be considered the formal portion of all things."[30]

---

[28] See the Appendix for a description of the Paris manuscript and a discussion of its probable date.

[29] "Clement of Alexandria ... defines an ideal form as λόγον θεοῦ (*logon theou*), the Word of God" (*Restoration*, 140). "[Origen] says that ... the forms of all things were in the Word, in the same way that things that will appear in the future are in seeds" (*Restoration*, 141).

[30] *Restoration*, 130.

Introduction

Light

"Light" is the most frequently occurring word in book 4. In this book, Servetus presents light as the basic stuff of the universe, both heavenly and earthly. These are some of the things that Servetus tells us about light:

1. Light is divine. Light is God, the spirit of God, and the Word of God. Souls and spirits are made of light.[31]
2. God's light contains the ideal forms of all things.[32] We know that form comes from light, because the earth was without form until God said, "Let there be light."[33]
3. It is not only immaterial ideal forms that are made of light — light is also the substantial, embodied form of all corporeal things. Light is the force that creates, sustains, and ultimately destroys all things.[34]
4. Light is the source of knowledge and understanding. It is "an effective way of knowing," the medium by which angels can contemplate God and prophets can see the future. Even on a more mundane level, "ideas themselves, which we grasp with our intellect, are like sparks of light and radiant images, illuminating the mind itself."[35]
5. And finally, light is the medium of communication between the divine and the created world.

   It is light, containing all things in itself, which links spiritual and corporeal things and makes them clearly visible to our eyes. The images in our souls are naturally luminous, there being a natural kinship of this light with external forms, with external light, and with the essential light of the soul itself ... From the soul's own light and from the light that enters it from outside, a single light is composed. For light often unites with light.[36]

---

[31] *Restoration*, 151, 162.
[32] *Restoration*, 143-144, 147, 149.
[33] *Restoration*, 151, referring to Gen 1:1-3.
[34] *Restoration*, 142-144, 152-154.
[35] *Restoration*, 143.
[36] *Restoration*, 147.

Splendour

The primary meaning of the Latin word *splendor* is brightness, brilliance, magnificence, and grandeur, and it is used in this way throughout *Restoration*. But in book 4, it is also used in a specialized sense, to mean a kind of cold light. Servetus is unlikely to have invented this usage, but it is not known where he may have encountered it.

In the "Origins of Natural Things" section of book 4, Servetus sets up a contrast between two kinds of light. The light of the sun (sometimes called just "light") is hot and dry, associated with daytime, the sun, and fire. Splendour is a kind of light that is cold and wet, associated with nighttime, the moon, and water.[37]

Since splendour is a kind of light, and forms are made of light, it follows that forms can be made of splendour. Servetus tells us that splendour is the form of water. The substance of the earth receives its form from "the splendour of water and the light of heaven."[38] All of this sets the stage for the revelation that splendour is one of the four basic building blocks of the universe.

> We may now conclude that there are four sources of natural things, two material and two formal. The material sources are the two kinds of matter already mentioned: the earthy and the watery. The formal sources are the light of the sun, which warms and dries, and the splendour of water, which cools and moistens.[39]

Having shown that all things arise from matter (the four elements) and form (the two kinds of light), Servetus concludes that, beneath the multiplicity of forms, there is a fundamental unity, just as the ancient philosophers taught.

The Perennial Philosophy

The perennial philosophy is the idea that there is a basic religious truth that is common to many, perhaps all, religions. Servetus is well known to have looked for religious truth in Jewish and Muslim

---

[37] *Restoration*, 152-154.
[38] *Restoration*, 161.
[39] *Restoration*, 161.

Introduction

writings as well as in Christian sources. In book 4 of *The Restoration of Christianity*, he widened his focus still further to examine the truth that can be found in the philosophies and religions of the pre-Christian ancient world. In this search he was guided primarily by the works of two Renaissance authors, Marsilio Ficino and Agostino Steuco.

In the Neoplatonism and Hermeticism presented by Ficino and Steuco, Servetus found several appealing features. They provided philosophical support for his theology. More importantly, the witnesses quoted by Ficino and Steuco formed part of a much broader tradition than had been imagined by most Christians. Servetus believed that the heart of this more universal tradition was the same as what one would find in Christianity if it were possible to strip away all of the error, corruption, and superstition that had attached itself over the centuries to the Christian Church.

Finding the traces of Ficino and Steuco in the works of Servetus requires some detective work, because Servetus did not mention them by name. Servetus used both authors' works principally as compendia of ancient and putatively ancient writings. For Servetus, only the most ancient authority counted, not the path of transmission. This belief was shared by both Ficino and Steuco. Like Servetus, they believed that the older the authority, the closer it was to the original divine revelation.

In his use of non-Christian sources, Servetus was continuing the project, begun in his earliest work *On the Errors of the Trinity*, of drawing upon the common wisdom preserved in other religions, in order to balance and correct the Christianity of his time. For Servetus, there was truth in Judaism and Islam, in ancient Greek philosophy and mystery religions, and in what he believed to be ancient wisdom from Egypt and Persia. To the end of his life, he sought to create a wider, more inclusive form of Christianity, in hopes that it would provide an attractive spiritual option for all people.

Ancient Wisdom and the Corpus Hermeticum

Ancient Greek and Roman polytheistic religion evolved in a syncretic manner. The ancient Greeks respected the gods of other cultures and were open to the study of the wisdom contained in their rites and myths. They boasted of the travels of their early philosophers and of the education these wisdom seekers had received in Egypt, Syria, Mesopotamia, and Persia. The Romans militarily conquered Greece and much of the Middle East, but were themselves conquered by their subject peoples' cultures and religions. There had long been a tendency within polytheism to picture the interplay of many deities as outward manifestations of a single underlying One. The ease with which polytheist societies engaged in syncretism may be partly attributed to the widely held belief that, at bottom, all divinities, by whatever name and in whatever guise, refer back to the same basic unified reality.

Among the teachings that fascinated the later pagan philosophers, and Christian philosophers as well, were sets of oracles from the East that claimed great antiquity, although the texts themselves were actually composed during, or only shortly before, the Christian era. These were the *Chaldean Oracles* (sometimes attributed to Zoroaster), the *Orphic Hymns* and *Rhapsodies*, the *Sibylline Oracles*, and the *Hermetica*. The antiquity of these texts was accepted without question in Servetus's time. Early in the seventeenth century, scholarly study, beginning with that of Isaac Casaubon, dated these works to the Hellenistic and early Christian period.[40]

The perennial philosophy was embodied for Servetus, above all, in the *Corpus Hermeticum*, a collection of writings attributed to a legendary figure called Hermes Trismegistus. The Hermetic texts were written in the second and third century CE, though they were believed to be much older. Augustine, in *City of God*, arranged pagan, Jewish, and Christian wisdom into a chronology and genealogy. Among the religious texts that Augustine thought to be the oldest were the *Hermetica*. He calculated that their supposed author, Hermes Trismegistus, was of a generation after that of Moses.[41] Servetus believed that Hermes Trismegistus had influenced Plato,[42] though in truth any influence must have been in the other direction.

---

[40] Isaac Casaubon, *De rebus sacris et ecclesiasticis exercitationes xvi* (1614), 70-87.
[41] Augustine, *De civitate Dei* 18.39.
[42] *Restoration*, 130.

Introduction

Hermes Trismegistus
from Pierre Mussard, *Historia Deorum fatidicorum* (1675)

The *Corpus Hermeticum* texts are written from a pagan perspective, but show signs of Christian influence. To those who believed them to predate Christianity, this appeared to be a powerful expression of the perennial philosophy — a set of writings composed by pagans in remote antiquity, that were yet compatible with Christian thinking.

The *Corpus Hermeticum* texts are written in the popular dialogue form and feature characters such as Hermes Trismegistus and his son Tat, Pimander (also known as Pymander or Poimandres), and Asclepius, the grandson of the Greek god of healing. In book 4, Servetus quoted extensively from the *Corpus Hermeticum* and from the related work *Asclepius*, which, although written in Greek like the *Corpus Hermeticum*, survived only in a Latin translation. Servetus found support for his idea of the omniform essence of God in Hermetic statements such as "[God] is, so to speak, many-bodied, since there is nothing in bodies that he is not."[43]

Marsilio Ficino and the Platonic Tradition

With the collapse of the Byzantine Empire and the fall of Constantinople, many learned Greeks headed west, bringing with them their manuscripts. In Italy they began to train Latin-educated scholars to read Greek and to appreciate this sizeable body of literature. Among these westerners was Marsilio Ficino (1433-1499), son of the personal physician of the Florentine ruler Cosimo de Medici. Influenced by the Byzantine philosopher Gemistos Plethon, Cosimo decided to establish a new Platonic academy in Florence. When, in 1456, he read *Platonic Institutes*, an early unpublished work by the young Ficino, he urged the author to study Greek so that he could read more Plato. In 1462 Cosimo gave Ficino an income and installed him in the villa which was to house the new academy.

It had long been a project of Christian scholastic philosophers, such as Thomas Aquinas, to make an accommodation between Christian theology and the thought of Aristotle. Ficino made it his personal mission to show that Christianity was even more consistent with the ideas of Plato. He translated the complete works of Plato into Latin (1484), wrote commentaries on many of the Platonic dialogues (1496), and translated and commented on Plotinus and other Neoplatonic philosophers. At the special request of Cosimo de Medici, he translated the *Corpus Hermeticum* (1471). In the midst of these translation projects he composed an apologetic work, *On Christian Religion* (1474), in which he expressed himself as moderately open-minded regarding religions other than Christianity.[44] This was followed by his own *summa theologica* and *magnum opus*, *Platonic Theology* (1482).

---

[43] *Restoration*, 132, quoting *Corpus Hermeticum* 5.10.

[44] Ficino, *De Christiana religione*, 4. As discussed in volume 1 of this series, everything that Servetus said about Islam in *On the Errors of the Trinity* can be found in *De Christiana religione*. See A.E1.45 (*On the Trinity and the Bible*, 415-416).

Introduction

Marsilio Ficino

In *Platonic Theology,* Ficino put forth a justification for seeking religious truth outside of Christianity. He called religion "that instinct which is common and natural to all peoples."[45] He asked, "What is more ancient than religion? And what is more widespread?" Just as people everywhere speak, but do so in different ways, Ficino wrote, "God is adored among all peoples in every century, although not with the same rites and in the same ways."[46] He found that the theology of Jews, Christians, and Muslims had much in common with the teachings of Plato, the Chaldeans, Orpheus, and Hermes Trismegistus.[47]

Ficino left his mark on Servetus's writing in several ways. First, there is information that Servetus gleaned from Ficino's works, principally *Platonic Theology*. *Platonic Theology* was one of Servetus's primary sources for information on the earliest Greek philosophers:

---

[45] Ficino, *Theologia Platonica* 14.9.2.
[46] Ficino, *Theologia Platonica* 14.10.10.
[47] Ficino, *Theologia Platonica* 18.1.

Introduction

Anaximenes, Pythagoras, Leucippus, Democritus, Parmenides, Diogenes, and Hipparchus. A supposedly very ancient source, the *Chaldean Oracles*, thought in Servetus's time to have been written by Zoroaster, was much quoted in *Platonic Theology*. Some of these quotations found their way into *The Restoration of Christianity*. Sometimes Servetus drew on Ficino's own words as well as on the works he quoted. For example, in *Platonic Theology*, Ficino quoted an Orphic saying, "Zeus, who appears as all things," to support his own claim that "God is omniform in essence."[48] Servetus combined Ficino's sentiment with the Orphic quote and presented it as though it were a single ancient pronouncement: "Orpheus said that God's essence is omniform, having all forms in itself."[49]

Another way that Ficino influenced Servetus is through his translations. Servetus made about thirty citations and references to the *Corpus Hermeticum* in book 4. Many, but not all, of the Hermetic quotations come from the (then standard) translation by Ficino. He also relied on Ficino's translations of works by Iamblichus and pseudo-Dionysius the Areopagite. Above all, Ficino was Servetus's guide to the works and the thought of Plato. Servetus used Ficino's translations of Plato's dialogues, which were published along with Ficino's commentaries and "epitomes" of the dialogues. Servetus's understanding of Plato was influenced by Ficino's interpretation, which highlighted the passages in Plato that were most compatible with Neoplatonist and Christian ideas.[50]

---

[48] Ficino, *Theologia Platonica* 2.11.1.

[49] *Restoration*, 138. But see A.R4.34 for a more detailed discussion of this matter.

[50] As a result, Servetus's claims about Plato may be quite puzzling at times. In a footnote in his Spanish translation of *The Restoration of Christianity*, Ángel Alcalá took issue with Servetus's claim that Plato — influenced by, among others, Zoroaster and Hermes Trismegistus — believed that there was "One, that is the prime being" that contains and sustains all things. Alcalá pointed out that Plato could not have read the works attributed to Zoroaster and Hermes that Servetus had in mind, because they were actually written hundreds of years after the time of Plato; that the opinions expressed by the characters in Plato's dialogues do not necessarily represent Plato's own beliefs; and that "An infinite personal god, through whom all beings share in the divine, is alien to Plato." Alcalá, *Obras Completas*, 5:220 n.28. See A.R4.18.

Introduction

Agostino Steuco's Perennial Philosophy

Besides Ficino, Servetus's guide to ancient wisdom was Agostino Steuco's *The Perennial Philosophy*. This work, in addition to setting forth the concept of the perennial philosophy, is loaded with quotations drawn from ancient writers, including many in whom Servetus was interested: Plato, the Chaldean oracles, Hermes Trismegistus, Porphyry, Proclus, Philo, Orpheus, Pythagoras, and others. (Helpfully, from the point of view of the scholar, the Latin translations of Greek quotations in *The Perennial Philosophy* were Steuco's own, which makes it possible to distinguish between Servetus's borrowings from Steuco and his use of translations from other sources.)

Agostino Steuco (1498-1548), born just before the death of Ficino, was a contemporary of Servetus. He was an Augustinian monk who, in the later stages of his life, worked as librarian for the Pope. He wrote a series of works in which he tried to show the truth of ideas from ancient pagan traditions. In the first, *Examination of the Old Testament according to Hebrew Truth* (1529), he argued, using Hermes, Zoroaster, Thales, Pythagoras, Plato, Porphyry, and many others, that the rituals of the Roman Catholic Church were of very ancient origin, going back through unexpected routes to the earliest revelations of God in the Old Testament. This work advanced his career and established him as a humanist champion of orthodoxy. But later works in which he further developed his syncretic views — *The Creation of the Universe* (1535) and *The Perennial Philosophy* (1540) — were not as warmly received. His critics believed that a sharp distinction had to be drawn between pagan and Christian thought and that it ought not be conceded that people could arrive at religious truth through reason alone, apart from Christian revelation. Because of Steuco's Vatican connections and his value to the church in combatting Protestantism, his syncretic books escaped actual condemnation until after his death.[51]

The *Perennial Philosophy* is Steuco's most systematic work. He began by asserting that perfect knowledge was given to the first

---

[51] Schmitt, "Perennial Philosophy," 524-527.

Introduction

Agostino Steuco

human beings in Eden, who benefited from direct association with God. After being expelled from paradise, Adam taught his descendants "the whole design of the created world." This perfect knowledge, attenuated through time into fables and dreams, has been supplemented by "a deep contemplation of things, which has ever been called philosophy."[52] Steuco defined the aim of philosophy as "nothing less than knowledge of God and the ability, in a way, to look at him directly."[53] Steuco tracked this philosophy back beyond the Greeks to the cultures of the ancient Middle East: Egypt, Persia, and elsewhere. Among these traditions, Steuco highlighted the teaching of Hermes Trismegistus, to whom he granted an authority and importance almost equal to that of Moses and whom he considered "the source of Greek philosophy."[54]

---

[52] Steuco, *De perenni philosophia* 1.1.
[53] Steuco, *De perenni philosophia* 10.9.
[54] Steuco, *De perenni philosophia* 1.10.

Introduction

Steuco's objective in all of this was to give extra support to Roman Catholic theology by tracing the path of God's original revelation through multiple pathways of tradition. However, by showing divine truth being carried by other ancient traditions alongside Judaism he, perhaps unintentionally, validated these other religions, which most Christians customarily regarded as false. Although many of the ancient texts that he employed in his genealogy of religious history were ultimately discredited, he remains an important link in an intellectual chain that runs from ancient syncretism to the twentieth century and beyond. It was Steuco who first coined the term "perennial philosophy."[55]

Steuco seems, in many ways, an odd source of inspiration for Servetus. Steuco was a strong supporter of the Pope, virulently anti-Protestant, and a critic of Erasmus. But Servetus looked for what he saw as the truth wherever he could find it. For, as he said in *On the Errors of the Trinity* when introducing the testimony of Muhammad, "greater trust is to be placed in one truth spoken by an enemy, than in a hundred of our own lies."[56]

The Jewish Tradition

In addition to the classical sources cited by Ficino and Steuco, in books 3 and 4 Servetus continued his exploration of Jewish sources, mostly through secondary works; he knew some Hebrew, but probably not enough to actually read a book in that language. His analysis of specific Hebrew words draws on Santes Pagnini's Hebrew lexicon. He was able to read Maimonides' *Guide for the Perplexed* in a Latin translation, and he found excerpts from the Targums and some rabbinic commentaries in Pagnini's *Isagoge* and Pietro Galatino's *On the Mysteries of Catholic Truth*. Servetus

---

[55] Nowadays, the expression "perennial philosophy" is probably associated most often with Aldous Huxley, who wrote a book by that name in 1945. Huxley credited the coining of the term to Gottfried Wilhelm Leibniz. Aldous Huxley, *The Perennial Philosophy* (1945; New York: HarperCollins, 2009), vii. See Schmitt, "Perennial Philosophy," 506.

[56] *Errors*, 43r.

mentioned other commentaries — those of Ibn Ezra and Rashi, and the compendium of commentaries on Genesis, *Bereshit Rabbah* — which he must have found in secondary sources, though these sources have not been identified.

Servetus's study of Jewish thought was aided by the work of the Catholic humanist and Hebrew scholar, Johannes Reuchlin (1455-1522). Reuchlin is best known for his long campaign to convince the Holy Roman Emperor of the scholarly and religious value of Jewish books, against those who thought that the destruction of Jewish literature would hasten the conversion of the Jews.

More importantly for Servetus, Reuchlin wrote *The Art of the Kabbalah* (1517). The Kabbalah was looked upon by some Christians in Servetus's time as a source of Jewish wisdom that could safely be appropriated by Christians. It is clear that Servetus read Reuchlin, for he made use of material from both *The Art of the Kabbalah* and *The Wonder-Working Word* (1494).

Johannes Reuchlin presents a document to Emperor Maximilian, explaining why Jewish books should not be burned
from Ulrich von Hutten, *Triumph Reuchlins* (1518)

Introduction

The Last Word

To study the works of Servetus is to become immersed in a world very different from our own. Each obscure allusion is an invitation to explore some fascinating byway of history or philosophy. This is particularly true of book 4, because it opens the door to a whole world of mystical and esoteric literature that retains its potency even today. We can sense Servetus's excitement as delved into these new sources and worked to integrate the new ideas into his world view.

But Servetus never forgot what he believed to be his God-given mission, and neither should we. In the end it was not about the riches of the Hermetic tradition, or the intricacies of the Hebrew language, or the intriguing web of correspondences that unite the elements of the earth, the human body, and the heavens above. As he said in the very first paragraph of *The Restoration of Christianity*, "The most important things, dear reader, are the recognition of God as he is revealed in substance, and the way in which the divine nature is actually communicated."[57] So as you, dear reader, engage with Servetus's words and Servetus's world —and we hope that you will — we remind you that, after all of its meanderings, book 4 ends with a statement of faith: "There is one source, one light of the Word, the omniform light, and the head of all, who is Jesus Christ our Lord, the source of all God's creations."[58] That, more than anything else, is what Servetus wanted us to know.

---

[57] *Restoration*, 3.
[58] *Restoration*, 162.

THE RESTORATION OF CHRISTIANITY

Books 3 and 4

DE TRINITATE
DIVINA LIBER TERTIVS
personæ Christi in verbo præfigurationem ostendens, visionem Dei, & verbi hypostasim.

CHristus Iesus Dominus & Deus noster, ex tam multis locis iam patefactus, calcar nobis addit, & animum roborat, vt maiora alia, quæ de ipso supersunt arcana, deinceps proferamus. Est verò summa tota, finisque nobis hic positus, manifestationis. Dei modum verum inuestigare, ac Christum in omnibus scopum proponere. Hoc itaque tertio libro, vt ad visionem Dei perueniamus, de verbi persona prius disseremus, in verbo ipso personā Christi ostendentes, vt totum sermonis arcanum sit Christi glorificatio. Ad hoc tendere dicimus Ioānis primum euangelium, vt gloriam Dei in facie Iesu Christi omnes videamus, vt eam gloriam in facie Christi videri ait Paulus.2.Cor.4.Et Ioannes ipse ait, Verbum illud caro extitit,& vidimus gloriam eius,Ioan.1. Verbum ipsum diuinū,quod initio erat apud Deum,nos vidimus.1.Ioā.1. Verbum erat λογός,idealis ratio, iam hominem referens. Id iam occultè referebat,in quo futurum erat, vt palā videretur:& vidimus,& testamur.Illam vidimus in facie Iesu Christi gloriam,quam olim super cherubim, intra caliginem & nubem lucentem, tenebræ non apprehenderunt. Illam vidimus Christi gloriam,quam ipse ab æterno habet apud Deum,Ioan.17. Iam olim in verbo apud Deum erat futuri hominis Iesu Christi exemplar,persona, & effigies.Et τὸ πρόσωπον ,hæc persona,hic vultus, hæc facies,hęc
homi

On the Divine Trinity

Book 3

Showing the prefiguration of the person of Christ in the Word, our vision of God, and the hypostasis of the Word

[92] Christ Jesus, our Lord and God, whom we have just now revealed in a great many Bible passages,[a] spurs us on and strengthens our spirits, so that we might bring to light the other remaining great mysteries about him. The whole object <u>and</u> goal set <u>for</u> us here is to investigate the true mode of the manifestation of God, <u>and to make Christ our aim in all things</u>. Therefore, in this third book, in order to attain our vision of God, we shall first examine the person of the Word, showing the person of Christ in the Word itself, <u>so that the entire mystery of the Word is the glorification of Christ</u>.

We say that the first chapter of the Gospel of John has this purpose: that all of us might behold *the glory of God in the face of Jesus Christ*, as Paul says in 2 Corinthians 4.[b] This <u>glory</u> is to be seen *in the face of Christ*. And John himself says, *the Word became flesh and we beheld his glory* (John 1).[c] <u>We have seen the divine Word, which in the beginning was with God</u> (1 John 1).[d] The Word, which was the λογος (*logos*) or ideal reason, now refers to a human

---

[a] In book 2.   [b] 2 Cor 4:6.   [c] John 1:14.   [d] John 1:1; 1 John 1:1-2.

being. It already had hidden reference [to Christ], in whom it was to be [made flesh] so that it could be clearly visible. *And we have seen this and bear witness.*[a] We have seen that *glory in the face of Jesus Christ,*[b] which was once [*seated*] *upon the cherubim,*[c] gleaming within *the gloom and clouds,*[d] *and the darkness did not overwhelm it.*[e] We have seen the glory of Christ which he himself has from eternity in the presence of God (John 17).[f]

In the beginning, the pattern, person, and likeness of the future human being, Jesus Christ, already existed in *the Word* that *was with God.*[g] This πρόσωπον (*prosopon*, person)—this person, this countenance, this face, this [93] representation of humanity in God—lies mystically hidden in all the passages of scripture that speak of image, face, and person. The prophets of old, called seers, only saw God by seeing Christ in God, or God through Christ. As he himself said, *Whoever has seen me, has seen God.*[h] Long ago when prophets saw the countenance of Elohim, they saw in the oracle of God the prototype and model of the future human being [Christ].[i] For what else could they have seen in God, *face to face?*[j] They saw there the very substance of Christ, just as we see the substance of God in Christ. The original exemplar of that archetype in heaven above was the human being, Christ Jesus.

Moses speaks about this likeness, shape, and image in God in Deuteronomy 4 and 5 and Numbers 12.[k] And in Exodus 20, the people heard Moses speaking,[l] but they did not see the image of Christ speaking. In these passages, תמונה (*temunah*, image or likeness)[m] designates the form,

Err, 86v

Err, 87r

---

[a] 1 John 1:1-2. [b] 2 Cor 4:6. [c] In many places in the Old Testament the Lord of Hosts is said to dwell or be seated upon or between the cherubim on the Ark of the Covenant. See, for example: Num 7:89; 1 Sam 4:4; 2 Kg 19:15; 1 Chr 13:6; Ps 99:1; Isa 37:16. [d] Joel 2:2. [e] John 1:5. [f] John 17:5. [g] John 1:1. [h] John 14:9. [i] See *Restoration*, 136-137 (book 4). [j] 1 Cor 13:12. [k] Deut 4:12; 5:4, 22; Num 12:6-8. [l] Ex 20:19-22. [m] Deut 4:12, 15; Num 12:8.

shape, likeness, and image of Jesus Christ that Moses saw. This is borne out by David's use of this word in Psalm 16, which is Psalm 17 in the Hebrew numbering: *I shall see your face, and I shall be satisfied when your image appears.*[a] Balaam saw this image from afar (Numbers 24). *I shall see him*, he says, *but I shall not look at him now, nor from nearby.*[b]

Err, 87r

All the prophets desired to see this shining face. Desiring this, David says in Psalm 79, *You who sit upon the cherubim, shine forth,*[c] appear in splendour. *Cause your face to shine*, make your countenance resplendent, *and we shall be saved.*[d] Psalms 4 and 43 relate the same thing about this face and countenance.[e] In the same way, in Psalm 88 one observes in God the face and countenance of Christ.[f]

Err, 87r

Isaiah saw this countenance *seated upon a lofty throne, but <u>the</u> face was veiled with wings* of fire (Isaiah 6).[g] What face would you say was there, <u>and</u> what feet, other than those of Christ? <u>They were not, of course, material limbs, but limbs resplendent in the light of God, and a prefiguration of Christ</u>. The same thing is proved in the vision of Ezekiel (chapters 1 and 10), as well as in the vision of Daniel (chapter 10) and the vision of the seventy elders in Exodus 24.[h] **[94]** Compare all these visions with the vision of John in the Apocalypse, chapters 1 and 4,[i] and you will say that they all saw the same thing in Christ, the same person and the same face.

This was not just a mask, <u>nor a mere created figure</u>, such as the sophists devised. For God wanted to reveal himself, to the glory of Christ. [The sophists] <u>recognize no true display of the substance of God, and thus no true communication of spirit,</u> as if God were incapable of this

---

[a] Ps 17:15. [b] Num 24:17. [c] Ps 80:1 (Ps 79:3 in Vulgate). [d] Ps 80:3, 7, 19. [e] Ps 4:6, 44:3. [f] Ps 89:15. [g] Isa 6:1-2. [h] Ezek 1 and 10 (entire chapter); Dan 10:4-20; Ex 24:9-11. See especially Ezek 1:4; 10:4; Dan 10:6. [i] Rev 1:12-20; 4:2-4, 6-8.

by himself, as if he could not have begotten Christ by himself, and as if he could only deceive those who saw [Christ] by means of a trick.

Was it then only a created figure that the prophets invoked, worshipped, and saw seated upon the cherubim, and that they wished to reveal? In Numbers 12 God teaches most plainly that Moses's *face-to-face* vision [of the deity] was *not some riddle*,[a] nor a substitute likeness, nor a mask, nor any other artificial image, but was God himself, although his face remained hidden. Irenaeus, in book 4, chapters 15 and 17 [of *Against Heresies*], says that the representation and the figure of Christ were in the Word.[b] The sophists even deny that God could have revealed a vision in the form of an angel, since they claim that it is impossible for an angel to have a visible form.[c]

But we shall show that [what was seen in these visions] was an angel and Christ. More than an angel, it was the true face of God, as is clearly established in Exodus 33 and in the previously cited chapter, Numbers 12.[d] At that time the radiant face of Christ was the face of God. A face shining by its own power, *greater than the splendour of the sun*[e] — shining not with a created but with an uncreated light. And it was the very same face that once shone in an angel, when the angel was clothed in the light of the Word.[f]

It is true that, because of sin, there was a kind of cloud or veiled darkness in visions of God until [the time] of

---

[a] Num 12:8. [b] The chapter numbers cited by Servetus are from Erasmus's edition of Irenaeus. Servetus's chapter 15 is *Adversus haereses* 4.7.1 (PG 7 990C-991A). Chapter 17 is *Adversus haereses* 4.7.4 (PG 7 993A). [c] Peter Lombard, *Sententiae* 2.8 (PL 192 667-668), says, "Many Catholic writers agree ... that angels are incorporeal, and do not have bodies united with them," though he notes that other writers disagree. [d] Ex 33:11; Num 12:6-8. [e] Acts 26:13. See also Matt 17:2. [f] Rev 10:1.

Christ. The vision [of the divine] in former times was not as clear as it is now. At that time God dwelt in darkness, and concealed Christ to some degree. Hence Daniel saw the image of *the Son of man*, beneath a veil of clouds (Daniel 7).[a] Zechariah beheld the same thing **[95]** in the darkness of night (Zechariah 1).[b] Christ said that formerly *the prophets and kings longed to see* this face, *and could not see it* clearly (Matthew 13 and Luke 10).[c] This longing can be found as well in Psalms 23, 26, 66, 67, 79,[d] and in 2 Chronicles 9.[e] Indeed it is a teaching of the Law that those wishing to bless someone should say, *may the Lord show his face to you* (Numbers 6).[f] In chapter 8, Isaiah waits for this face.[g] For since the face he had seen in chapter 6 was veiled and hidden,[h] afterwards, in chapter 8, he says that this face may be revealed in the future. Habakkuk waits for the same face in chapters 2 and 3.[i]

Err, 87v

John reports that *these* and other things *were said by Isaiah* and other prophets *when they beheld the glory* of Christ (John 12).[j] Could it be that this glory of Christ in God was only a created apparition? This is what the Arians would say. The human Christ had his *glory* in God *before the world began* (John 17).[k] Isaiah plainly speaks about the divine glory and splendour of Christ, and he proves that Christ himself is *the splendour of glory*,[l] or the gloriousness shining forth in God (chapter 60 and 66),[m] just as Christ is called *the bright reflection of* [God's] *glory* in Hebrews 1.[n] Thus did his splendour radiate (Habakkuk 3).[o] The splendour that Paul saw glittering

Err, 87v

---

[a] Dan 7:13. [b] Zech 1:8. [c] Matt 13:17; Luke 10:24. [d] Ps 24:6; 27:7-9; 67:1; 68:3 (67:4 in Vulgate); 80:3, 7, 19. [e] 2 Chr 9:23: "All the kings of the earth sought the presence (or face) of Solomon," where Solomon is a type of Christ. [f] Num 6:25. [g] Isa 8:17.
[h] Isa 6:1-2. [i] Hab 2:3; 3:2. [j] John 12:41, referring to Isa 6:3. See also Ezek 1:28; 3:12. [k] John 17:5. [l] Heb 1:3. [m] Isa 60:1-3, 19-20; 66:18-19. [n] Heb 1:3. [o] Hab 3:4.

Err, 87v   in the face of Christ *surpassed the splendour of the sun* (Acts 9 and 26).[a] What was formerly called seeing the Lord *face to face*,[b] has been revealed to us in the gospel as the face of Christ. For the gospels and epistles teach that God was seen in Christ. Otherwise, [God] was not seen, and could not have been seen (John 1, 5, and 14, Hebrews 11, 1 John 4, and 1 Timothy 6).[c]

Jacob's vision <u>teaches</u> the same thing <u>very clearly</u>. He says that <u>in the night</u> he *saw Elohim face to face* (Genesis 32).[d] <u>[Jacob] shows that this face</u> was the face <u>and countenance</u> of the human being Christ when, in the following chapter, he says to his brother Esau, "*I have seen your face, as if I had seen <u>the face of Elohim</u>, the countenance of Elohim*, which I saw this night."[e] **[96]** Christ teaches the same thing by using the verb ["to see"] in the past tense: "*Whoever has seen me has seen the Father*,"[f] not a mask, not a fictitious spectre. The prophets of old saw the Word of God, as Irenaeus and Tertullian tell us.[g]

Err, 88r

Err, 88r   God *has revealed his Word at the proper time*.[h] The grace which now has been openly granted to us, was given to us through Christ *before the world began*.[i] For, *before the world began*, God contained in himself the pattern of Jesus Christ — his substance, his light, and his spirit — the grace which he was going to give to us through [Christ]. Christ himself, the Word itself, <u>is</u> made manifest, as Peter and John tell us (1 Peter 1 and 1 John 1).[j] For Christ was previously foreshadowed in the Word, within darkness and clouds. The Word represented Christ, and he who was represented then was the face of God. Paul says that the human being Christ was an εικονα (*eikon*, image),

---

[a] Acts 9:3; 26:13.   [b] For example: Gen 32:30 (Jacob); Ex 33:11, Num 12:8, Deut 34:10 (Moses); Deut 5:4 (all Israel).   [c] John 1:18; 5:36-39; 14:6; Heb 11:1-3; 1 John 4:12; 1 Tim 6:16.   [d] Gen 32:30.
[e] Gen 33:10.   [f] John 14:9.   [g] Irenaeus, *Adversus haereses* 4.20.8 (PG 7 1037C-1038B). Tertullian, *Adversus Praxean* 14 (PL 2 170C-172B).
[h] Titus 1:3.   [i] Titus 1:2.   [j] 1 Peter 1:20; 1 John 1:1-3.

the true *likeness of* the invisible *God*, and that *God's glory was known in the face of Jesus Christ* (2 Corinthians 4).ᵃ [This face] is recognized, I say, because the glorious face of Christ was shining forth in God. Note Paul's words: when the face of Christ is seen, God can be seen in his glory. That very [face] is "*the glory which I had with you before the world came to be*" (John 17).ᵇ

Err, 88v

Consider this: it is not the deity but the human being who seeks to be glorified according to that glory, which he formerly had with God. This man was then already glorious in God, and desired by all, not an apparition created in God. It was his face that Moses and the prophets desired to see. *They saw* him in another way *and rejoiced*, as Christ says of Abraham (John 8).ᶜ They saw his back, but not his face (Exodus 33).ᵈ To see him from behind is like seeing him with his face covered. Terror overwhelmed them when they turned their eyes to this face, and they *feared* that they *were going to die* (Exodus 3 and 20 and Judges 13).ᵉ Because of Adam's sin the face of God was hidden, and before it stood *a flaming sword* (Genesis 3).ᶠ He who had previously been visible to Adam afterwards became invisible. Sin caused *the face of God to be hidden, the cloud* of his *anger* having been thrown over it (Isaiah 59 and Lamentations 3).ᵍ

Err, 88v

Under the Law, visions [of God] were terrifying, alarming, **[97]** and frightening, and made Moses and Elijah hide their faces (Exodus 3 and 1 Kings 19).ʰ But now that these terrifying visions have been taken away, Christ speaks graciously to us (Hebrews 11).ⁱ At one time God showed himself to us in anger, but now he is reconciled to us through Christ. The veil of the inner [sanctuary of the divine] oracle, like the veil on the face

---

ᵃ 2 Cor 4:4, 6.   ᵇ John 17:5.   ᶜ John 8:56.   ᵈ Ex 33:20-23.
ᵉ Ex 3:6; 20:19; Judg 13:22.   ᶠ Gen 3:24.   ᵍ Isa 59:2; Lam 3:43-44.
ʰ Ex 3:6; 1 Kg 19:11-13.   ⁱ Heb 11:39-40.

of Moses,ᵃ meant that the glory of God, and the true pathway of the saints, was not yet revealed (Hebrews 9).ᵇ But now, the temple curtain having been torn,ᶜ we are allowed to gaze upon the *unveiled face* of the Holy of Holies, that is, to see the celestial face of Christ, which to [the Hebrews] was veiled (2 Corinthians 3 and 4).ᵈ For us there is no other covering than the flesh of Christ which contains in substantial form the entire deity of the Father (Hebrews 10 and Colossians 2).ᵉ That flesh, which was torn like a veil by the Jews in the Passion, has revealed at the resurrection his true divinity and celestial glory. Thus Moses beheld the veiled features of Christ's face, but not his true face.

They longed, said Christ, *to see what you see, and did not see it.*ᶠ *The light gleamed in the darkness, and the darkness did not overwhelm it* (John 1).ᵍ *He made the darkness around him his hiding place* (Psalm 17 and 2 Samuel 22).ʰ In those days God *dwelt in darkness* (2 Chronicles 5 and 6).ⁱ For that reason when John says *the darkness did not overwhelm it*, he indicates that they had all been in darkness, since that glorious face, shining in the darkness, was hidden from them. <u>In these passages</u>, every human nature who, because of Adam's sin, is deserving of the darkness of hell, is included in the word "darkness." In the same vein, Luke 1 says, *to bring light to those [who sit] in darkness*. And Matthew 4: *The people who were sitting in darkness have seen a great light.*ʲ Christ himself says in John 12, "*I have come as a light into the world, so that everyone who sees and believes in me, may not remain in darkness.*"ᵏ The face of God, hidden to [those in darkness], was revealed to us. For

Err, 88v-89r

ᵃ 2 Cor 3:7, 13.   ᵇ Heb 9:6-15.   ᶜ Matt 27:51; Mark 15:38; Luke 23:45.   ᵈ 2 Cor 3:14-16; 4:3-6.   ᵉ Heb 10:20; Col 2:9.   ᶠ Matt 13:17; Luke 10:24.   ᵍ John 1:5.   ʰ Ps 18:11; 2 Sam 22:12.   ⁱ 2 Chr 5:13-14; 6:1.   ʲ Luke 1:79; Matt 4:16, quoting Isa 9:2.   ᵏ John 12:46.

it was truly said, *God was manifested in the flesh* (1 Timothy 3).[a] Isaiah says much the same thing, calling God hidden, in chapter 45.[b] For the countenance of Christ lay hidden within the shadow of the Father.

Then Christ *dwelt in the hiding-place of the Most High,* and *in the shadow* **[98]** *of the Almighty* (Psalm 90).[c] *There was the hiding-place of his strength* (Habakkuk 3).[d] And Deuteronomy 33 is in agreement with this.[e] For at the time when the Law was handed down there was a concealment, when the countenance of the one who was speaking was not seen.[f] Nevertheless, he has now been clearly shown to us. For it was foretold: *the glory of the Lord shall be revealed, and all flesh shall see it.*[g] [*Thus says the Lord God:*] *"It is I who was speaking, here I am."*[h] And *they shall see eye to eye.*[i]

Err, 89v

Err, 95r

Christ, the God of Israel, was previously hidden, but *afterward was seen upon earth, and lived among human beings* (Baruch 3).[j] Baruch is speaking about the *Wisdom of God,* the visible Word that *appeared on earth, dwelling among human beings,* in the days of the patriarchs and Moses. There was a divine light and a human face, just as in the light of your mind you can see a human face. This is the light of God's glory, which was the light of the Word. The Word is the shining and now visible splendour of *the face of Christ,* as Paul teaches in 2 Corinthians 3 and 4.[k] David taught the same thing, saying *the light of the countenance of Elohim,* that is, the light of the face of Christ (Psalms 4, 43, 66, 88 and 89).[l] Who could be so unfamiliar with the true meaning [of these passages] as to say, like the sophists, that all of the light and glory of Christ was a deceptive mask, a conjurer's trick, and an

---

[a] 1 Tim 3:16. [b] Isa 45:15. [c] Ps 91:1. [d] Hab 3:4. [e] Deut 33:12 and 33:27 speak of God as a shelter or refuge. [f] See Ex 33:20-23. [g] Isa 40:5. [h] Isa 52:6. [i] Isa 52:8. [j] Baruch 3:37. [k] 2 Cor 3:18; 4:6. [l] Ps 4:6; 44:3; 67:1; 89:15; 90:8.

The Restoration of Christianity

imposture? If [that light and glory] was merely a created apparition, and that [apparition] was what was revealed, it then follows that Christ was an apparition.

Err, 89r

If you wish to learn more about the glory of Christ, rise up to the cherubim and seraphim, and contemplate Ezekiel's [vision of] wheels and creatures.[a] For in all of them the image of Jesus Christ, which is itself the glory of God, is represented as a person and shines out in substance. Above the wheels and animals, Ezekiel saw Christ, a vision of *the glory of the Lord*.[b] The same creatures were seen, and the same *sound of many waters* [was heard] in Ezekiel as in the Apocalypse of John.[c] The reference to Christ is always shown by these things.

Err, 89r

The angels were heralds of the glory of Christ, as shown by their words, repeated in Isaiah 6, Luke 2 and Revelation 4.[d] The angels, with their human faces, foreshadowed Christ. When Christ was seen in an angel, the messenger of the Father was shown in advance. **[99]** The true messenger who was to come, the *angel of great counsel*,[1] was prefigured there. After Adam's sin, God placed the cherubim[e] before the oracle of the face of Christ. In the same way the cherubim seen in heaven veiled, or hid, both the face of the oracle and their own faces.[2] The pattern for [the cherubim] was revealed to Moses for the construction of the tabernacle, and was also shown to Solomon, so that he might make golden cherubim.[f]

A cherub is generally said to be an eminent figure.[3] The figure is understood by its eminence to be human, and wings add further angelic excellence. According to Hebrew etymology, with the first letter [כ] being considered servile,

---

[a] Ezek 1:5-14 (creatures); 1:15-21 (wheels).   [b] "The glory of the Lord" occurs several times in Ezekiel: see Ezek 1:28; 3:12, 23; 10:4, 18; 11:23; 43:4, 5.   [c] Rev 4:6-8 (creatures); Rev 1:15; 14:2; 19:6 (sound of waters). Cf. Ezek 1:5-14 (creatures); 43:2 (sound of waters).
[d] Isa 6:2-3; Luke 2:13-14; Rev 4:8.   [e] Gen 3:24.   [f] Ex 25:18-22; 1 Kg 6:23-28.

כרובים (cherubim) are said to be like parties to a lawsuit or like the great and illustrious.[4] In the same way a king is called *a mighty cherub*.[a] The cherubim were shown in the heavens, whenever there was strife [on earth], and their fiery countenances demonstrated that God had become angry. The *wrath* of God *blazed like fire*.[b] For this reason the seraphim are also called fiery, aflame, and burning.[c] These cherubim, like the seraphim seen by Isaiah, were a kind of hidden flame in the likeness of a human being, veiling and shadowing their faces with their wings.[d] They did this not only because it was not granted to the angels to behold the divine splendour without Christ, but also to prevent the blazing light of the face of Christ from being seen by the Jews of that time.

Moses saw in God the image and pattern of Christ, as depicted in Exodus 25, Acts 7, and Hebrews 8.[e] For the pattern that he saw there, which is described in Exodus 25 and mentioned in the preceding chapter,[f] is Elohim, that is, Christ. David saw the same image of Christ above the cherubim (2 Samuel 22).[g] He *gave to his son Solomon this pattern* and likeness (1 Chronicles 28).[h] He calls it the pattern and likeness *of all the things which he* had seen *in his spirit*.[i] And [David] says, *he made me understand all the works of that pattern*. And he says, *all these things were written by the hand of God*.[j] But what can more properly be said to be written by the hand of God, than that which was expressed and given a [visible] shape in himself?

Err, 89r-v

To [the Hebrews of that time], however, [Christ] was a figure behind a veil. *The wings of the cherubim concealed* and *overshadowed the oracle* of Christ himself (Exodus 25

Err, 89v

---

[a] Ezek 28:14.   [b] Ps 89:46. See also Isa 9:19; Ezek 22:21, 31.
[c] In Num 21:6-8 and Deut 8:15, a seraph is a fiery serpent.
[d] Isa 6:2.   [e] Ex 25 (entire chapter); referenced in Acts 7:44, Heb 8:5.   [f] Ex 24:9-11.   [g] 2 Sam 22:11.   [h] 1 Chr 28:11-19.
[i] 1 Chr 28:12.   [j] 1 Chr 28:19.

Err, 89v   and Hebrews 9).ᵃ Even though this writing and shadowing **[100]** present a picture of a temple made of stone, nevertheless the true temple is the body of Christ (John 2).ᵇ The comparison of that pattern to Christ is made clear in Hebrews 9.ᶜ In summary, *all things* that are in the Law *are a foreshadowing of the body of Christ*, as the apostle to the Colossians and the Hebrews teaches.ᵈ For the Jews every [contact with the divine] took place through angels, and was a foreshadowing of Christ. Christ was prefigured by the angels.

Err, 89v   The angels are often called gods by the Jews, although what they call gods are not the invisible <u>gods</u> of the tritheists,⁵ but <u>are actually</u> God and Christ (1 Corinthians 8).ᵉ The glory of God is seated on the cherubim, which means that Jesus Christ is superior to the angels. For he is *the Lord of glory* and *sits on his glorious throne* (1 Corinthians 2 and Matthew 25).ᶠ And he *will come with* splendour, *majesty*, and *glory* (Mark 8 and Matthew 16).ᵍ The glory and majesty of the Lord, which is described in Exodus 40,ʰ is the very thing that, departing from the cherub and coming to Christ, is said to have gone up from the cherub to a much loftier place (Ezekiel 9).ⁱ Set above the heads of the cherubim was the throne, the seat of Christ, encircled [by a rainbow] (Ezekiel 1 and 10).ʲ For Christ is far superior to the angels.

Err, 67r   In the letter to the Hebrews, Christ is compared to the angels so that the Jews, to whom the angels appeared as God, might thereby be able to understand that Christ, who was prefigured in the Law as superior to the angels, is the true God above the angels.ᵏ The divinity of the

---

ᵃ Ex 25:20; Heb 9:5.   ᵇ John 2:19-22.   ᶜ Heb 9:11-28.   ᵈ Col 2:17; Heb 8:5.   ᵉ 1 Cor 8:4-6.   ᶠ 1 Cor 2:8; Matt 25:31.   ᵍ Mark 8:38; Matt 16:27.   ʰ Ex 40:34-35.   ⁱ The glory of the Lord departs from the temple and rises above the cherubim in Ezek 9:3; 10:4, 18.   ʲ Ezek 1:26-28; 10:1. See also Rev 4:2-4.   ᵏ Heb 1:1-4.

Book 3

angels had only a ministerial character, in the shadow <u>and</u> prefiguration of the true deity of Christ. This is why Paul calls it superstition when anyone, under the pretext of that divinity, introduces a religion of angels (Colossians 2).[a] For that reason, John says that we should avoid all images, even though they might possess some appearance of deity. Christ alone *is the true God* (1 John 5).[b] *There is no other name under heaven by which we are to be saved* (Acts 4).[c] The truth of Christ shining forth for us casts out the shadows. *The glory of the Lord*, which appeared so often by means of angels, in the cherubim and in the cloud,[d] is now *revealed* in the face of Christ (Isaiah 40 and 46).[e]

Err, 89v-90r

When we know Christ **[101]**, because we turn our eyes to him, *we all see* in him *the glory of God with his face unveiled* (Isaiah 66 and Habakkuk 2).[f] We recognize that [*glory*] *in the face of Jesus Christ*,[g] which once, among the Jews, was foreshadowed by angels. The Jews saw an angel in God, and God in an angel; we see Christ in God and God in Christ. They saw *an angel ordaining* all things according to the Law, and, throughout the Law, speaking as God (Acts 7, Hebrews 2, and Galatians 3).[h] An angel is called the face of God (Exodus 33).[6] Having seen an angel, Jacob is said to have seen the face of God (Genesis 32).[i] [The place was called] Peniel [the face of El] because the face and person of Christ were foreshadowed there by an angel. In those days, the name of God, whose dwelling place was said to be among the cherubim,[j] dwelt among the angels in the person of Christ. Exodus 23 says that the name of

Err, 89v

Err, 90r

---

[a] Col 2:18. [b] 1 John 5:20. [c] Acts 4:12. [d] "The glory of the Lord" appears about 30 times in the Old Testament, including: Ex 16:10; 24:16; 40:34-35; Num 16:42; 1 Kg 8:11; 2 Chr 5:13-14 (the glory of the Lord appears in the cloud); Ezek 9:3; 10:4, 18 (the glory of the Lord rises above the cherubim). [e] Isa 40:5, 46:13. [f] Isa 66:18-19; Hab 2:14. See also 2 Cor 3:18. [g] 2 Cor 4:6. [h] Acts 7:53; Heb 2:2; Gal 3:19. [i] Gen 32:30. [j] 1 Chr 13:6; 2 Sam 6:2.

God dwelt in an angel.^a At that time it dwelt in shadow, but now it dwells in Christ through his body (Colossians 2).^b The angel prefiguring Christ took on the person of God, and was called God; as *the angel said* to Jacob, *I am the God of Bethel* (Genesis 31).^c An angel said to Moses, *I am the God of your fathers* (Exodus 3).^d And an angel in the person of God spoke and appeared to Abraham⁷ (Genesis 18 and 22) and to Hagar (Genesis 16 and 21).^e

Err, 61r

Thus Origen says, in his eighth homily on Genesis, based on chapter 22: "I believe that just as Christ appeared among us humans as a human being, so also he appeared among angels as an angel."^f What Origen said is true, for angelic substance was a sharer in the light of the Word, and in the Word the person of Christ was assumed by an angel. The angel about whom Ezekiel speaks in chapter 43 was also Christ: *A man standing next to me said to me, "The inner court is the place of my throne, the place of the soles of my feet, where I will dwell in the midst of the children of Israel forever."*^g <u>That man</u> was a prefiguration of Christ, by which an angel made himself both God and a human being, just as Christ is both God and human, <u>and dwells in the inner court of our heart.</u>

<u>In those days</u> angels with human faces allowed themselves to be worshipped (Numbers 22 and Joshua 5).^h Now, however, **[102]** since Christ, whom the angels prefigured, is revealed, they worship him and are our *fellow servants* (Revelation 19 and 22).ⁱ At one time God was worshipped

---

^a Ex 23:20-22. ^b Col 2:17. ^c Gen 31:13. ^d Ex 3:6, 15.
^e Gen 18:1-15 (angel or angels predict the birth of Isaac); Gen 22:11-18 (angel tells Abraham not to sacrifice Isaac); Gen 16:7-13 (angel predicts the birth of Hagar's son Ishmael); Gen 21:17-18 (angel predicts future greatness of Ishmael). ^f Origen, *In Geneseos*, homilia 8 (PG 12 208A). ^g Ezek 43:6-7. ^h Num 22:31 (Balaam bows his head and falls on his face before the angel); Josh 5:13-15 (Joshua falls on his face and worships "the commander of the Lord's army").
ⁱ Rev 19:10; 22:9.

in the form of an angel, but now he is truly worshipped in Christ alone. When God was worshipped in the form of angels, they were a foreshadowing of Christ. Just as when the Jews heard the voice of an angel, they were hearing the voice of God (Exodus 23),^a so also for us [Christians], the voice of Christ is the voice of God (Acts 12).^b Christ *speaks the words of* the Father (John 3).^c Just as, when we see [Christ, the Father is seen,] so when we hear [Christ], the Father is heard (John 14).^d The bread of Christ's body is the bread of God (John 6) and his blood is the blood of God (Acts 20).^e We are *justified through Christ*^f by God's justice, and are made *the body and members of Christ*.^g We are the congregation of God.

Err, 90v-91r

The prefiguration of the person of Christ in the Word becomes abundantly clear, because humankind is said to be made *in the image and likeness*^h of God — <u>in the form and shape of God, which is the meaning of the Hebrew words</u>. For in Genesis 1 [God] says, *in our image* and *in our likeness*, that is, according to the form and shape of that image, shared by God, the Word, and the angels. God says "our," using the plural, and "image," not "images," using the singular. For there was only one <u>personal</u> image or face, <u>which was</u> the person of Christ in God, also shared by the angels.

You may remember that I said earlier that it is the property of speech and wisdom to represent something.ⁱ The Word was the representation of Christ. *The Word*, as a person, *was with God and was* itself *God*.^j <u>The angels, sharing in the light of the Word, were assigned the task of shaping things</u>. Therefore Jesus Christ himself is the true pattern and the original image, or prototype. In the begin-

---

^a Ex 23:20-22. ^b Acts 12:7-11. ^c John 3:34. ^d John 14:9.
^e John 6:51-57; Acts 20:28. ^f Gal 2:17. ^g 1 Cor 12:27. ^h Gen 1:26. ⁱ *Restoration*, 47 (book 2). ^j John 1:1.

ning we were created in his image. So also in baptism we are born anew and regenerated <u>in his image</u>. I am speaking of the real, visible image in the inner self, as I shall show later. But for now, our discussion concerns the external image [of God].

Based on <u>the clearest</u> scriptural references, the ancient Hebrews <u>maintained that</u> a visible image <u>was seen</u> in God <u>himself</u>. <u>This was taught by</u> Philo, Eusebius, Jerome,[8] **[103]** Petrus Alfonsi,[a] Paul of Burgos,[b] and <u>many</u> other Jews who converted to Christ. The earliest Christians maintained the same thing, as can be seen in Irenaeus and Tertullian, who both say that there was a human form and shape in the Word itself.[c] This was accepted even before Moses, and among foreigners, as Job and his companions teach. In the book's final chapter, Job saw the form of God with his mortal eyes: "*I heard of you with the hearing of my ear, but now my eye <u>sees</u> you.*"[d] <u>What is the meaning of "now my eye sees you"? It means, as Isaiah says in chapter 6, I have seen God the king with my own eyes.</u>[e] <u>And in the last chapter of 1 Kings [the prophet] Michaiah says, *I saw Jehovah sitting on his throne.*</u>[f]

On the subject [of the image of God], consider what Eusebius Pamphilus says in book 5 of *Proof of the Gospel* and book 7 of *Preparation for the Gospel*. The body of

---

[a] Petrus Alfonsi, *Dialogi* 1 (PL 157 541B-543C). Petrus Alfonsi (né Moses Sephardi) converted to Christianity in 1106. He was a physician to King Alfonso VI of Castile and for a time was court physician to Henry I of England. He was also an astronomer and translator of works from Arabic to Latin.   [b] Paul of Burgos, *Dialogus* [*Scrutinium scripturarum*] 1.10.7. Paul of Burgos (c.1351-1435, né Solomon ha-Levi) was a rabbi of Burgos, converted to Christianity c.1390. He studied theology at the University of Paris. He was bishop of Cartagena and archbishop of Burgos.   [c] Irenaeus, *Adversus haereses* 4.7.4 (PG 7 992B). Tertullian, *Adversus Praxean* 14-16 (PL 2 170C-176A).
[d] Job 42:5.   [e] Isa 6:5.   [f] 1 Kg 22:19.

Book 3

Adam was formed in the image of God before the soul was breathed into him. Therefore it was the image of a body.[a] In terms of appearance, a man was first formed in the image of God, then a woman was formed. Paul teaches this in 1 Corinthians 11, <u>where he speaks about the image of the appearance [and glory of God]</u>.[b] The image and likeness of the first human being, formed in the image of God, contains the image and likeness of both the soul and the body.

Although, morally speaking, the first man is said to be the image of God in innocence and righteousness; and although the soul, in its likeness to God, is a kind of intelligent mind, nevertheless, in [the account of] the formation of humanity, [the words] צלם (*tselem*, image) and דמות (*demuth*, likeness) refer to the image of the whole [human being], even the visible shape, <u>as the meaning of these [Hebrew] words clearly indicates</u>. Furthermore, Christ himself, in his entirety, is called the likeness and shape of God. The meaning of *tselem* is shown in Daniel, <u>chapter 3</u>, where it is said of Nebuchadnezzar that the *tselem*, that is, *the form, of his countenance was changed*.[c] Also, Psalm 72 (Psalm 73 according to the Hebrew numbering): *You will despise their tsalmam*,[d] that is, their faces or countenances. This clearly shows that *tselem* refers to external form. *Tselem* is also used of the form and corporeal image of a statue in Numbers 33, 2 Kings 11, and many other places.[e] Ezekiel 1 and 8 and Isaiah 40 show the same thing about [the Hebrew word] *demuth*.[f] The pattern, according to which **[104]** humankind was first formed, is *demuth*,[g] which

Err, 91v

---

[a] Eusebius, *Demonstratio evangelica* 5.7 (PG 22 379C-D); *Praeparatio evangelica* 7.17 (PG 21 558B-559A).   [b] 1 Cor 11:7-8, referring to Gen 2:21-23.   [c] Dan 3:19.   [d] Ps 73:20. *Tsalmam* צלמם is the plural of *tselem* צלם. It is usually translated as "images."   [e] Num 33:52; 2 Kg 11:18. See also 2 Chr 23:17; Ezek 16:17; Amos 5:26; Dan 2:31-35; etc.   [f] Ezek 1:5, 10, 13, 16, 22, 26, 28; 8:2; Isa 40:18.   [g] Gen 1:26.

Ezekiel saw [in his vision]. <u>Could it be that *demuth* was a demonic creature in whose image man was made?</u> By means of the true form and shape of Christ, which was in God, humanity was made to resemble God, even in the body; so much so that even a dead body is said to be in the image of God. Using these same words, *tselem* and *demuth*, [it is said that] Adam fathered children *in his own image and likeness*, <u>just as he himself was formed *in the image and likeness* of God</u> (Genesis 5)[a] — <u>hence there was a</u> similarity of form.

Irenaeus and Tertullian teach that the <u>very</u> body of Adam was formed in the image <u>and likeness</u> of God.[b] After the era of the ancient Hebrews, in the time of the first Christians, Philo taught the same thing in book 1 of *Questions on Genesis*, which Eusebius Pamphilus cites in book 7 of *Preparation for the Gospel*. "Nothing mortal," he says, "can be compared to the supreme Father as his image, but [the image] is conveyed by means of the Word, as if by <u>a kind of intermediary God</u>."[c] In his book *On Agriculture*, Philo also says, "The human soul was made and shaped according to the <u>ideal form and</u> image of the first, archetypal Word."[d] <u>He also teaches about the form of the soul and the image of the face in his book *Women Should Not Behave Shamelessly*.</u>[9] <u>And in his book *On the World*, he says that there is an old saying that divinity, which made humankind in its own image, frequently appeared in human form.</u>[10] Therefore, in terms of both his body and his soul, Adam was made according to the pattern, form, shape, and image of Christ.

---

[a] Gen 5:3; see Gen 1:26.   [b] Irenaeus, *Adversus haereses* 5.1.3, 5.15.4, 5.16.1 (PG 7 1123A-B, 1166B-C, 1167A-B). Tertullian, *Adversus Praxean* 12 (PL 2 167C-168C).   [c] Eusebius, *Praeparatio evangelica* 7.13 (PG 21 546 B-C), quoting Philo, *Questions on Genesis* 2.62 (not book 1). The incorrect citation came from Eusebius.   [d] Eusebius, *Praeparatio evangelica* 7.18 (PG 21 559B-D), paraphrase of Philo, *On Planting* (*De plantatione*) 1.5.20 (often considered book 2 of *On Agriculture*).

But although "let us make" [humankind] and "our" [image]^a could be understood literally to refer to angels—because, <u>in a certain sense, even</u> angels could contain within themselves the ideal form of humanity—nevertheless, in the mystery [of the Word], Christ is always understood to be foreshadowed by angels.[11] [In the Old Testament, angels] are spoken of in the person of Christ, just as more excellent qualities are ascribed to David and Solomon than could reasonably belong to them. Because the mystery is implicitly understood, things may be said about them that are not actually due to them.^b

In Exodus 33, "*My face shall go before you,*"^c in its literal sense, is said about an angel,^d **[105]** although the true face is Christ, who was the Son, the companion of the Israelites on their journey (1 Corinthians 10).^e Indeed, he who said, "*Let us make humankind [in our image and likeness]*" was Christ, that is to say, Elohim, the person of the Word, who was the person of God. And [Christ] spoke to the angels, just as in numerous places [in the Old Testament], the angels also spoke as gods. To the angels he said, "*Behold Adam who is as one of us.*"^f And also, "*Let us go down,*" etc.^g In the Law all things took place through the agency of angels, and these angels were called gods. Hence some have taught that there are other gods above the gods of the Old Testament.^h From this derives the heresy of Simon Magus, Cerdo, Marcion, and others,ⁱ who denied that the God of the Law is the father of Jesus

Err, 91r

---

^a Gen 1:26.   ^b See *Restoration*, 60 (book 2).   ^c Ex 33:14. Usually translated as "My presence will go with you," but rendered as *facies mea* ("my face") in both the Vulgate and Pagnini.   ^d That is, the word *Elohim* is used. See A.R3.11.   ^e 1 Cor 10:1-4.   ^f Gen 3:22.   ^g Gen 11:7. From the story of the Tower of Babel: "Let us go down and there confuse their language, that they may not understand one another's speech."   ^h "Gods," not God, because *Elohim* is plural.
ⁱ On Simon: Irenaeus, *Adversus haereses* 1.23.1-4 (PG 7 670B-673A). On Cerdo and Marcion: Irenaeus, *Adversus haereses* 1.27.1-2 (PG 7 687B-688B).

Christ, because they perversely understood the God of the Law to be an angel.¹²

Others have imagined that God himself is corporeal by nature, since inherent corporeal forms are attributed to him throughout the Law. In this regard, Onkelos the Chaldean, in his version [of the Torah], and Rabbi Moses [Maimonides] the Egyptian in his *Guide for the Perplexed*,ᵃ contort themselves in various ways in order to remove these [corporeal] forms from God. But all of these things are accepted by us [Christians]. And all this perplexity is easily removed by Christ. For he himself is <u>truly</u> the face, image, likeness, and form of God, containing in himself real corporeal forms. He himself is God of gods and God of the angels. It should be noted that in this regard an artful method has arisen using a variety of ways of interpreting the scriptures. It is something of a mystery that in the Old Testament, unlike the New, scripture assigns such [corporeal forms] to God. It is significant that in the Old Testament <u>you</u> often read about God's hands, eyes, face, and feet being seen by corporeal eyes. Nothing of this sort can be found in the New Testament. Indeed the opposite [is found]: *God is spirit.*ᵇ

Err, 91v

The reason for this is <u>obvious</u>. [In Old Testament times] the person of Christ was represented as being with God. There was then no real distinction between the Father and the Son. These corporeal forms, which are now in the Son, <u>were then</u> attributed to God himself. As a result, angels in the form of God and angels in the form of Christ were interchangeable in [Old Testament] writings. If this was Cyprian's understanding, he rightly made use of this ancient truth, when he said that **[106]** [in the Old Testament] God, an angel, and Christ were

Err, 92r

ᵃ Maimonides, *Guide for the Perplexed* 1.27, citing *Targum Onkelos* (Aramaic translation of the Torah).   ᵇ John 4:24.

spoken of as the same being. For in book 2 of *Against the Jews* he shows that in many [passages of scripture], the angel who spoke to Abraham and others, and was seen by them, was also God and Christ.[a] All of this <u>can actually be gathered from a single passage</u>: Exodus, chapter 3. For it was Christ who said *"I will be who I will be,"*[b] when the angel appeared and spoke as the voice of God.[c] Paul makes the same observation in Galatians 3: *The Law* was given from God *by angels through the hand of a mediator.*[d] The glory of Jesus Christ is so great that his person was prefigured in God, angels, human beings, a lamb, a calf, a serpent, a tree, a rock, and other things. If these great mysteries of Christ had been understood in former times, no one would ever have claimed that angels created the world and that they were the gods of the Old Testament.[e] For in their ministry they acted as a foreshadowing of Christ, not only at creation, but in other events that followed later.

Err, 92r

Others made God and the ideal form two separate principles, although the ideal form itself was the appearance of the Word, as well as the divine form. It is a wonderful concept: the wonder-working Word.[13] God created by means of the Word, and the person of Christ was the one creating. God created through the Word, creating through his very self, that is, through a manifestation of himself produced by his utterance. God manifested himself in creation and shared himself with

Err, 92r

---

[a] Cyprian, *Adversus Iudaeos* 2.5 (PL 4 699C-700B).   [b] Ex 3:14 (Pagnini). Often translated in the present tense, as in the Vulgate: "I am who I am." However, the future tense used by Pagnini is probably a more accurate rendering of the Hebrew.   [c] In the story of Moses and the burning bush (Ex 3:1-4:17), the terms Angel of the Lord, God (Elohim), and Lord (Yahweh) are used interchangeably.   [d] Gal 3:19.
[e] See Irenaeus, *Adversus haereses* 1.24.4 (PG 7 676B); Isidore, *Etymologiae* 8.5.3, 8.5.12-13 (PL 82 298B, 299B).

his creatures, so that, prior to sinning, Adam innocently gazed upon the form of God and received a pure spirit. After [the first] sin, the face of God was hidden from humankind behind an embroidered veil, which was not to be opened until the coming of Christ.[14]

Under the Law, Christ did not allow himself to be clearly seen. He was only visible as if *through a latticed window* (Proverbs 7 and Song of Solomon 2).[a] Zechariah chapter 3 teaches that the embroidery <u>of the veil of Christ is to be opened</u> for us.[15] For there, God says about Christ, "*I am engraving his inscription; I am uncovering what has been carved.*"[b] The Hebrew verb פתח (*patach*) literally means to carve, as with a sharp tool, in order to uncover and expose a hidden figure. Thus God uncovered himself by showing us Christ. The Chaldean translator [in his Aramaic rendering] translates *patach* in <u>nearly</u> the same way: to reveal or **[107]** uncover the face of Christ.[c] For <u>there</u> the Targum Jonathan has הא אנא גלי חזייתהא[d] (*ha aena gele chezijathaha*), that is, "Behold, I reveal, or <u>I</u> uncover, a vision of [Christ]."[16]

Err, 113v

Err, 113v-114r

To briefly summarize, in their narratives and prophecies about Christ, both the Law and the Prophets very often include the words face, image, hidden, concealed, habitation, and shelter.[e] Because all these things were written about him in *the Law and all the Prophets* (<u>as Christ says in Luke 24 and Matthew 11</u>),[f] the spirit of the Lord artfully carved them in engraved letters, so that, beneath the silver engraving, the golden Word would lie

---

[a] Prov 7:6; Song of Sol 2:9. [b] Two different translations of Zech 3:9: first Pagnini, then Sebastian Münster's *Hebraica Biblia*. [c] Targum Jonathan (Zech 3:9). [d] In the 1553 printing of *Restoration*, the first letter of חזייתהא is incorrect – it is פ instead of ה. It is correct in *Errors*, 113v. [e] In Latin these words are rhyming pairs: *faciem, imaginem; reconditum, absconditum; habitaculum, umbraculum.* [f] Luke 24:27, 44; Matt 11:13.

Book 3

hidden. In God's mysterious plan, all these things were foreshadowed, as a kind of cover, by historical and ritual types, just as Christ himself was foreshadowed in God. By analogy to the higher mysteries, there was, in the lesser mysteries of the Law, a foreshadowing prefiguring Christ. Therefore the [divine] plan of foreshadowing came from [heaven] above to [the world] below. In God there was a shining Word; it shone, however, in darkness and shadow.

Err, 114r

<u>In the beginning</u> [the Word] was like the shadow of Christ, not only because it prefigured Christ, but also because diminished light is called shadow. It was <u>like</u> diminished light <u>because of Adam's sin, and</u> because [the light] did not shine for <u>the Jews</u> as it does for us. The patriarchs spoke of the Word as if it were corporeal. For there was a substance shining in the cloud with <u>the likeness of a corporeal being,</u>[a] <u>although there was no corporeal matter in it</u>. You will <u>readily</u> comprehend the mode of divinity in the cloud, as well as in the heavenly dew <u>of the begetting of Christ</u>, when you have learned about the universal and omniform essence of God, in the next book.[b]

If you are able to believe that God could truly beget out of himself a human son, <u>then</u> you will have no difficulty in believing <u>these things</u>. Thus it is now time for a plain and simple consideration of Jesus Christ in God the Father. In the preaching of Paul and of the other apostles, we hear of nothing but the *one God, who is the Father, and Jesus Christ* his son.[c] You must keep in mind all the distinctions, and the various ways of speaking, to know whether it is the Word or the Son that is being discussed. For these words mean different things. **[108]** If you can point out to me any place [in scripture] showing that the Word was ever called the Son, I will admit defeat.

Err, 93v

---

[a] For example, Ex 13:21-22; 14:19; 33:9-10; Num 12:5; Deut 31:15.
[b] *Restoration*, 128-133 (book 4).   [c] 1 Cor 8:6.

Therefore I will say, along with the scriptures, that what was once the Word is now the Son. And the person of the Son was once in the Word.

The person of the Son was correctly spoken of by the ancients. However, the sophists, not understanding this, distorted "persons" to mean something different. Thus they have made up metaphysical, incorporeal, <u>and</u> invisible persons – <u>or what are</u> foolishly <u>called</u> persons. But their abuse of words is as nothing compared to their abuse of God himself, whom they <u>carved up</u>, mutilated, and tore to pieces <u>in different ways</u>. Listen instead to what scripture teaches about persons, so that you might realize [the extent of] their abuse.

Err, 36v

The <u>outward</u> appearance, face, and presentation of a human being is <u>always</u> called a "person," in scripture <u>and elsewhere</u>, as when we say, "this person is beautiful." This is the way "person" is generally understood in Romans 2, Colossians 3, Acts 10, and 1 Peter 1: *God is no respecter of persons,*[a] that is, he has no regard for outward differences, such as whether someone is *male or female, slave or free, Jew or Greek,*[b] rich or poor. This idea is advocated in 1 Samuel 17, Leviticus 19, Deuteronomy 1, and James 2, where we are taught *not to take into consideration the person of the poor or the countenance of the mighty.*[c] See also 2 Corinthians 1, 2, 3, 4, 8, 10, and 11.[d] Outside of scripture, the meaning of the word προσωπον (*prosopon*, person) in Greek, or of *persona* in Latin, is so well known, that some evil demon must have instigated all of the tritheists to foist upon us these [three] invented invisible beings in place of persons.

---

[a] Rom 2:11; Col 3:25; Acts 10:34; 1 Pet 1:17 — all passages dealing with the idea that God shows no partiality or, as the KJV has it, "God is no respecter of persons."   [b] Gal 3:28. See also 1 Cor 12:13, Col 3:11.   [c] Lev 19:15. Similar ideas are expressed in Deut 1:17; 1 Sam 16:7 (not 1 Sam 17); James 2:1-7.   [d] 2 Cor 1:11; 2:10; 3:7, 13, 18; 4:6; 8:24; 10:1, 7; 11:20. These are all places where the word προσωπον (*prosopon*, person) is used in Greek, usually with the meaning of "face."

Book 3

In Hebrew this matter is clear. What we call a person, they call a face. Reader, examine in the original sources what "the person of the Word" meant to the first Christians.

Err, 37r

Likewise the [Hebrew] scriptures have <u>the same</u> way of speaking about <u>a person</u>. One being is said to put on the person of another. <u>In this way</u> the companions of Job, having taken on the role of God, wished to speak and pronounce judgement as if they themselves were gods.[a] Angels speak in the person of God throughout the Law. Pseudo-apostles once spoke in the person of the apostles, and *Satan* speaks in the person of a good angel when he *transforms himself into an angel of light*.[b] Wisdom itself, an angel, **[109]** David, and other prophets often speak in the person of Christ.

Err, 93v-94r

In the same way, we say that the Word, in the person of Christ, was at one time the Son, and that Christ was at one time with the Father in the person of the Word. Christ is the person of the Word and the Word is the person of Christ, but there is only one person and only one face. What shone forth in the Word, and in Wisdom, is Christ himself. Similarly, if you see me face to face, and also see me in a mirror, you see only one person. Given this, the parable of Wisdom in Proverbs 8 can be readily understood.[c] The person of Christ is shown there, saying that he was formed from eternity. [Wisdom] was a prefiguration of Christ, a reflection and an expression [of God]. <u>This generation was a thought and manifestation in God, leading to the begetting of Christ</u>. Wisdom speaks there in the parable, in a figurative manner. For Wisdom takes on the person of Christ, who was formed in God from eternity, and was begotten and created as an expression [of God]. He is said to be created, because he participates in creation. He was begotten as a person, as [God's] personal son. Thus he was formed as a person.

Err, 94r

---

[a] Job 13:7. [b] 2 Cor 11:14. [c] Prov 8:22-31.

Having understood the person of the Word and the mode in which it is manifested, it will now be easy to say what remains to be said about our vision of God. With Christ as my teacher, I am compelled to present a vision of God, which the world does not understand. Thus I may call them blind, who *having sight do not see, and having understanding, do not understand*[a] God. But you, Christian reader, are gaining a true understanding and vision of God, which, you will <u>realize</u>, you can obtain through Christ, and which you will receive entirely from him. For God in himself is completely incomprehensible. He can neither be seen nor understood, unless you consider that within him there is some visible form, as Christ teaches (John 5).[b] This, as has now been revealed, is the face of Christ, and the person of the Word. When [God] willed it, a great and divine majesty appeared in that face — on the mount, in the temple, or in some other place — so that his face alone, with its wondrous power, could arouse those who saw it.

In heaven this [face] is now <u>far</u> more glorious, as it was in the vision of Paul,[c] when **[110]** the human [Christ] was glorified *with that glory which* the Word once *possessed with God* (John 17).[d] *The Word*, which *was with God, and was God* himself,[e] was the person of Jesus Christ. Through him the God of glory wished to be seen, is seen, and will always be seen. <u>As</u> you see the light in the body of the sun, so in the very body of Christ the apostles saw God shining. They saw him with their outward eyes. You see him with inward ones. <u>For what light could have been seen, transfigured in the face of Christ and</u> *shining brighter than the sun*,[f] <u>other than uncreated light itself?</u> Those abstract ideas about God, of which the sophists boast when apart from

---

[a] Matt 13:13.   [b] John 5:36-39.   [c] Acts 26:13.   [d] John 17:5.
[e] John 1:1.   [f] Acts 26:13; see also Matt 17:2.

Book 3

him, are mere nothings, or illusions rather, when in the presence of God.

What Christian of sound mind would make the Turks, Saracens, and other nations equal to us <u>in their vision of God, or</u> in forming a conception of God? Making a comparison to this matter, Peter, in book 2 of Clement's *Recognitions*, relates ideas which he had formed about Jerusalem and Caesarea, before he had ever seen those cities. Later, after seeing them, he realized that everything he had thought about them was wrong.[a] We, who see God through Christ, can prove beyond a doubt that the imaginings of others about God are false. For how could a human being ever imagine God, before he made himself visible? He is far more hidden than the cities which were the objects of Peter's imaginings.

The mind fails when it thinks about God, because he is incomprehensible. The eye does not see him, because he is invisible. The ear does not hear him, nor has it ever heard him, except when he has spoken in a human voice. The hand does not touch him, because he is incorporeal. The tongue cannot describe him, because he is indescribable. No place can hold him, because he is unbounded. Time does not measure him, because he is immeasurable.[17] In fact he transcends everything, surpassing every intellect and mind.

<u>Some people have taught</u> that God can be defined only by saying what he is not.[b] For if you contemplate light or any other thing known to us, you will certainly say that God is not light, but is beyond light; nor is he essence, but is beyond essence; **[111]** nor is he spirit,

---

[a] [Clement], *Recognitiones* 2.62-2.65 (PG 1 1277-1279). See also Augustine, *De Trinitate* 8.9 (PL 42 954-955), on remembering Carthage and imagining Alexandria.   [b] For example: Philo, Maimonides, Plotinus, Proclus, pseudo-Dionysius the Areopagite, Clement of Alexandria, Basil, Gregory of Nyssa, John of Damascus.

but is beyond spirit. God is beyond anything that can be thought. This approach to knowing God is false, since it does not teach what God is, but rather what God is not. No one knows God who does not understand the mode in which he chose to reveal himself to us. The mode is clearly set forth for us through the holy oracles. The sophists do not believe in [this mode], because they refuse to see God in Christ.

Nevertheless, this is the most certain truth of the teaching of Christ, which is wholly consistent with the vision of God. We are unable to form a true idea of God himself or of any other being, unless we can observe in it a face or some image. No idea can be said to affect the mind by representing something to it, unless a likeness of that thing is presented to the intellect by means of a mental image. Aristotle's saying, "observing a mental image is necessary for understanding," is well known.[a] Likewise, Paul teaches, *now we see in a mirror* (1 Corinthians 13).[b] Seeing [a mental image] is the same as understanding something by seeing it in a mirror.

Let our opponents now answer Paul: in what mirror do they see God? Let them tell us what image [their mirror] reflects, or what likeness that mental image has, which they envision when they form their idea of God. For certainly that mental image, whatever it may be, places before them a perceptible appearance or likeness. If they had allowed themselves to be taught true philosophy, or rather true wisdom, by God himself, they would already be used to calling up the vision of God that is always found in the holy and divine words [of scripture]. There is no idea of God, or angels, or anything else, that is not based on a vision, even what is called an inward vision, which exists only in the mind's eye.

---

[a] *Auctoritates Aristotelis*, "De Anima" no. 167; *On the Soul* 3.8 (432a).
[b] 1 Cor 13:12.

Book 3

<u>Some may</u> object that the philosophers had an idea of God, because Paul says: *The invisible attributes of God,* such as his power, divinity, justice, and other things attributed to God, *can be understood from created things* (Romans 1).[a] There is no need for any other answer, since Paul himself expressly **[112]** teaches that *the invisible attributes of God* can even be comprehended by means of common knowledge. Certainly we know general things about God and have common <u>ideas</u> based on other things, as Paul himself concludes. From the greatness of a deed we deduce the power of the doer; from conduct, we deduce justice; and similarly for the other [ideas] that we hold. From the things [in this world] that reflect divinity or hidden power, we deduce that there is something more divine, wiser, and more powerful. These are *the invisible attributes of God,* commonly accepted by people of many nations, <u>which Paul mentions</u>.

By means of syllogisms, we logically conclude from effects that there is one first cause. From motions we conclude that there is a prime mover.[b] Nevertheless, Aristotle never had a specific, <u>unique,</u> or abstract idea about this. These [inferences from created things], says Paul, are what can be known about God. However, God himself cannot be known <u>from this, especially when we have no definite knowledge of his will</u>. On the contrary, Aristotle's entire discourse on cause and motion[c] is nothing but a rearrangement of visual mental images in the brain. Because of this [the Greek philosophers] are said to have known about God in some way. This is because they impressed a mental image of motion on him by means of syllogisms, <u>and gathered a number of predicate terms [for their syllogisms] which are rightly assigned to God</u>.

Err, 103r-v

---

[a] Rom 1:20. [b] See Aristotle, *Physics* book 8 and *Metaphysics* book 12.
[c] Aristotle discusses motion and its causes in *Physics.*

The Restoration of Christianity

But truly, we can go beyond all this. Anyone who has been accustomed to drink water from the divine fountains [of the scriptures] will immediately recognize the truth that flows from them like light. For God wanted to be shown to the world <u>and to be seen</u> through his Word. *Whoever sees* Christ, *sees the Father*,[a] and no one sees him except in Christ.[b] If Jews, Turks, and other non-Christians now see God as we do, what [special] vision of God did Christ bring us?

Therefore, Christian reader, you must become acquainted with the visible appearance of God — <u>the true θεοφανίαν (*theophaneia*, manifestation of God)</u> — and *perceive God's glory in the face of Jesus Christ* (2 Corinthians 4).[c] <u>Then</u> you will come to know God, whom you have never known before and whose appearance you have not yet seen (John 5).[d] **[113]** In this passage [the Greek word] ειδος (*eidos*, form) means the appearance, the form, the shape, and the face of God. We are taught here that we cannot see God, except in the face of Christ. Here the divine teacher is alluding to what is written in Exodus 20 and Deuteronomy 4.[e] For although the people of Israel in ancient times heard voices, and many of them saw the appearance of someone who spoke with Christ's voice, in more recent times those who do not acknowledge Christ, neither hear God's voice nor see his appearance. Similarly, today the sophists do not see or hear anything at all. For the voice of Christ is the voice of God, just as a vision of Christ is a vision of God. God is known and seen by believers in the face of Christ. If only he would show me, without a veil, that visible countenance that Moses saw *face to face*![f]

Err, 103v

If God clearly showed himself to me, I would see the face that [even] Moses did not see: nothing other than the <u>glorious</u> face of Jesus Christ. This is the manifestation

Err, 103v (margin, first occurrence)

---

[a] John 14:9. [b] See John 14:6. [c] 2 Cor 4:6. [d] John 5:36-39.
[e] Ex 20:19; Deut 4:12. [f] Ex 33:11.

Book 3

of the invisible God by the visible Word. It is said to be the visible image of the invisible God. This is why Christ is called the face of God. Whatever allows a thing to be seen and known is called its face. Therefore we must agree, purely and simply, that God is seen in the face of Christ. As Paul says, God is seen through Christ.[a] *Whoever sees Christ sees the Father.*[b] *And no one has ever seen him, except through the Son* (John 1, 5, 6, 8, 12, and 14).[c]

Err, 103v

Note that here we are always speaking about that vision of God which can be granted to mortals in this world. For in the world to come we will see God differently. <u>Then we will see him just as he is. Now we see him [only] as he shows himself to us</u>. No intellect can now attain that future vision, nor does it arise in the human heart. [Of course] we are speaking here of an inward vision, not an invisible illusion.

Our adversaries, using an imaginary illusion, <u>contend</u> that the first being is now seen by means of the second. How can this be? How can this invisible and unintelligible being, which is more unknown than the Father himself, ever lead us **[114]** to a true understanding and vision of <u>the Father? The tritheists</u> have never understood the intent of the Gospel message, which so often <u>mentions</u> a vision of God, seen *eye to eye*[d] through Jesus Christ, and never before seen or known. How <u>[then] are we to</u> understand that God was truly revealed in the flesh? What is it that God promised [when he said] that in the future, we would all see him *eye to eye*? Will God be seen on earth? Beware, reader, lest you be led to accept a meaning far from [its true sense] and, with the sophists, misuse the word "to see." But Christ, who was not a sophist, said to <u>all</u> the apostles, *now you have seen the Father* (John 14).[e] John

Err, 47r

---

[a] Col 1:15. [b] John 14:9. [c] John 1:18; 5:37; 6:46 (no one has ever seen the Father); John 8:19; 12:45; 14:9 (whoever sees Christ sees the Father); John 14:6 (no one comes to the Father except through Christ).
[d] Isa 52:8. [e] John 14:7.

said the same thing about the rest of the disciples (1 John 2).^a What they saw, <u>however</u>, was nothing other than the face of Christ, in which the deity of the Father was reflected. Consider with what incomprehension Thomas and Philip asked Christ for a vision and manifestation of the Father; and Christ's response to the thinking behind the questions (John 14).^b

Err, 104r   When Christ says <u>there</u> that the Father is seen through him, do not <u>think</u> that he was speaking frivolously. Call it a mental vision, an idea, a thought, an understanding, or what you will. Allow me to speak in the same way. God was never before seen, as Christ himself says. Otherwise, Christ would have offered nothing new. He would merely have uttered an empty boast [when he said] that the Father is seen through him. And John would have spoken falsely when he said, *we beheld the glory* [of God], whom *no one has ever seen*.^c

Err, 104v   [The disciples] saw nothing other than the glorious face of Jesus Christ. By means of God's art, this syllogism holds true: Formerly, God was seen by visual examination of the countenance of Elohim; and this [countenance] is now the face of <u>Jesus</u> Christ; therefore, God is seen in the face of <u>Jesus</u> Christ. Truly and properly, Christ is now in God in substance, just as *the Word was God* himself *and was with God*.^d Always keep in mind what the sight of [God's] countenance was like under the Law, in comparison to the face of Christ. You must admit that God is now seen more clearly. Take care not to forget this. Hear him now calling out to us from heaven: **[115]** *when you see me you see* God; <u>*when you see me you see the Father*</u>.^e Lift up your mind's eye and see. If God had the power to place a sign in the world by which the light of God could properly be seen, this certainly was the sign he placed.

---

^a 1 John 1:1-3 (not 1 John 2).   ^b John 14:5-11.   ^c John 1:14, 18.
^d John 1:1.   ^e John 14:9.

Book 3

Perhaps you will object that it profits us little to see this outward face. My reply is that the very essence of eternal blessedness is to see because you believe (John 6 and 17).[a] As one look at [Moses's] serpent of bronze [was enough to cure the bite of fiery serpents], one look [at Christ] cures every sting of the devil (John 3).[b] But you are looking at his face in an unworthy manner. However, once you believe, you will never turn your mind's eye away, and you will realize how greatly this benefits you. For only this vision will lift you completely up to him in heaven, where the light of his countenance, illuminating your darkness, will cleanse you of dangerous error. *They looked upon him and were enlightened* (Psalm 33).[c] *Make your face shine upon your servant* (Psalm 118).[d] *Lift the light of your countenance over us* (Psalm 4).[e] *You will see and be enlightened* (Isaiah 60).[f] Did not Christ call those eyes blessed which saw him?[g]

Err, 90r

Err, 112r

Many prophets are said to have seen God himself face to face. If God is not seen in the face of Christ, they must have seen more than the apostles saw. And, consequently, Christ was talking nonsense when he claimed that, for this reason, the apostles were more blessed than the prophets.[h] But the apostles really saw, as we ourselves now see, *the glory of God* revealed *in the face of Christ*.[i] Indeed, the prophets saw [God] behind the veil of an angel, and in shadow. An angel, appearing as God, prefigured Christ for them. It profited some [of the apostles] little to see Christ only with outward eyes, because they did not believe in him, though they saw him.[j] But it is far different now to see, with inward eyes, the face of Christ shining in heaven. This cannot happen without faith.

---

[a] John 6:40; 17:24; see also John 11:40.   [b] John 3:14-15, referring to Num 21:4-9.   [c] Ps 34:5 (Pagnini).   [d] Ps 119:135.   [e] Ps 4:6.
[f] Isa 60:19-20.   [g] Matt 13:16.   [h] Matt 13:17.   [i] 2 Cor 4:6.
[j] John 6:36.

Those who are <u>truly</u> reborn in him see Christ <u>dwelling</u> deep within themselves. As Paul says, this inward vision *gloriously transforms us into* Christ **[116]** (2 Corinthians 3).^a To the inner self, the light of the face of Christ is eternal glory, and the enjoyment of divine blessedness. The salvation of Christ *is the salvation of* [the psalmist's] *countenance* (Psalm 41) *and the illumination of* [God's] *countenance* (Psalm 43).^b This vision has great power, if it is followed by illumination of the mind. And the vision itself is enjoyment of the divine. The eternal blessedness to come is full enjoyment of the divine and a vision of divine light, which is union with God. The vision of the face of Christ, which exists in us, now makes us sharers in his eternal blessedness. Examine that face, gloriously transformed on the mountain [of transfiguration].^c In this vision, light itself is seen: *God is light*, and Christ *is the light of the world*.^d This light illuminates the soul of the beholder and gloriously transforms it <u>into the likeness of Christ</u>.

Err, 105v   From what has been said, it is evident that Christ is called not only the image of God, but more than an image. For it is an image when there are two things, formed in a similar way, one of which is called the image of the other. But in Christ there is something more. If the angel Gabriel were to come to me, in the form of an eagle in flight, would I say, "This is the image of Gabriel"?[18] Even if it is called an image, it is more than an image. It is a kind of likeness representing, and also containing, the substance [*hypostasis*][19] itself. In this way the Word, the person, or the countenance of Elohim, was more than an image. It was the very face of God; it was God himself. It was a kind of likeness or form containing the very being of God.

In a similar way, Christ is now more than an image. He is, as the Apostle says, the *likeness of the* [divine] *essence* itself

---

^a 2 Cor 3:18.   ^b Ps 42:11; 44:3.   ^c Matt 17:1-8; Mark 9:2-8; Luke 9:28-36.   ^d 1 John 1:5; John 8:12.

(Hebrews 1).[a] He is the imprint of the hypostasis of God, engraved on the divine essence. In Psalm 16 and Deuteronomy 4, David and Moses call this תמונה (*temunah*, image or likeness). Pay attention to the meaning of the word "image," when Moses says that they *did not see the image* of [God] when he was speaking.[b] That image is what David later wishes for us.[c] For if you accept the word "image" [in the psalm] as having the same meaning [as it has in Deuteronomy], you will have understood it correctly. That very image was the form of the face [of God]. The image was an ειδος (*eidos*, form), a manifestation of a being by means of a visible form (John 5).[d] [117] In the same sense Christ is called εικον (*eikon*, image), the image of God, the likeness of God (2 Corinthians 4 and Colossians 1).[e]

Err, 105v-106r

In the same way, χαρακτηρ (*charakter*, imprint or representation)[f] is a kind of imprint, an engraving, the shape of the [divine] hypostasis; that is, of the existence, essence, or substance of God. For God subsists in [Christ] alone. The vision of God is attested from all of these things: [likeness, image, form, imprint]. For I am said to see God by seeing the imprint of his likeness, just as I would be said to see Gabriel by seeing the eagle. Otherwise, God would not be able to reveal himself to us in visible form. <u>What sophist is so insane that he would take away this power from God? As if God were a feeble blockhead, who can neither make himself known nor communicate with humanity. But if [God] was willing and able to manifest himself to humanity,</u> he accomplished this through our looking behind the veil of the [divine] oracle and seeing the revealed face of Jesus Christ. Just as the countenance of the sun appears in the midst of boundless and inacces-

Err, 106r-v

---

[a] Heb 1:3.   [b] Deut 4:12. In the Vulgate, *temunah* is translated as *forma* (shape or form). Servetus follows Pagnini in using *imago* (image).
[c] Ps 17:15.   [d] John 5:37.   [e] 2 Cor 4:4; Col 1:15.   [f] Heb 1:3 – the only occurrence of this word in the New Testament.

Err, 106v   sible light, so too, in the midst of the heights and depths of God, his oracle appeared in the person of Jesus Christ. Here I pass over any mention of the metaphysical images and invisible imprints which the tritheists place among their [divine] beings. For these are ridiculous fantasies, unknown to scripture, which can neither be perceived nor understood.

[The tritheists] object that I offer humanity no idea of God, angels, or souls. My response is that I am offering a clear and understandable vision. In the next book, we will show the true essence of all of the ideas in our soul, declaring it to be the essence of light.[a] That light, which we see in the face of Jesus Christ through the illumination of the Spirit, we declare to be God himself, seen by us through Christ. We say that this [illumination] is a clear idea of God in us, and that God is seen by us in Christ. *God is light*[b] — the same light that we see in the face of Jesus Christ. Is this not the true vision and knowledge of God through Christ? We will also show that the substance of angels and of souls derives from the substance of light, and that it <u>is visible in</u> the ideal form of a human being. Otherwise how were those disembodied *souls* seen, which John *saw under the altar* in Revelation 6?[c]

[118] Nothing can be seen, either in this age or in the future, except by means of light. [In John's vision] the shape of an entire human being was seen shining in [that person's] soul, since the soul can contain the <u>true</u> ideal form and shape of a human being, as Irenaeus teaches in book 2, chapters 33, 63, and 64 [of *Against Heresies*].[d] Philo teaches, in the work cited above, that the soul is formed according to the image and pattern of the

---

[a] *Restoration*, 151-153 (book 4).   [b] 1 John 1:5.   [c] Rev 6:9.
[d] Irenaeus, *Adversus haereses* 2:19.6, 2.33.5, 2.34.1 (PG 7 774A-C, 833B-834B, 834C-835A). The chapter numbers cited by Servetus are from Erasmus's edition of Irenaeus.

Word.ᵃ <u>Therefore, the soul can be seen in the ideal form of a human being. But an angel can easily exist both in the ideal form [of a human being] and in other forms</u>; and can be seen, <u>always</u> by means of light, just as God can be seen in Christ by means of light.

The sophists, however, see invisible things. Instead of visions they have illusions. Christ has been made unnecessary for them, because they do not see God any differently than before [the Incarnation]. But true Christians understand, and will always understand, that the manifestation of God himself was meant to be visible to the eye. We have no doubt that God is seen through Christ. We know that Christ rebuked Thomas and Philip because they were anxious to seek God through other paths, visions, <u>inquiries</u>, and manifestations. He testified that every path to <u>getting to know and see</u> God was in himself, declaring that he himself was *the way* (John 14).ᵇ Thus, from eternity, God has established and willed that he should be visible in Christ alone. He wants us constantly to look into this mirror, and to be illuminated in the spirit by this, so that our illuminated spirit, containing this light, is transformed to the same glory that Christ possesses, becoming glorious like Christ (2 Corinthians 3 and 4).ᶜ

This is a true idea of God, which I profess to have through Christ. With this I delight in God and I worship God in spirit—not separately from Christ, but with the same delight with which I delight in Christ, and the same worship with which I worship Christ. For, as [Christ says], *whoever sees me, sees the Father*;ᵈ [that is] whoever delights in me, delights in the Father, and whoever worships me, worships the Father. <u>What is worshipped in spirit ought</u>

Err, 108r

ᵃ Eusebius, *Praeparatio evangelica* 7.18 (PG 21 559B-D), paraphrasing Philo, *On Planting* 1.5.20.   ᵇ John 14:5-11.   ᶜ 2 Cor 3:18; 4:6.
ᵈ John 14:9.

to be seen in spirit. Otherwise Christ would say to us, "*You worship what you do not know*,"ᵃ just as the sophists worship him, whom they do not know. Christ is *the way and the light*.ᵇ One must approach God on the way that shines through Christ, worship God, and **[119]** see God, who is the light.

But the tritheists have not entered on this path. Following an invisible path, they worship an *unknown God*,[20] or, rather, a three-headed monster. Without realizing it, they dream about a three-headed Cerberus,[21] a tripartite God. These three beings, enclosed in one being, are like three [geometrical] points contained in a single point.ᶜ They reduce every divine substance to something like a geometrical point. They claim that God himself is like a point many times repeated on the same plane, and that there are three points in one simple point.[22] Apart from Christ, is this not how the sophists see God? Is this not the idea of God that they are so proud to hold?

Err, 108v

If the natural splendour of God shines in the face of Christ, and if the substance of deity *dwells bodily*ᵈ in the flesh of Christ, is not God seen there? How is God—revealed once in the Word and now in the flesh—seen *eye to eye*,ᵉ then and now? See and believe, reader, or else woe to you!

So that this vision of God might be better established in us, more needs to be said about the hypostasis of the Word. But we have already sufficiently shown that it was the visible and substantial Word, substantial light, and the countenance of Elohim—although the latter was hidden in a cloud. There was a [divine] oracle subsisting and shining in a fiery cloud.ᶠ It was said to be *the glory of the Lord* and his majestyᵍ in the cloud. This was the very

---

ᵃ John 4:22.   ᵇ John 14:6 (the way); John 8:12 (the light).   ᶜ See *Restoration*, 41 (book 1), 129 (book 4).   ᵈ Col 2:9   ᵉ Isa 52:8.
ᶠ Ex 14:24; Deut 5:22; Ezek 1:4.   ᵍ Isa 2:10, 19, 21; 1 Chr 29:11.

oracle that was protected and concealed by angels' wings,[a] the oracle through which God answered Moses.[b] This was the oracle in the concealed [inner court] of the house [of the Lord],[c] just as Christ was hidden in the shadow of the Omnipotent.

Err, 105r

The Hebrew word confirms the meaning of "oracle." For from the word דבר (*dabar*, word), which is λογος [in Greek], comes דביר (*debir*, oracle or Holy of Holies),[23] which is the oracle of the temple (Psalm 27, 1 Kings 6, and 2 Chronicles 3, 4, and 5).[d] Christ is the true oracle through whom we receive answers from God. He is the mercy-seat, through whom and in whom God is graciously disposed toward us. He is the covering which protects us from every evil, and on account of **[120]** which we are blessed and protected from sin. Just as Christ himself is now the oracle, so previously he was in the temple and in the tabernacle. And before that, the person of Christ was the oracle who gave answers to Adam, Abraham, Moses, and others.

Err, 105r

See how beautifully the entire Law portrays John's [doctrine of the] Word: not only as the oracle in the cloud, but also in the light of the countenance of Elohim, and so on. From the Law, one can deduce that it was the hypostasis of the Word in the cloud that <u>was</u> the seed of the begetting of Christ. The substance of the <u>archetypal cloud</u> was the substance of the <u>Word</u>. It was the substantial dew that watered the soil so that Christ would one day sprout forth (Psalm 71, Isaiah 45, 55, 61, Ezekiel 17, Hosea 6).[e] Hence Christ is called the Branch of God (Isaiah 4, Zechariah 3 and 6, and elsewhere).[f]

---

[a] Isa 6:2; Ezek 10:5. [b] Ex 24:16. [c] 2 Chr 29:16. [d] The word דביר (*debir*) is used for the Holy of Holies, or innermost sanctuary of the Temple, in Ps 28:2; 1 Kg 6:5, 16, 19-23, 31; 7:49; 8:6-8; 2 Chr 3:16; 4:20; 5:7, 9. [e] Ps 72:6; Isa 45:8; 55:10; 61:11; Ezek 17:5-6; Hos 6:3. [f] Isa 4:2; 11:1; Jer 23:5; 33:15; Zech 3:8; 6:12.

[The Law] attests to the same hypostasis in the form of a cloud. For throughout the Law, God is said to have appeared and to have gone before the children of Israel in *a pillar of cloud by day and a pillar of fire by night*.[a] [The Latin Bible] uses the word *columna* (pillar) to translate the Hebrew word עמוד (*ammud*), which means "firmness" and "consistency." It is derived from the Hebrew verb עמד, meaning "stood" or "stood firm." [The usual translation] "pillar" is inappropriate in this context, nor is the idea of a pillar <u>at all</u> relevant there. Rather, God appeared at that time in the consistency, or essence, of a cloud or of fire. The cloud, the fire, and the light were all the same substance. <u>The cloud was not, I say, elemental, of dark, created matter; rather it was super-elemental, of uncreated matter, shining from within. God was in the fire, and the fire was God himself</u>.

<u>Now you will say it follows</u> that, if such was the hypostasis of the Word, then its substance was corporeal and divisible. <u>But it does not follow. If God is in corporeal things, and brings corporeal things into himself, it does not therefore follow that he himself is corporeal. For God himself, in his essence, is the omniform mind. In your soul there are forms of corporeal and divisible things. These are also in God. In him they are essences, in you they are [merely] accidents</u>.[b] God, incorporeal and imperceptible in himself, <u>is presented to us in a miraculous way</u>. He showed himself to us perceptibly through the Word, and in the Word was the Spirit. <u>This does not prove</u> **[121]** <u>that there is a body in God, but rather shows the ineffable and omniform nature of his mind. The wonderful power of his intellect is such that the nature of a body can shine in it</u>. The following book will <u>clearly</u> teach that there are visible forms in God, which are indivisible and unchanging.[c]

---

[a] Ex 13:21-22; 14:24; Num 14:14. [b] See A.R4.49. [c] *Restoration*, 138-139, 147-149 (book 4).

<u>God is not divisible, nor is the substance of the Word,</u> since what is divisible is perishable.[a] Certainly there is nothing incorporeal, like an imaginary point, in the nature of things. Nor, despite what the natural philosophers teach, can anything be formed from <u>such</u> points.[24] The substance of angels is not like a point, nor is the substance of souls. The substance of the spirit of God, from which angels and souls emanate, is not like a point. Rather, it is like the elemental substance <u>of [God's] breath</u>, of which it was the elemental archetype <u>in the divine mind</u>. In the substance of God that was shown to the world, which is the substance of the Word and of the Spirit, there are no parts. Nor can one speak of any division in it, such as is found in created things. Parts and divisions are spoken of in the substance of God, according to the distribution of the [divine] economy.[25]

God divided up the Spirit that was in Moses and gave portions of it to seventy men.[b] Also, at the sending forth of the Holy Spirit [to the apostles], tongues of fire were dispersed, and each received a portion.[c] In the partition of spirit—each portion of which, as scripture says, is God—the division does not destroy the substance of the Holy Spirit.[d] In keeping with its source, the light radiating from the sun is coarser than the light of God, which is much finer. The former can be destroyed, the latter cannot <u>be destroyed</u>. Compared to the light of the Word and the Spirit, everything in the world is coarse matter, which is divisible and penetrable. The light [of God] *pierces even to the division of soul and spirit,* as Paul bears witness.[e] The light of God penetrates and fills the very substance of an angel or a soul, just as the light of

---

[a] "Everything divisible is perishable" (*Omne divisibile est corruptibile*) is a medieval scholastic philosophical maxim, adapted from Aristotle, *On the Heavens* 3.6 (305a).   [b] Num 11:24-25.   [c] Acts 2:3-4.
[d] See 1 Cor 12:4-11.   [e] Heb 4:12.

the sun penetrates and fills the air. The light of God also penetrates the light of the sun and sustains it from within. As the form of forms,[26] this light penetrates and sustains all the forms in the world.

[122] We shall say more later about spirit and light. For now it will suffice to say that the true substance in the Word was <u>the visible hypostasis that brought to life that ideal form, the human being [Christ], as the next book will explain.</u>[a] <u>In the Word was the ideal form of the human Christ, and also the substantial seed of his begetting.</u> This man could not have been said to be *truly the Son of God*,[b] if God had simply created him in Mary, without making use of the normal manner of begetting from the substance of the father. <u>The substance of the seed, the substance of God that was revealed to us, was in the Word. And somehow, by means of the Word</u>, God was given a body and made human. He who was once prefigured is now an actual [man].

John the Evangelist <u>reports</u> that he *had touched* the substance of *the Word with* his *hands*.[c] Paul teaches that *deity dwells bodily in* Christ.[d] The ancient theologians[27] spoke of the corporeal Word in bodily terms, as something perceptible, tangible, and visible. You will admit that the incarnate Word is tangible and palpable, once you agree that, in [all] other things, what is felt and touched is not pure matter, but rather a tangible form <u>and</u> a palpable shape. Thus, what is felt and touched is the whole thing, [both matter and] form.[28] <u>Let no one be amazed if we say with John that, in Christ, deity may be touched by our hands, since Paul declares that, in other situations, it can almost be touched (Acts 17)</u>.[e] Let no one be amazed when we say that the Word of God, which was to be formed

---

[a] *Restoration*, 149-150, 162 (book 4).   [b] Matt 27:54.   [c] 1 John 1:1.
[d] Col 2:9.   [e] Acts 17:27.

into a body, previously had a corporeal form, since the evangelists bear witness that *the Holy Spirit* also *descended in bodily form.*[a] This was not impossible for God, who wished to <u>reveal</u> his Word <u>by</u> begetting Christ. <u>God wished to appear in a corporeal mode and was able to do so. God also *came and stood* in corporeal form right before Samuel (1 Samuel 3).</u>[b] The way [to understand the appearances of God] is easy, as we will [now] show.

The hypostasis of the Word is proclaimed at the beginning of the Gospel of John. He says that [the Word] "was," and also teaches that it was visible.[c] John saw that, in earlier times, <u>the human</u> Jesus Christ already existed. Daniel saw him in a vision, *coming with clouds of heaven.*[d] <u>Earlier,</u> he directed the four wheels in Ezekiel's vision,[e] *rode on a horse among* Zechariah's *myrtle trees,*[f] and *sat on a throne* in Isaiah's vision.[g] **[123]** He presided over every age. And since this was the artistry of a <u>thinking and</u> speaking God, he called it λογον (*logos*). It was the spoken Word. It is as if a word breathed from your own mouth were to contain the ideal form of a human being, by which all things come into being.

Err, 116v

In earlier times Christ presided over the world. The <u>proverb</u> of Solomon introduces Wisdom, presiding in the person of [Christ].[h] David reveals the very same thing to us by his use of the word *Yah*, bidding us to praise Christ in his name, which is יה (*Yah*),[29] that is, existence, essence, hypostasis. Psalm 67 says: *Exalt him riding through the wilderness,*[30] *in his name Yah.*[i] And Psalm 101: *A people yet to be created will praise Yah,*[j] <u>that is</u>, the existence who is Christ. Christ himself teaches about the same hypos-

Err, 115v

---

[a] Luke 3:22; see also Matt 3:16, Mark 1:10.   [b] 1 Sam 3:10. (Here Servetus, following Pagnini, called this book 1 Samuel. He usually refers to this book as 1 Kings, as in the Vulgate.)   [c] John 1:1, 14.   [d] Dan 7:13.   [e] Ezek 1:20-21.   [f] Zech 1:8.   [g] Isa 6:1.   [h] Prov 8:22-23. See also Wisdom 7:22-30.   [i] Ps 68:4.   [j] Ps 102:18.

tasis when he says, [*Before Abraham was*] *I am*; from the beginning I am the eternal first being, existing in God.^a

So that you may understand the various stages in the manifestation of <u>God and the grace of Christ</u> that have been made for us, you must first <u>bear in mind, reader</u>, that God in himself, infinitely surpassing everything, is to us incomprehensible, unimaginable, and incommunicable.

Err, 119r Base your idea of [God] on this: None of us can see him, unless he accommodates himself to us and appears in a form that is within our ability to perceive. Similarly, we cannot have communication with him in our spirit, unless he accommodates himself in some way as a spirit like ours, inwardly perceptible to us. This divine mode, about which we will speak later,^b is the Holy Spirit within us. For now, we are only seeking the mode of manifestation and vision of God that was prior [to the incarnation of Christ]. He was set before us as a kind of divine appearance, as we have shown in many places, and as Christ himself points out in John 5 and 14 and elsewhere.^c

Next, <u>bear in mind</u> the mode in which God visibly revealed himself to Adam in a friendly way.^d But later, having hidden himself because of [Adam's] sin, he entered into the spirits of human beings in various ways, without being seen. He always practiced mercy toward humanity, in whom he had instilled natural law by an inborn breath

Err, 119r of deity. At times he also revealed himself through speech, **[124]** just as I might make my voice heard among those who do not see me. In various modes, God <u>rallied</u> unhappy [human] nature, held captive by Satan, <u>to his side</u>. In this way, at the time of the giving of the Law [to Moses on Mount Sinai], God was revealed to the entire [Hebrew] people by his audible voice.^e

---

^a John 8:58.   ^b In book 5.   ^c John 5:45-47; 14:6. See also Mark 12:26; Luke 16:31; 24:44-45; John 1:45.   ^d Gen 3:8.   ^e Ex 19:9, 19.

Book 3

From Adam to Abraham, [God] spoke to <u>many</u> people in the same way. Another mode of revelation, vision, began with Abraham (Genesis 15).[a] After Adam, God was seen first by Abraham,[b] and by no one else before him. <u>From this you can gather that this vision was an extraordinary gift</u>. This privilege was given to the first patriarch, and then to his successors, the holy prophets, <u>who therefore were</u> called seers. *God spoke* to them *at various times*[c] through visions: to some in dreams, to some face to face, revealing himself in different ways. However, these visions, in which foreshadowing was presented by an angel, were always veiled.

At last [God] was revealed to us, shining in spite of the darkness, and seen with his face unveiled. *The Word was made flesh and we beheld his glory.*[d] We saw *the glory of God in the face of Jesus Christ.*[e] We saw Christ, and in him we saw the Father. In him we saw the light, God himself shining. Would that we could remain steadfast in this vision, so that vision, and the glorification that even now makes us sharers in the glory to come, might lead us to that vision of future eternal blessedness, through Jesus Christ our Lord.

Err, 99v

---

[a] Gen 15:1 (the word of the Lord comes to Abraham in a vision).
[b] Gen 17:1 (the Lord appears to Abraham and speaks with him).
[c] Heb 1:1.   [d] John 1:14.   [e] 2 Cor 4:6.

DE TRINITATE
DIVINA LIBER QVARTVS,
Nomina Dei, eiusq́; essentiam omniformem manifestans, & rerum omnium principia.

VIso iam Christo, & viso in eius facie patre Deo, non abs re fuerit hoc libro quarto, diuinorum nominum significationem exponere, vt nos, qui Christum Deum nostrum profitemur, in eo diuinam manifestationem melius ostendamus. Essentiam Dei omniformem nunc omnes cognoscemus, veterum sententijs concinnè satis explicatam: rerúq́; principia in lucem proferemus, summis philosophis hactenus incognita. Nomina deitatis insigniora sunt אלהים & יהוה. Et est Elohim pluralis numeri, quo nomine, vt cõmuniore, est primò vocatus Deus. Nomen vero Iehouah est magis Deo peculiare. Tam nomen Iehouah, quàm Elohim, mysteria Christi in seipsis continent, Iehouah in essentia, Elohim in apparentia. Nomẽ illud Iehouah essentiam significare plerique tradunt, alij potius generationem. Verũ nos & ea & alia eo nomine comprehendi dicimus, & essentiam potius: nec essentiam simpliciter, sed essentiantem essentiam, seu esse facientem. Non est Deus instar puncti, sed est substantiæ pelagus infinitũ, omnia essentians, omnia esse faciens, & omnium essentias sustinens. Cabalistis sua circa id nomen secreta relinquimus, hoc dicentes, quòd, vt iod cum scheua puncto nobis indicat, est futurum piel, significationis actiuæ, à radice היה, seu potius היה, mutando iod in vau, & voces paruas

Iehouah.

uas

On the Divine Trinity

Book 4

Revealing the names of God, his omniform essence, and the origins of all things

[125] Now that we have seen Christ, and seen in his face God the Father, this fourth book offers an opportunity to explain the meanings of the divine names, so that we, who profess Christ to be our God, might more clearly show the divine manifestation that is in him. <u>We will now all learn about the omniform essence of God, which has been amply and elegantly explained in the thoughts of ancient writers. And we shall bring to light the origins of things, hitherto unknown to the greatest philosophers.</u>

The most well-known names for <u>the deity</u> [in the Hebrew scriptures] are אלהים (*Elohim*) and יהוה (*Yahweh* or *Jehovah*).[1] And [the word] *Elohim* is plural in number.[2] God was called by this name first, as it was commonly used [among various peoples].[3] However, the name Jehovah is applied particularly to the God [of Israel]. The names Jehovah and Elohim both contain, in themselves, the mysteries of Christ. Jehovah is [God] in essence, while Elohim is [God's] visible appearance.

[*The Names of God*]

{Jehovah}

Err, 100r-v   Many say that the name Jehovah signifies God's essence, while others <u>prefer to</u> say that it refers to [God's role in] generation.[4] Indeed, we say that <u>both of</u> these meanings are included in the name [Jehovah], or rather in his essence. For it is not simply essence, but essentializing <u>essence: that is</u>, essence that causes things to exist. God is not like a [geometrical] point.[a] Rather, he is an infinite sea of substance, essentializing all things, making all things exist, and sustaining the essences of all things.

Err, 100v   We leave the secret knowledge about this name to the Kabbalists, noting only this:[5] that the *yod* [in the tetragrammaton יהוה], <u>pointed</u> with a *shva*, indicates a future, active verb, of the conjugation *pi'el*, from the Hebrew root הוה (*havah*). This, in turn, derives from היה (*haya*) by changing *yod* to *vav*, and the short vowels **[126]** into long ones, as frequently happens. This [change] is happening here, since the middle letter [*vav*] <u>is pointed with *dagesh*</u>,[6] although <u>here</u> [the verb] is of the *pi'el* conjugation, in which *vav* cannot be used as a consonant, only as a vowel. Since this *vav* is a vowel, unless there is some elision, each syllable of the name [Jehovah] must have been pronounced by the Hebrews. This name is ineffable to them, and thus cannot be spoken, unless you say it by pronouncing the syllables separately: Ye-ho-wah. But whether you say it in this way, or with a consonantal *vav* as we do,[7] and whether you say Jehovah or Jova, it is <u>well known</u> that, <u>in ancient times, many spoke the name aloud</u>.[8]

Indeed, in other [Old Testament passages] the name [Jehovah] often appears in conjunction with another word, as in Genesis 22 and Exodus 17, <u>where</u> one place is

---

[a] See *Restoration*, 41 (book 1), 119 (book 3), A.R3.22.

called *Jehovah yireh* (Jehovah will be seen),[a] and another is called *Jehovah nissi* (Jehovah is my banner).[b] Similarly, in Jeremiah 23 and 33, we have *Jehovah sidqenu* (Jehovah our righteousness),[c] and in Judges 6, *Jehovah shalom* (the peace of Jehovah).[d] That is: God is vision, God is exaltation, God is righteousness, God is peace — all through Christ. Thus, reasoning according to the future tense of a *pi'el* verb,[e] [the name] Jehovah means: he will essentialize, he will cause to be. Not only does God himself cause [things] to be, but he also creates another creator. For the Father caused the all-creating Son to exist, and essentialized the Son who essentializes all things, so that the Son himself would be the fountainhead of essence. *Err*, 100r

We are taught that this is the true meaning of the word, on the authority of Jehovah himself, who reveals his name to Moses in Exodus 6.[f] In this passage, because [God] was going to accomplish great things, and was going to grant the power of doing these things to a human being [Moses], he says that his name is Jehovah, the name of him who created so much, and created another creator. The Patriarchs did not know this name, although the names *El* and *Shaddai* were known to them. [God] says, "*I was seen by Abraham, Isaac, and Jacob under the name El-Shaddai, but I was unknown to them by my name Jehovah.*"[g] Previously God had appeared to the Patriarchs, and had revealed himself to them under the name El-Shaddai (Genesis 17, 28, 35, and 48), always saying to them, "*I am El-Shaddai.*"[h] *Err*, 100v-r

From the meanings of these names in the Exodus passage, much more can be conveyed by the name Jehovah.

---

[a] Gen 22:14. The base meaning of the Hebrew verb ראה is "to see," hence "the Lord will be seen." However, in this verse it is often translated as "the Lord will provide."   [b] Ex 17:15.   [c] Jer 23:6; 33:16.   [d] Judg 6:24.   [e] See A.R4.5.   [f] Ex 6:2-8.   [g] Ex 6:3.
[h] Gen 17:1; 28:3; 35:11; 48:3.

Err, 100v-101r

The word שדי (*Shaddai*) is **[127]** from the root שדד (*shadad*), which means to destroy, and the noun שד (*shad*), destruction or devastation. Hence God is called *Shaddai*, the destroyer, or he who has the power to destroy everything.[9] This is clearly shown in Isaiah 13 and Joel 1: כשד משדי (*ke-shod mi-shaddai*), which means "like destruction from the destroyer."[a] Here our translator renders "destroyer" as "Almighty."[10] Similarly [God] is called *El*, that is, powerful.[11] Thus we have *El Shaddai*, a powerful destroyer. It was under this name that God appeared to Abraham, saying, "*I am El-Shaddai*" (Genesis 17). Because of this, Abraham had the courage not to fear others, and walked blamelessly with God, considering himself to be always in the presence of God Almighty. When Abraham was angered by his enemies, God comforted and supported him, saying, "*Walk with me, and be blameless.*"[b]

Indeed God says to Moses, in chapter 6 [of Exodus], "Although I appeared to your forefathers under the name El-Shaddai, and although they knew that I had destroyed Sodom and Gomorrah, nevertheless I did not reveal to them that I was Jehovah. They did not yet fully know me as the essence-maker, or the one who causes things to exist through another, who gives the power of performing miracles to others, as I now do for Moses himself against the Egyptians."[12] No one before Moses had been given the power to perform miracles, and so the significance of the name [Jehovah], conveying all this about God, had been known to no one, even though the name had been heard by the Patriarchs. The Patriarchs did not fully know whether Christ was Jehovah, with such great power of essentializing all things, or Jehovah was Christ, and was thus the power that was to essentialize.

---

[a] Isa 13:6; Joel 1:15. [b] Gen 17:1.

Furthermore, the perfect name for the essentializer or creator was <u>revealed</u> from the <u>beginning</u> of the world, from the first passage in which that word [Jehovah] begins to be uttered by the Holy Spirit. For during the six days of the work [of creation] God was not called by that name—just as Christ was not while he was active on earth—but only when he rested in heaven. Once creation had been completed, God rested and gave the power of essentializing, creating, and generating to those whom he created. **[128]** Jehovah was then said to create or essentialize through another (Genesis 2).[a] There God is said to be essentializing essences, so that those can, in turn, essentialize others. [God] himself is the source of all essence, the source of light, *the source of life,*[b] *the father of spirits,*[c] and *the father of lights.*[d] He essentializes the heavenly spirits. From him flow the essential rays of divinity and the essential angels, who, in turn, pour essence into other beings. God himself is in them, and the light of his Word shines in them.

Thus the Father assigned to Christ all the power of essentializing, so that he could essentialize all things. *All things are* and *are held together through* Christ and *in him,* as Paul teaches.[e] [Christ] bears, carries, and *upholds all things by the word of his power* (Hebrews 1).[f] *All things are held together <u>in him</u>,* both *in heaven and on earth* (Colossians 1).[g] The angels were made sharers in Christ's deity, and this is written about in the Law.[h] Through angels God sends out his light, and this light is God himself. And Christ himself, whom the angels serve, is the dispenser of God's light, sending it out from his substance: <u>sending the Spirit out from his own substance.</u> He sends out the

Err, 101v

Err, 102r

Err, 102r

---

[a] The name Jehovah (*Yahweh Elohim*) is used for the first time in Gen 2:4, immediately after the verse in which God rested on the seventh day. Before that, the name Elohim is used. [b] Ps 36:9.
[c] Heb 12:9. [d] James 1:17. [e] Col 1:17. [f] Heb 1:3. [g] Col 1:17.
[h] For example, Ps 103:20.

Spirit by means of angels, and this spirit is God himself. The essence of God, the very spirit of God, divinity itself, the very light of God, always shines there. For this reason he is called Jehovah Zebaoth (Lord of Hosts),[13] that is, he who creates his own armies, or the essence of warfare. Jehovah endows all the heavenly hosts and armies with the splendour of his essence. Although [scripture] says that there are innumerable thousands of infinities and myriads of myriads [of angels],[14] Jehovah is <u>nevertheless</u> in all of them (Psalm 67 and Daniel 7).[a] This is why the <u>divine</u> name is always in the names of angels: because [God's] essence is in them.[15]

[*The Omniform Essence of God*]

The <u>universal and omniform</u> essence of God essentializes human beings and all other things. His spirit was implanted in us from the beginning, and afterwards more abundantly poured into us. God therefore has within himself the essences of infinite thousands, and the natures of infinite thousands. These are distinguished from each other, not metaphysically, but in an ineffable way. From this we draw a conclusion opposite to what the trinitarians sophistically teach. For they **[129]** set up three invisible metaphysical beings in one essence and nature, like three [geometrical] points in a single point.[b] We, on the contrary, say that there is one [divine] being only, which contains the essences of infinite thousands and the natures of infinite thousands. Not only is God infinite in terms of the number of beings to whom he communicates, but also in terms of the modes of his deity. The divine modes <u>in [all] things, pre-formed in God from eternity</u>, are inef-

---

[a] Dan 7:10; Ps 68:17. The most reliable reading of Ps 68:17 is, "The chariots of God are twenty thousand, thousands of thousands," though some texts say "angels" instead of "chariots." On the problems with the text of Psalm 68, see A.R3.30. [b] See *Restoration*, 41 (book 1), 119 (book 3), A.R3.22.

fable. However, we will now explain <u>those modes</u>, at least as far as human frailty will permit.

There is a single primary divine mode, which is the source of the others. This is the mode of the fullness of substance, the divine mode without measure,[a] present only in the body and spirit of Jesus Christ. <u>It is a twofold mode, and hence there are said to be two persons</u>. It is a mode of manifestation in the Word, and a mode of communication in the Spirit[b]—a corporeal <u>mode</u> and a spiritual <u>mode</u>. Both of these are modes of substance, essentializing other beings in body and spirit: the source of all life, all light, and all spirit. <u>This is God's eternal plan for all things, and his manifestation by means of that mode, from which come</u> all other modes, like branches from a trunk, sprouts from a root, or shoots from a vine.

There is another divine mode of spirit given according to measure: one [measure] to us, and another to the angels. Further, one spirit is innate, and another, over and above, is given by grace. Each of these is manifold, in accordance with a distribution made by Christ. The final [divine] mode is in each and every thing, according to its own specific and individual ideal form. This is the lowest [mode] of all. Nevertheless, there is some divinity in all things. These are the modes of divinity that are in us, in our present state. There will be more and loftier [modes] after resurrection, which we will not touch upon here.

For the moment, regarding this final mode, <u>which is now</u> in individual things, and speaking simply of the essence of God, we say that the essence of all things is God himself. God encompasses and contains all things.[c]

---

[a] John 3:34.   [b] See the opening paragraph of *Restoration*: "The manifestation of God himself through the Word, and his communication by means of the Spirit, both become substance in Christ alone" (*Restoration*, 3).   [c] *Corpus Hermeticum* 8.5. Unless otherwise noted, all references to *Corpus Hermeticum* in the footnotes are to the Ficino translation.

<u>God</u> **[130]** *upholds* and *carries* us (Isaiah 46 and 63).[a] He *gives life to all things* (1 Timothy 6).[b] *In him we live, move, and have our being* (Acts 17).[c] *All things are held together in him* (Colossians 1).[d] <u>All things are from him, through him, and in him.</u>[e] All things are in him. He gives existence to things, and he is the formal [pattern] of all individual forms. Because he contains in his essence the ideal forms of all things, he may be considered the formal portion of all things. And, by a special dispensation applicable to ourselves alone, we are said to be sharers in the divine nature. He is <u>our</u> portion, and a portion of our spirit. This is not like earthly possession of land, but is a possession which is heavenly and divine, so that we may rightfully say, *the Lord is my portion* and *my share* (Psalm 15 and 72).[f] Through Christ, a share of the divine spirit is distributed to us and we all receive this share from his fullness, just as, long ago, it was said that a share of the spirit of Moses was distributed to others.[g]

God is said to be in all other created things, not by means of a gift of the spirit, but in another, more general way. Thus he sustains the essence of all things, so that any created thing whatsoever, left without this sustenance, reverts to nothingness, just as it came from nothing. The ancient Hebrews and the philosophers taught this very thing. Among the Hebrews, Rabbi Moses [Maimonides] the Egyptian says in book 1, chapter 68 of his *Guide for the Perplexed*:[h] "In the Creator is everything that is," and he himself is in all things, to help and sustain them, "by that mode which is called splendour" or secondary light.[16] [Abraham] Ibn Ezra teaches the same thing in [his commentary on] Genesis,[17] as do all the other [Jewish

---

[a] Isa 46:3, 63:9.   [b] 1 Tim 6:13.   [c] Acts 17:28   [d] Col 1:17.
[e] See Rom 11:36, Col 1:16.   [f] Ps 16:5, 73:26.   [g] Num 11:24-25.
[h] Maimonides, *Guide for the Perplexed* 1.68 (in modern editions, section 1.69).

commentators], and the prophets themselves. All of the ancient philosophers agree with this. It is now the proper time to hear what they have to say.

In *Parmenides*, *Cratylus*, and *Phaedo*, Plato asserts, based on Pythagoras, Anaxagoras, and other more ancient [philosophers], and on the wise Zoroaster and [Hermes] Trismegistus, that there is One, that is the prime being, and that all things are contained and held together in the One.[18] Only the One is beautiful and good in itself. Other things are not called beautiful and good, except by participation in the One.[a] And they are more beautiful the closer they come to it. The One is [131] the sole ψύχωσιν (*psychosin*, animator) of the world. It is a kind of νοῦν (*nous*, mind), ἔχουσαν (*echousan*, containing) in itself all of the natures of the world. For in it all things are held together and διακοσμοῦσαν (*diakosmousan*, set in order).[b] Hence the world is called κοσμος (*kosmos*, the universe). In *Cratylus* Socrates calls God φυσέχην (*physichin*, natural), the essence of nature, because God ὀχεῖ (*ochei*, carries) and ἔχει (*echei*, contains) φύσιν (*physis*, nature) itself.[19] In the natural order, all motions lead back to one prime mover, all natures to one nature, and all lives to one primary life, through which and in which all other things live and move.

God himself, all the ancient theologians say, shed light on everything coming out of chaos.[c] And by drawing out disordered matter from [chaos], he introduced bright and visible forms, in the likeness of his own beauty. Being himself beautiful and good, he first made the light, beautiful and good like himself, and then all the other things, beautiful and good, as described in Genesis. For

---

[a] Plato, *Phaedo* (100c-d). [b] Plato, *Cratylus* (400a), quoted in Steuco, *De perenni philosophia* 1.5, 4.8. [c] Ficino, *Theologia Platonica* 10.7.2. See Plato, *Timaeus* (30a, 69b).

the Hebrew word טוב (*tov*) means beautiful and good.[a] Iamblichus, Macrobius, and Philo, citing very ancient [philosophers], say that the mind is the mother of the forms of all things, and contains in itself the ideal forms of things, putting on things the stamp of its own deity:[b] that is, spirit and light. For within itself it contains the light which forms all things, and the spirit which it breathes into things. Zoroaster teaches the same thing in *The Oracles of Wisdom*, which [in Greek] is called μαγικά λογια (*Magika Logia, The Magical Oracles*).[c]

The oracle of Apollo, cited by Porphyry in book 10 of *On the Praise of Philosophy*,[20] clearly says that God himself is the form, the soul, and the spirit of all things.[d] But he cannot be perceived, even by angels, unless he decides to make himself seen in some way. This was the inscription on [the statue of Isis], the Egyptian goddess of Wisdom, as cited by Plutarch in "Isis," as well as by Proclus: "I am everything that has been, that is, and that shall be. No mortal has yet drawn aside my veil."[e] It is Wisdom who truly contains everything in herself. As Seneca writes, "God is all that you see and all that you do not see." Lactantius also cites Seneca.[f] On this subject Plotinus, in his book "On Providence," says that the eternal mind,

---

[a] *Tov* is the word used in Genesis 1 when God looks at the things he has made and sees that they are good. See Gen 1:4, 10, 12, 18, 21, 25, 31.   [b] Iamblichus, *De Mysteriis*, 245-246 (cites Heraclitus). Macrobius, *In Somnium Scipionis* 1.2 (cites Plato); quoted in Steuco, *De perenni philosophia* 1.6. Philo, *Questions on Genesis* (cites Moses); quoted in Eusebius, *Praeparatio evangelica* 7.18 (PG 21 559A-B).
[c] Steuco, *De perenni philosophia* 1.7. The title *Magika Logia* is from Steuco, *De perenni philosophia* 9.15.   [d] Steuco, *De perenni philosophia* 3.14.   [e] Plutarch, *Moralia*, "Isis and Osiris" 9, and Proclus, *Platonic Theology* 7.21; both quoted in Steuco, *De perenni philosophia* 2.6.
[f] Seneca, *Quaestiones naturales*, 1.pref.13, quoted in Steuco, *De perenni philosophia* 6.2. Steuco also cites a similar passage in Lactantius, *Divinae institutiones* 2.9, which refers to Seneca, *De beneficiis* 4.7.1.

Book 4

[132] <u>in which all things are held together and which is itself unmoved, sets everything in motion; and that it contains the natures of all things.</u> [Plotinus also says] "This world is the shadow and likeness" [of the eternal mind].[a]

In his sacred discourse in *Pimander*, [Hermes] Trismegistus, the father of ancient philosophy, <u>sings thus:</u> "God is the nature of all things, the glory and the source of all things,"[b] and "he in whom all nature is held together."[c] To [his son] Tat, he says, "All things are one God,"[d] and "he is, so to speak, many-bodied, since there is nothing in bodies that he is not."[e] And later he says, "God originates, encompasses, and contains all things."[f] In effect, he is all things. And this idea is in [Hermes'] book *The Beautiful and the Good Are in God Alone*. "All things," he says, "are in God and depend on him."[g] In the same book he says, "God is all things"[h] and "God, who creates all things, makes all things similar to himself,"[i] just as "every agent produces something similar to itself."[21] In *Asclepius*, he says, "God is everything in all things and the omniform varieties [of all things]."[j] He says that the Word of God is the archetypal world, "the archetypal light, and the archetype of the soul."[k] And "In <u>all things</u>, there shines some image of God."[l] Hence he sings in the hymn in *Pimander*, "Holy is God, whose image is all of nature."[m] To his son Tat, he says, "There is nothing in the nature of things that does not display some likeness of divinity."[n] All around

---

[a] Plotinus, *Enneads* 3.2.1-3 and 3.8.11, quoted in Steuco, *De perenni philosophia* 1.17, 1.19. "On Providence" is *Enneads* 3.2 and 3.3.
[b] *Corpus Hermeticum* (CH) 3.1.   [c] CH 3.4.   [d] CH 12.8 ("All things are one").   [e] CH 5.10.   [f] CH 8.5, quoted in Steuco, *De perenni philosophia* 7.9.   [g] CH 9.9, quoted (along with the title *The Beautiful and the Good Are in God Alone*) in Steuco, *De perenni philosophia* 8.10.   [h] CH 9.9.   [i] CH 9.5.   [j] *Asclepius* 34.   [k] CH 2.12, quoted in Steuco, *De perenni philosophia* 1.10.   [l] CH 5.2.
[m] CH 1.31.   [n] CH 5.9 ("There is nothing in the nature of things that he is not"). See also CH 12.23.

us we observe with our own eyes <u>the omniform</u> image <u>of God</u>,[a] which is the image of light <u>in all things</u>, presenting itself and imprinting itself on us.

In Acts 17 Paul <u>teaches the same thing: God can almost be touched in everything, since he is implanted in every single thing. [Paul]</u> quotes [the poet] Aratus: "We are the offspring of the Divine," and of the race of God,[b] as Pythagoras says.[22] For we have in us the seeds of deity, <u>which are truly innate in us, because the divine spirit is in us from birth</u>. In the same chapter [of Acts], <u>the Apostle</u> says that in God himself *we live, move, and have our being*.[c] <u>In him we breathe.</u> Our life and our breath are <u>in</u> him,[d] <u>and we depend on him</u>. For this reason early philosophers said that Jove is air or is [to be found] in the air in which we live,[23] since in the air there is divine, life-giving breath. Aratus, whom Paul cites speaking of Jove, also said, **[133]** "Everything is full of Jove."[e] And "Whatever you see is Jupiter; wherever you go is Jupiter."[f]

[The ancient Romans] spoke of [God] as Jove, which follows the tradition of the ancient Hebrews, who called God *Jova*. [The Hebrew] *Jova*, which is indeclinable, is turned, by means of an inflection, into *Jovem* [the accusative case of the name of the Roman god *Jovis*].[24] *Jova*, however, is the way יהוה (*Jehovah*) is pronounced, since the *shva* is silent at the beginning [of a word], and the pronunciation of the aspirate is omitted, which happens not infrequently in that language.[25]

---

[a] Ficino, *Theologia Platonica* 11.4.14.   [b] Acts 17:28-29. "We are the offspring of God" and "We are of the race of God" are two different ways of translating Acts 17:28: the Vulgate uses the word *genus* (race), and Erasmus's New Testament uses *progenies* (offspring).   [c] Acts 17:28.   [d] Paraphrase of Acts 17:25.   [e] Aratus, *Phenomena*, line 3. The poem is quoted in Steuco, *De perenni philosophia* 3.13, 3.16, and *Enarrationes in Iob* 9.   [f] Lucan, *Pharsalia* 9.580. In Steuco, *Enarrationes in Iob* 9, this line appears immediately after the quotation from Aratus. Steuco does not identify the source as Lucan, so Servetus may have interpreted this as another line from Aratus.

Book 4

[Hermes] Trismegistus, speaking about the Spirit to Asclepius, says, "The spirit of God fills all things and gives life to all things," and "The world feeds bodies, while the spirit feeds and sustains souls."[a] In his third discourse [Hermes] says that the spirit, which gives life to all things, proceeds from a sacred source.[b] He says that the soul maintains its connection with, and its dependency on, its origin,[c] just as light and heat depend on their source. David expresses this same thought in Psalm 103: when God withdraws his spirit, souls die.[26] Likewise, all the Platonists[27] affirm that God is the soul of the world[d] and that the spirit of the universe sustains all things and gives them life. I shall soon say more about this universal essence and the ideal forms of all things. But first I will say something about <u>the word</u> *Elohim*.

{*Elohim*}

[*What Exists from Eternity*]

So that we may <u>give a more reliable account of</u> the name Elohim, we must look into what has been said about God, as the name Elohim must be consistent with that.

According to the *Bereshit Rabbah*, or *Great Genesis*, the ancient Hebrews taught that these <u>seven</u> things have existed from the beginning of the world: the Messiah, the throne of God's glory, the city of Jerusalem, the garden of Paradise, the souls of the just, the Law, and Israel.[28] Truly, the throne of deity, the seat of glorious majesty seen by Isaiah, has existed from the beginning, with the Messiah himself (Isaiah 6).[e] This is <u>shown to us</u> in Deuteronomy 33, Jeremiah 17, Psalm 92, and Psalm

---

[a] *Asclepius* 16, 18, quoted in Steuco, *De perenni philosophia* 2.3.
[b] *Corpus Hermeticum* 3.1, quoted in Steuco, *De perenni philosophia* 2.3.   [c] *Corpus Hermeticum* 10.14, quoted in Steuco, *De perenni philosophia* 2.3.   [d] Plato, *Timaeus* (30c).   [e] Isa 6:1.

102, all of which speak of the throne and the seat of God, <u>unchanged</u> from the beginning [of the world].^a This is *our holy place*, prepared *from the beginning*, as Jeremiah says.^b It is the garden of celestial paradise and *the heavenly city of Jerusalem*.^c And Christ says that *a kingdom has been prepared for* us *from the beginning*, as well as the [*eternal*] *fire* **[134]** of retribution with which the wicked are to be punished (Matthew 20 and 25 and Isaiah 30).^d

<u>Bear in mind</u> the sense in which the Hebrews <u>said</u> that the Messiah existed from the beginning—not in the manner proposed by the trinitarian sophists, but because <u>his</u> person and visible form was in God. <u>Hence Rabbi Isaac ben Arama [in his midrashic commentary] on Genesis said, "Before the sun was created, the name of the Messiah was there, already seated on the throne of God."</u>^e <u>If only our sophists held this point of view.</u> The Hebrews prove, from <u>a passage in</u> Deuteronomy, chapter 33, that from the beginning, the Law was in the right hand of God.^f And because the Law is said to have been *written with the finger of God* in God's book,^g [they say] that it was brought down to earth from heaven.^h They also assert that Israel existed from the beginning, because it is said that *the people of old*, that is, the eternal people, *were established* from the beginning (Isaiah 44)ⁱ and *engraved on* [*the hands of*] *God* (Isaiah 49).^j Likewise they demonstrate that the earthly Jerusalem was founded in the beginning (2 Kings 19, Isaiah 37 and 49, and Psalm 86).^k

---

^a Deut 33:27; Jer 17:12; Ps 93:2; 103:19.   ^b Jer 17:12.   ^c Heb 12:22.   ^d Matt 20:1-16 (parable of the vineyard); Matt 25:31-46 (separating the sheep and the goats); Isa 30:33.   ^e Isaac ben Moses Arama, *The Offering of Isaac* 47, translated in Galatino, *De Arcanis* 3.17.   ^f Deut 33:2.   ^g Ex 31:18 (written with the finger of God); Deut 31:24-26 (written in a book).   ^h Ex 32:15-16; Neh 9:13.   ⁱ Isa 44:7.   ^j Isa 49:16.   ^k 2 Kg 19:25; Isa 37:26; 49:14-16; Ps 87:5.

Book 4

But since these were foreshadowings of a very different truth, [and] since we [Christians] are implanted substantially in Christ by the eternal spirit, we can more truly claim to be, in a special way, sharers in Christ from eternity. The spirits of those reborn in Christ are in Christ in substance, recorded in the book of glory. They possess eternity, that is, they have a share in Christ's eternal spirit. For they possess a portion of the substance of his spirit or substantial breath. Thus it is fitting that the kingly throne of Christ is adorned and attended upon by those chosen for all eternity. This extends to what Christ says to the apostles: *You have been with me from the beginning; your names are written in heaven.*[a] *You are the people of old, engraved in God.*[b] [God's] *throne has been from the beginning.*[c] There could never have been talk of a heavenly city at that time, unless there were citizens in that city.[d]

Behold how great is the power of the eternity of Christ, and how much of his eternal deity is shared with us according to special forms and spirits. Indeed, not only the spirits of the just, but also those of other human beings, and **[135]** the luminous forms of all things, exist from eternity in God, as we will soon say about ideal forms. This applies especially to the elect, predestined in Christ himself,[29] who are in number twelve times one hundred and forty-four thousand thousands of thousands (Revelation 21).[30] For these *there are many* homes, or *mansions*,[e] prepared from eternity, and a spirit prepared for each of them in God.

Also existing in God from the beginning, and seen around the throne of majesty, are cherubim and seraphim, and heavenly powers, principalities, and authorities, having various duties, together with their thrones, as Paul

---

[a] John 15:27, Luke 10:20. [b] Isa 44:7. [c] Ps 93:2. [d] See Heb 12:22. [e] John 14:2-3.

and Daniel say.[a] There are also, as Daniel says, countless myriads of legions of attendant spirits and ministering angels.[b] Ezekiel saw [many] beings in God in chapters 1 and 10, where he says that he *saw visions of gods*.[31] In the last chapter of 1 Kings, Michaiah saw similar visions, as did David in 2 Samuel 22.[c] Ezekiel attests that *the sound of the words* of God *was like the sound of an army*, and Daniel attests in chapter 10 that God's voice is *like the sound of a multitude*.[d] Such great majesty was seen and heard in the multitude, in which shone the splendours of the faces of Christ, or, as the Hebrews have it, the splendours of the faces exhibited by the angels, and the various faces of the cherubim and seraphim,[e] with so many flashing eyes[f] and so many forms of deity.

[*The Plurality in God*]

So many things seen and heard in heaven by Adam, Abraham, and others, could not be called anything else than Elohim, gods; Adonim, lords; or Adonai, my lords. Jacob saw and recorded this plurality in God, saying that gods were revealed to him (Genesis 35). And Abraham said, "gods made me a wanderer" (Genesis 20).[g] From these passages it is clear that Elohim contained many things in himself. In fact, Elohim was God. The form [of Elohim] was Christ, together with a multitudinous ministry of angels. In summary, Elohim contains divinities,

---

[a] Col 1:16; Dan 7:9. A listing of the ranks of angels is found in [Dionysius the Areopagite], *De coelesti hierarchia* 6.2 (PG 3 203A-206A). See *De coelesti hierarchia* chapters 7-10 for further discussion of the powers and duties of the different ranks of angels. [b] Dan 7:10.
[c] 1 Kg 22:19; 2 Sam 22:7-16. [d] Ezek 1:24; Dan 10:6. [e] Ezek 9:3; chapter 10; 11:22 (cherubim); Isa 6:2, 6 (seraphim). [f] Dan 10:6 (eyes like flaming torches); Ezek 1:18 (eyes on Ezekiel's wheels); Ezek 10:12 (cherubim covered with eyes). [g] Gen 35:7: "Elohim appeared to him." Gen 20:13: "Elohim made me wander from my father's home." In these verses, the word Elohim is used with a plural verb.

Book 4

or splendid forms: blessed gods, or the faces of gods. The name [Elohim] was first applied to God, and then to other beings who displayed illustrious forms. **[136]** When angels were sent on a ministry, they assumed a divine persona, under the person of Christ, and were therefore called gods.

Concerning this name [Elohim] the trinitarians are wildly incoherent. For they assert that the word "gods" is predicated of the three beings [of the Trinity], as if these were three gods, which they themselves deny. <u>Was it these three gods who</u> caused Abraham to become a wanderer, <u>and who</u> appeared to Jacob? <u>If they admit that there are three and that they are gods, it follows that there are three gods</u>. Besides, the Jews would never concede that these three beings exist in God. So that they <u>could</u> avoid the idea of a plurality in God, they <u>attributed</u> the use of a plural noun to linguistic tradition, claiming that there is nothing mysterious about it. But if they were to acknowledge the true Messiah, they would recognize that the mystery of God, Christ, and the angels was made clear in the word Elohim, which is sanctioned throughout the Law. <u>For</u> the customary use of the plural [in Hebrew] did not happen by chance, nor could it have arisen in the sacred language without an element of mystery.

What is more, in addition <u>to the passages already cited</u>, where gods [Elohim] caused [Abraham] to become a wanderer and gods [Elohim] appeared [to Jacob], plural words are used in several other places [in the Hebrew scriptures]. [Elohim] are called *holy gods* in Joshua 24, *living gods* in Jeremiah 10 and 23, and *gods who judge* in Psalm 57.[a] In 2 Samuel 7, gods, that is, the heavenly powers — God, Christ, and the angels — *went to redeem [the Jews]*.[b] Indeed, now that Christ alone contains, in himself, all that

---

[a] Josh 24:19; Jer 10:10; Jer 23:36; Ps 58:11. In these verses, as in Gen 20:13 and 35:7, the word *Elohim* is used with a plural verb.   [b] 2 Sam 7:23.

is *his and the Father's*, along with the majesty *of the angels*, as Jesus himself attests in chapter 9 of Luke,[a] he is rightly called Elohim, possessing divinity in all of its forms.

It is open to question whether the name Jehovah should be assigned to Christ. However, there is no doubt that in the Law an angel is called Jehovah.[b] Therefore, Christ is far more worthy [of that name], <u>particularly</u> since that name is given to the angel [who appears] in the form of Christ. Just as, in the beginning, Elohim and Jehovah were the same — because God was the Word — so too are they now, since Christ has been raised to his original glory. Nevertheless, when Christ was active on earth, the name [Jehovah] was not assigned to him by the prophets, and **[137]** Christ claimed for himself [at most] the deity of Elohim.[32] But now he is the true Jehovah, who causes all things to be and sustains them, and grants the power of performing miracles. He is the source of the light which forms all things, and pours the ideal forms of things into our minds; <u>for</u> the ideal forms were previously in the Wisdom of God, which <u>now</u> is Christ himself.

{*The Ideas or Forms of All Things Are in God*}

We have several times come upon the term "ideal forms." Since an understanding of these produces a deeper knowledge of Christ, and of the essence of God and a revelation of his names, we must now speak about them.

[*Ideal Forms*]

The images, or representations, of all things were in God from eternity — in wisdom itself, in the Word <u>of God</u> itself — as they were shining in the world of archetypes.

---

[a] Luke 9:26.   [b] There is no place in the Bible where an angel is specifically called Jehovah/Yahweh (usually translated as "the Lord"), but sometimes the Angel of the Lord speaks in the voice of the Lord. See, for example, Gen 16:7-13, Ex 3:2-4, Judg 2:1-4, Judg 6:11-22.

For God saw all things in himself, by his own light. He saw the ideal forms of all things within himself, as though they were shining in a mirror. From the beginning of the world this was the accepted teaching about the wisdom of God, recorded in sacred literature. This doctrine, handed down from their ancestors, was taught to the Greeks by the Chaldeans and the Egyptians. This is what Job, Moses, David, Solomon, and others taught in holy scripture. The same thing was taught to all the Greeks, from Orpheus to Plato, by Zoroaster and [Hermes] Trismegistus—chiefly by Trismegistus.[a] In both *Pimander* and *Asclepius* he teaches that, in the first patterns of the world, the shining forms of all things were contained in the Word of God; and that the first architect of the world possessed a kind of innate wisdom, filled with the ideal forms and origins of all things.[b]

[*Wisdom: The Maker and Form of All Things*]

These words are written about the wisdom in God himself: God observes every single thing, sees all things under heaven, and regulates each thing, as taught long ago, in Job 28.[c] For more about this wisdom, describing how everything existed from the beginning with God, see the Proverbs of Solomon, chapter 8.[d] It is spoken of in the same way in Baruch, chapter 3,[e] and more extensively in Ecclesiasticus[f]—that is, the book of Jesus son of Sirach—and in the book of Wisdom. There Wisdom is called *a unique and manifold spirit,*[g] containing all things. We are taught that *Wisdom is the maker of all things,*[h] like an architect who contains in himself an idea of a future

---

[a] Steuco, *De perenni philosophia* 7.8. See also A.R3.27.
[b] Ficino, introduction to book 1 of *Corpus Hermeticum*. See also *Corpus Hermeticum* 1.8-9.   [c] Job 28:24.   [d] Prov 8:22-31.
[e] Baruch 3:32-37.   [f] Ecclus 1:1-10.   [g] Wisdom 7:22.
[h] Wisdom 7:22.

[138] house. In chapter 8 [of Proverbs], Wisdom itself says, *In God's presence I was a multitude,*³³ *and I was daily his delight*;^a that is, a multitude of <u>ideal forms</u>, with their delights, producing every single thing.

<u>Wisdom is everything that was, everything that is, and everything that will be.</u> Wisdom itself was the λογος (*logos*): the miraculous design, in which <u>all things</u> shone visibly. The Word of God is God's wisdom. The light of Christ's face is for us the light of understanding, and the ideal form of all things. It is the visible and audible word of God, both in terms of sense perception and intellectual understanding. From the words we speak, the sense of hearing perceives this or that idea, just as the eye perceives by vision. But the Word of God contains at once all things that are seen, heard, and understood, indeed all that is perceived by the other senses as well.

[*The Omniform World*]

The Word of God was called by the ancients the omniform <u>world</u>, the archetypal world, the intellectual world. Trismegistus, after the sermons to Asclepius and to his son Tat, is taught by Mind that there is an omniform world in God, that this lower world was created in its likeness, and that in God there exists the ideal form of the world, which expresses the forms by means of individual bodies.^b <u>In this way</u> all things exist and are contained in God. Orpheus said that God's essence is omniform, <u>having all forms in itself</u>.³⁴ This is <u>shown to us</u> in this way: he sustains the forms of all things. And to sustain them, he sees them in himself, as they appear in his own light.^c We call these appearances ideal forms.

<u>There is another reason why</u> human beings conceive the likenesses of things according to divine images: because

---

^a Prov 8:30.   ^b *Corpus Hermeticum* 11.16.   ^c Steuco, *De perenni philosophia* 1.28.

God himself places the likenesses and the ideal forms in their minds. This is what Mind teaches Trismegistus in the passage cited above, speaking to him as to a friend: "Consider how many things you know. Then contemplate God, who possesses all knowledge in himself. Thus, unless you <u>make</u> yourself like God, you cannot understand God. For like is understood by like."[a] Therefore, the likenesses and ideal forms of things are in God. If they are in us, we too become like God. <u>Seneca writes to</u> **[139]** <u>Lucilius: "God has within himself the patterns of all things, their quantities and measures. He is filled with the shapes that Plato calls unchangeable ideal forms."</u>[b]

But let us seek no further for confirmation of this. For all these things are amply proven in holy scripture, once we come to understand, through Christ, the special character of the light of God, which makes all things visible and bright. <u>In the Word was shining the life of every [human being] (John 1).</u>[c] The ideal forms of the things to be created were in the mind of God before the things themselves were created. God knew all kinds of things and viewed them in his own light, saying, *Let the earth bring forth living creatures according to their kinds*[d] and *<u>let the earth bring forth plants according to their kinds</u>*.[e]

In the same way, when we are planning to build a house, a city, or any other thing, we form ideas in our minds, which <u>themselves</u> are from the light of God, <u>or</u> are like the light of God. This reasoning powerfully inspired Timaeus of Locris, Archytas, and Plato.[f] We think about things that are communicated to us by divine wisdom, which, as Philo says, are <u>in us</u> *an emanation of the glory of God, a radiance of eternal light, and a spotless mirror,*

---

[a] *Corpus Hermeticum* 11.20. [b] Seneca, Letter to Lucilius 65.7, quoted in Steuco, *De perenni philosophia* 6.5. [c] John 1:4. [d] Gen 1:24.
[e] Gen 1:11. [f] Ficino, *Theologia Platonica* 11.3.9 (Archytas); 3.2.6, 5.13.13 (Plato and Timaeus).

reflecting all things in us as *his image* (Wisdom 7).ᵃ Also, Jesus the son of Sirach, having studied *the books of his forefathers*, in which, he says, *was no small or contemptible teaching*,ᵇ teaches that there is a wisdom in God, in which God himself, as if by his own light, *saw and numbered* all created things, every *drop of rain* and all *the sands of the sea*.ᶜ This same *wisdom, poured* into us,ᵈ gives us a clear understanding of things.

[Ideal Forms in God's Book]

This tradition of the Hebrews is plain to see. In *On the Allegorical Interpretation of the Laws*, which is based on the teachings of the Torah, Philo proves the existence of ideal forms, explaining the words of Moses, *Blot me out of your book*.ᵉ Here Philo says, "Moses calls the word of God a book, in which the existences of all things are written down and engraved."ᶠ Psalm 138 (in the Hebrew Bible, Psalm 139) renders this beautifully. The prophet David says to God, *In your book all* these *things were written down, when none of them as yet existed*.ᵍ <u>Consider what it means to say that all things were written in God's book before they existed.</u> In Psalm 55: *You have numbered my wanderings; all things are in your book*.ʰ In Psalm 49 God says, **[140]** *I know that all [the birds] and all [the beasts] of the field are with me*.ⁱ One of the ancients, Plato, writes to Dionysius [Dionysius II, tyrant of Syracuse], "all things are always present to the king of the universe."ʲ <u>In the Book of Revelation John teaches that the books of God, in which all things are written, will be opened so that</u>

ᵃ Philo, *Questions on Genesis* 1.57, citing Wisdom 7:25-26; quoted in Eusebius, *Praeparatio evangelica* 11.14 (PG 21 886A).   ᵇ Ecclus, Prologue.   ᶜ Ecclus 1:1-2.   ᵈ Ecclus 1:9.   ᵉ Ex 32:32.   ᶠ Philo, *On the Allegorical Interpretation of the Laws* 1:19, quoted in Steuco, *De perenni philosophia* 1.26.   ᵍ Ps 139:16 (Pagnini).   ʰ Ps 56:8 (may be Ps 56:9 or 56:9-10 in different versions of the Bible).
ⁱ Ps 50:11.   ʲ Second Platonic epistle (312e), quoted in Steuco, *De perenni philosophia* 2.3.

Book 4

judgement can be passed on all [the dead] according to these writings—an enormous volume filled with ideal forms and writings.[a]

[*Ideal Forms in the Church Fathers*]

The earliest disciples of the church held the same opinion about ideal forms. In book 2, chapters 3 and 21, Irenaeus says that there were "preformations of all things in God." He said that God preformed all things in himself, and "took the pattern and form of all things from within himself." And in book 4, chapter 37, he says that God "took from himself the substance of created things, the patterns of the things he made, and the forms of the adornments in the world." There he also says, "the Word of God contains what are, in effect, designs of things [to come]."[b] In *Against Praxeas*, Tertullian says that before the creation of the world everything existed in the wisdom of God, arranged and made according to his plan. "The only thing lacking was that these things could not be openly perceived or grasped in material form."[c] Similarly, in *Against Hermogenes*, Tertullian says that wisdom contains the likenesses of all things.[d]

In books 4 and 5 of *Stromata*, Clement of Alexandria, approving [Plato's] discussion of ideal forms, defines an ideal form as λόγον θεοῦ (*logon theou*), the Word of God. He says, "There is a region of God which is difficult to grasp, which Plato, who was taught by Moses himself,[35] called the χώραν ἰδεῶν (*choran ideon*), the region of ideal forms, which contains everything in the universe."[e] He also says, "The mind of God is the region of ideal forms,"

---

[a] Rev 20:12.   [b] Irenaeus, *Adversus haereses* 2.3.2, 2.16.3, 4.20.1, 4.20.11 (PG 7 718A, 760B-C, 1032B, 1041C). The chapter numbers cited by Servetus are from Erasmus's edition of Irenaeus.
[c] Tertullian, *Adversus Praxean* 6 (PL 2 161A-B).   [d] Tertullian, *Adversus Hermogenem* 20 (PL 2 215B).   [e] Clement of Alexandria, *Stromata* 5.3, 5.11 (PG 9 31B, 111A).

and "A human being contemplating ideal forms almost becomes a god."[a] In that way, souls, existing separately, are visible gods when they associate themselves with divine, or ideal, forms. In *Exhortation to the Heathen*, [Clement] says that we are, from the beginning, born in God himself, since all things existed in the Word.[b] There is nothing wondrous in this: if [scripture] says that the Word was born [in the beginning], then it is saying that we, too, in some way, were also born at that time. Generation is discussed there in terms of personal likeness. The same thought is found in book 7 of *Stromata*. He says, "The Word of the Father is first of all, before anything that is born, the teacher of all those who are formed in it."[c]

Origen, in his **[141]** third homily on the Song of Songs, says that the patterns of all things were in the heavens, so that just as God made humankind in his own image, he also made other creatures according to other celestial images.[d] And all the things that are visible in the world were at one time in God invisibly (Hebrews 11).[e] In his homily on John, chapter 1, [Origen] says that life, light, and the forms of all things were in the Word,[f] in the same way that things that will appear in the future are in seeds. Behold the true teaching, which was known to the first Christians, just as it was to the ancient Hebrews and the most eminent philosophers. Augustine, in question 46 of his book *83 Questions*, as well as in many passages in *The City of God*, says that an ideal form is a λογόν (*logon*), a thought or imagination of the mind.[g] Thus in God the λογός (*logos*) was truly an ideal thought, representing an image.

---

[a] Clement of Alexandria, *Stromata* 4.25 (PG 8 1363C). [b] Clement of Alexandria, *Adversus gentes* 1 (PG 8 62B). [c] Clement of Alexandria, *Stromata* 7.2 (PG 9 411A). [d] Origen, *In Canticum canticorum*, 3.12 (PG 13 173A-C). [e] Heb 11:3. [f] Origen, *In evangelium Ioannis* 1.22 (PG 14 55D-58A). [g] Augustine, *De diversis quaestionibus LXXXIII* 46.2 (PL 40 30); *De civitate Dei* 8.6 (PL 41 231), 10.14 (PL 41 292).

[Ideal Forms in Ezekiel's Vision]

Ezekiel's vision, in chapters 1 and 10, confirms that this is the way ideal forms function in God. For in that vision there are wheels full of living and seeing eyes, just like those shining in the animals and their various faces.[a] Even though the prophet saw, in this mysterious way, only four faces there, nevertheless all other things always shine out in God. God himself is full of eyes with which he contemplates, present in himself, all things that are, and were, and will be. There are infinite eyes and infinite fountains in the one essence of God. For according to the Hebrew way of speaking,[b] the eyes of God [may be called] living fountains[c] which pour into everything, in which all things are seen reflected *as in a mirror*[d] and in which all things exist. Here is the book of God's writing, which contains the existences of all things,[e] even, as Christ says, *the hairs of your head.*[f]

Now let us explain the vision of Ezekiel, since until now it has been poorly understood.

In [the vision] there is a fiery chariot coming *out of the north*,[g] to incinerate the city and drive the Jews swiftly into exile in Babylon. This chariot was sent by God through Christ, as explained in chapters 10 and 43.[h] God in his anger declares that [the Jews] must be compelled to go

---

[a] Ezek 1:18, 10:12 (wheels with eyes), 1:5-14, 10:14 (creatures with four faces).   [b] The Hebrew word עין (*ayin*), a common word meaning "eye," can also be used to mean "fountain." See, for example, Deut 8:7; 33:28; Prov 8:28. Servetus could have found this information in Pagnini's *Thesaurus*.   [c] Ps 36:9; Prov 13:14 (fountain of life); Jer 2:13; 17:13 (fountain of living waters).   [d] 2 Cor 3:18.   [e] See, for example, Ex 32:32-33; Ps 56:8; 139:16 (God's book); Ps 69:28; Phil 4:3; Rev 3:5; 20:12 (book of life).   [f] Luke 12:7; Matt 10:30.   [g] Ezek 1:4: "a whirlwind was coming out of the north, a great cloud with raging fire engulfing it."   [h] Ezek 10:18-19 (the glory of the Lord departs from the temple); 43:1-5 (the glory of the Lord comes back to fill the temple).

to Babylon by violence and suffering inflicted by fiery wheels, urged on by [creatures who are] partly humans, partly oxen, partly lions, and partly eagles.[a] [The Jews] are shown that they will bear various afflictions, **[142]** and be tormented by human beings, by beasts of burden, by wild animals, and by birds [of prey].[b] The wheels, called deprivations or removals, are sent to carry the people [into captivity].[36] <u>A sound was heard like the sound of devastation,</u> *<u>like the sound of an army</u>*.[c] All [the wheels] were full of eyes, watching attentively lest any captive escape. They emitted a brilliant light, to prevent King Zedekiah <u>himself</u> or any of his [attendants and soldiers] from escaping by fleeing in the night.[d] The wheels, together with the creatures, moved quickly in every direction,[e] lest anyone escape by any path.

This was a terrifying vision of the wrath of God, aimed at the impious, similar to the vision in Revelation 4,[f] in which <u>God</u> showed his anger to the followers of the Antichrist. However, he is pleased with the others, who give glory to him, and carries them up to heaven in an angelic chariot.[g] There, too, are *creatures full of eyes*, who carefully watch over <u>Christ's</u> elect, lest any of them perish.[h] These creatures also guard us from all harm from human beings, beasts, birds, and wild animals. All those eyes are always on Christ—eyes in which all things are reflected, but especially the elect, who are recorded in a special *book of life*,[i] and reign in a special kingdom.

---

[a] Ezek 10:9-17 (creatures); Ezek 12:11-16 (exile).   [b] That is, the man, ox, lion, and eagle in Ezekiel's vision.   [c] Ezek 1:24.   [d] Ezek 12:12-14 describes the capture of the king and scattering of those who try to help him.   [e] Ezek 1:17; 10:11.   [f] Rev 4:6-8 describes four creatures—a lion, a calf, a man, and an eagle—with eyes all around. These creatures are related, but not identical, to the creatures and wheels in Ezekiel 1 and 10.   [g] Matt 24:31.   [h] The creatures in Rev 4:6-8 are full of eyes.   [i] Phil 4:3; Rev 3:5; 20:12.

Book 4

[*Patterns and Reflections in the Light of God*]

The way to think about a pattern in God can be demonstrated by thinking about [patterns in] other things. For if God made a microcosm [for example, a human being] according to the image of <u>some</u> pattern, that pattern was already in God. Everything in the entire universe is contained in this microcosm. Therefore, the pattern of the universe was in God. Indeed, this single pattern of a human being contained all things in itself, just as all things exist in Christ, and just as in a single soul there are patterns of many things. Also, when God commanded certain things to be made, he displayed, <u>visible</u> in himself, their clearly defined forms (Exodus 25, Numbers 8, Ezekiel 40, and 1 Chronicles 28).[a] All of these [patterns] were seen shining in the light of God when God opened himself or <u>revealed</u> himself in some way. This is not difficult [to understand], for it is natural and appropriate for God. By means of light he brought all things to life.

[143] These [patterns], and everything else, were formed in the light of the Word of God for the glory of Christ. For there are no other ideas in God or in Christ himself. Here I would gladly ask <u>my opponents</u> whether they believe that the ideas that they call qualities are now present in the soul of Christ. In the afterlife, in blessedness, there will be for us no qualities or ideas other than God's love, which brings things to life for us in their own individual forms. For this is a special property of [God's] light. It is an effective way of knowing, if you think about it carefully and understand well how angels can see the future in God, with no masks interposed between God

---

[a] The chapters listed here all contain detailed instructions, or patterns: Ex 25 (the Ark, table, and lampstand for the tabernacle); Num 8:1-4 (the arrangement of lamps in the tabernacle); Ezek 40 (the temple to be built in the restored Israel); 1 Chr 28:11-19 (Solomon's temple).

and themselves. Thus all theologians acknowledge that angels see [all things] in the Word.³⁷ Therefore the ideal forms of [all] things are in the Word.

Samuel, who *was called a seer*,ᵃ saw in God what Saul was searching for in the past and what would happen to him in the future (1 Samuel 9 and 10).ᵇ Micaiah saw in God what would happen in the coming battle: *Israel was to be scattered* and Ahab was to be killed (last chapter of 1 Kings).ᶜ While he was in Babylon, Ezekiel saw in visions of God, in the Spirit, and in God himself, everything that was happening in Jerusalem (Ezekiel 8).ᵈ In a vision of God Balaam saw what was going to happen in the future, *in much later times* (Numbers 24).ᵉ And similar things in Jeremiah 1, Ezekiel 1, Amos 1, and in many other passages.ᶠ For the prophets were called seers because they saw—within themselves, in the Spirit, in God—the future appearing visibly in his light. Sometimes this was by means of an internal vision. At other times it was an external one, as God himself says (Numbers 12).ᵍ This light is so widely diffused that ideas themselves, which we grasp with our intellect, are like sparks of light and radiant images, illuminating the mind itself and presenting likenesses of all things to us in the divine light. For without light nothing whatsoever can be given form, depicted, or seen.

Now consider further evidence based upon the eye, which proves these ideas about light in the clearest way. The visible likenesses brought before a mirror and then reflected back to the eye from any object, are like sparks of light, which display the precise form and image of the object [144] seen in the mirror. Thus, by the magnificent

---

ᵃ 1 Sam 9:9.   ᵇ 1 Sam 9:20, 10:2-9.   ᶜ 1 Kg 22:17-20.
ᵈ Ezek 8:3-16.   ᵉ Num 24:14-24.   ᶠ There are prophecies in Jer 1:4-19; Ezek 1:4-28; Amos 1; and elsewhere in all three books.
ᵍ Num 12:6-8.

artistry of God, something that is not corporeal contains within itself the bright image, form, and likeness of every corporeal thing, as it truly exists in the incorporeal light of God, in which all things in the world shine out. In God there are no bodily parts, but [God is] like rays of light reflecting the bodily forms of all things, as if they were reflected in a mirror. Thus, without any actual partitioning or division of God, there are, in his boundless light, infinite rays shining out in an infinity of ways. Indeed all of these rays, and their mirror-like way of representing things, have a heavenly origin.

Moreover, in order to perceive, by means of a parallel drawn from everyday life, how it is possible to see things to come in God himself, you should consider the following analogy. If, after you have formed an idea of something, you inwardly reflect upon this idea, as if in the mirror of your mind, you might say that you can see this thing, even though it be absent <u>or</u> dead. This is because the light of your mind contains in itself the physical image of the thing, like the appearance of light reflected in a mirror. I use the terms "physical image" and "natural kinship" so that you will <u>soon</u> understand [what I am telling you] based on the physical and substantial form of things themselves. The light of the divine Word, *in whose light we see light*,[a] as the Prophet [David] says, contains the images and ideal forms of things. The light of the Word is quite properly said by Trismegistus to be "the archetypal light," and "the archetype of the soul."[b] For there could not be in our soul any light containing images of things, unless that light was like the original light from which souls emanated, possessing the ideal forms of the bodies they were going to shape. Indeed, not only souls themselves but even the

---

[a] Ps 36:9.   [b] *Corpus Hermeticum* 2.12, quoted in Steuco, *De perenni philosophia* 1.10.

substantial forms of other things contain the ideal form of the whole, which they send to [be reflected in] a mirror, imitating the original primal light, in which all things have been shining and continue to shine.

If it were granted to anyone to see clearly the very essence of God, or the entire splendour of Christ, that individual would behold, in [God], everything that is, was, and will be, all things shining in <u>him</u> as forms. [145] But this is not given even to angels, except in part, and in the form of reflected knowledge, which is directly known only by Christ. In this way an angel can see more things in God than another being, and is able to instruct others about things to come, as is clear from the visions of Daniel and John [of Patmos].[a]

[*Substantial Forms*]

It follows from all this that, in both divine and human ideal forms, there are not only patterns but also substantial forms. For in ideal forms there is a system of reference and correspondence to nature, as well as a natural kinship with substantial forms. Not only are all things shown <u>in</u> light, but the existence of all things depends on light. And the Word, *in which all things exist*, is light (John 1 and Colossians 1).[b] God, who sees all things in himself, sustains all things. And he sustains them by means of the ideal form of each one. Plato teaches this, following Anaxagoras and Trismegistus.[c] After him, Plotinus and Proclus, the interpreters of Plato, taught that in divine ideal forms there are not only patterns but also essential forms, from which all created things derive.[d]

---

[a] Dan 8:15-26; 9:20-27 (the angel Gabriel); Rev 1:1; 14:6-9. [b] John 1:1-5; Col 1:17. [c] Steuco, *De perenni philosophia* 1.5, 1.10, 2.5, 7.9, 7.15. [d] Ficino, *Theologia Platonica* 11.4.7.

Book 4

[Seedbeds of Light]

The vital powers of things originate in the light of God, and are then found in created light and in the elements.[a] This created light is like an offshoot of the primal light. It acts as a seedbed, containing the formative properties of things, and the vital forces implanted in the substantial forms themselves. In the soul there is also a seedbed of imprints of light. By reason of that same light and an ideal form, any seed contains the formative property of the thing that will grow from it; just as the Word of God, which <u>was</u> the seed of Christ, contained in itself <u>the formative plan and the vital powers of all things</u>. [The Word] itself is the primal element, the primal seed, from which power is disseminated to all elements and seeds. Hence in *Pimander* Trismegistus says, "The will of God, containing the Word and contemplating in itself the beautiful world according to the pattern of the elements of nature, adorned everything else with its own elements and the seeds of life."[b]

Such excellent plants and animals, with their own forms, could not have been produced so precisely, <u>in such a consistent way</u>, from such tiny seeds, unless there was **[146]** preexisting in them a divine ideal form and formative plan. The soul could not have generated the truth on its own, by turning to itself, unless it had an innate seedbed of divine truth. Therefore, both in the soul and in other things, there is a seedbed of light that comes from the substantial seed of the Word, in which was the light and life of all things. Like a seed tossed upon the earth, the Word of God, which was the seed of the begetting of Christ, generates all things by an imprint of itself, and causes them to grow, bringing everything to life with spirit

---

[a] "Elements" in this context means the four classical elements: earth, air, water, and fire. According to Aristotle, all matter was composed of these elements.   [b] *Corpus Hermeticum* 1.8.

and light. This is a marvelous analogy <u>to the unique seed of the Word</u>. Just as all generative things first conceive a seed in themselves and transfer it to an embryo outside themselves,[38] so, too, the seed of the Word was in God before his Son was conceived in Mary. What makes this argument so potent is that the begetting of Christ is the model and prototype of all other generation.

The primal cause worked *a priori*, from cause to effect. We ourselves, however, reverse the process of deduction, moving backward from perceptible objects. We reason *a posteriori*, from effect to cause. This is the *a priori* deduction: <u>that</u> just as in God there was first a generative seed, which became the real Son of God, so, in other generation, the Creator wanted to preserve the same order. The substantial seed of Christ was truly in God, and in it were the vital plans and model forms of all things.

[*The Natural Kinship of Light*]

The substantial forms of things are made from created light, and they possess the formative imprint of uncreated light. Just as all things, corporeal and spiritual, take their existence from light, so all things are seen outwardly in light, and all things are conceived of inwardly in the light of the intellect. What is true [of uncreated light] is also true of created light, by analogy and by the second type of reasoning [*a posteriori*]. Hence, as Plato said beautifully in *Timaeus*: "Ideas themselves, that is, intellectual concepts, have a natural kinship with the things they express."[a] There is truly a kinship of light, which teaches that the forms of things are made from light. This is the **[147]** meaning of "natural kinship" and "natural image."

The forms of things are made from light. From this light, images which appear in a mirror enter the eye and are transmitted all the way to the soul. These are rays of

---

[a] Plato, *Timaeus* (29b).

the same formative light sent to the intellect, which is also light. Thus, penetrating a luminous medium, they imprint upon it the luminous image of an external object. This image naturally refers to the thing itself, because of the natural and formative imprint, kinship, and participation of light. The light of your mind, with which you picture me within yourself, has a <u>kinship</u> to my form as it is seen by you. <u>And</u> my form has imprinted its mark on your soul. It is light, containing all things in itself, which links spiritual and corporeal things and makes them clearly visible to our eyes. The images in our souls are naturally luminous, there being a natural kinship of this light with external forms, with external light, and with the essential light of the soul itself. <u>And</u> the essential light of the soul contains the original seedbed of the images. This is formed by the imprint of deity and the light of the Word, in which is the original pattern of all things. Hence the images that are located in the soul naturally manifest themselves to the soul itself, whenever <u>the soul</u> reflects upon them. Nor is there is any need for another new idea. Rather, from the soul's own light and from the light that enters it from outside, a single light is composed. For light often unites with light.

[*Transformation and Truth*]

Separation [of lights] can also occur; or one may be destroyed while the other remains, as when the form of a thing is destroyed while the matter remains. Although the images that enter the soul may change, yet the mind, that is, the primary substance of the soul, remains the same.

"Temporal things," as Parmenides says, "participate in the eternal ideal forms" to which they are related.[a] However, when these things change, the divine mind does not change. This is no more difficult than [understanding]

---

[a] Ficino, *Theologia Platonica* 11.4.15.

that Christ's human nature, <u>which was united with the divine,</u> underwent transformation, while his divine nature remains forever the same. In this world the transformation of forms and bodies is so fluid that they never remain the same. Therefore, **[148]** as Timaeus concludes, there must be other things, which remain whole and pure, above those that are defective or imperfect in their parts.[a] Imperfect things must be judged in relation to those that are perfect. Hence this Platonic paradox: Bodies do not truly exist, and in <u>bodies</u> there is no truth. For if you say, "This is Socrates," before you finish speaking, the man you just now pointed to has already ceased to exist. Therefore, he does not exist when you present him as Socrates. There is no truth in bodies; otherwise, [truth] would change when bodies change.[b] Therefore truth exists only as an idea in the mind, and God alone is truth. This statement of Timaeus also follows: "The intelligible world has always existed and never began to be, while the sensible world is always coming into being and never exists."[c]

There is no time given [to us] in which we can say, "This is the world." For even before you finish speaking the world has changed. Therefore, this world is the *vanity of vanities*,[d] something that does not exist [in its own right], but arises out of something else. It is the likeness and shadow of the intelligible world.[e] However, there is no truth in a thing that does not exist. Therefore, there is no truth in this world, and anyone possessing truth is *not of this world*.[f] If somehow there appears to be truth

---

[a] Ficino, *Theologia Platonica* 11.6.7; see Plato, *Timaeus* (30c).
[b] Ficino, *Theologia Platonica* 11.6.3; see Plato, *Timaeus* (49d-e).
[c] Ficino, *Theologia Platonica* 11.6.11; see Plato, *Timaeus* (51e-52a).
[d] Eccl 1:2, 12:8, quoted in Ficino, *Theologia Platonica* 11.6.12.
[e] Ficino, *Theologia Platonica* 11.6.4, 11.6.11; see Plato, *Timaeus* (37e-38b) and Plato's allegory of the cave in *Republic* (514a–520a).
[f] John 8:23; 17:16; 18:36.

in these things, it is but a likeness and *a passing shadow*^a of the truth. For truth is the unchanging and spotless purity of any nature. <u>This is the truth in the thing itself, the thing that exists. There is another truth, a truth in the mind, in the words that correspond to the thing that exists.</u> Truth is the eternal Word of God, which contains eternal patterns and the plans of all things. <u>However you look at it, Christ is truth.</u>

From this it also follows that there is an ideal form within an ideal form, *like a wheel within a wheel*,^b an eye within an eye, or a light within a light. In God, one ideal form of a human being contains an infinite number of ideal forms, just as one ray of light contains an infinite number of points of light, in which God eternally contemplates everything that belongs to this human: *sitting down, standing up, lying down*,^c all movements and all the parts of the body, even *the hairs* **[149]** *of your head*.^d In Psalm 138, David, contemplating all things that are thus contained in God, says that [God's] watching over these things is wonderful and beyond human comprehension.^e Nevertheless this is not difficult for God, as the following reasoning shows. If in our soul there are potentially—and at times actually—separate ideal forms of the parts, changes, and actions of a human being, why would we not say that all of these always exist, [not just potentially, but] actually, in God? Furthermore, there are not distinct things in God. Rather, all beings shine in his light, as an infinite number of appearances in an infinite number of ways. And every single being exists in the ideal form of light, in which they all shine, all of them present to God and contained in him.

---

^a Ps 144:4.   ^b Ezek 1:16.   ^c Ps 139:2-3.   ^d Matt 10:30; Luke 12:7.
^e Ps 139:6.

[Christ Is the Substantial Form of Deity]

I have discussed patterns at some length so that you, reader, may understand that, without any change in God, the first pattern has been shining in his essence from eternity. This is the pattern of Christ, the head and originator of all things, the living pattern and the source of all life. He was the first and greatest substantial mode of divinity: understanding, living, and pouring life into things. All things that are now in God were naturally arranged in order by him before creation. He alone is the first, the Son and the heir. He alone is begotten by God. Not only was Christ first in rank in God, but God revealed Christ alone in substance. God manifested himself in Christ alone. In accordance with the [divine] plan, he generated Christ from himself, with all the *fullness of deity* flowing out from Christ to others. In every way that you can conceive, the entire *fullness of deity was in the body* of Christ.[a]

You must consider [Christ's] deity separately during the time that he was living in the form of a human being, and say that he was Jesus Christ, who was at that time *in the form of God*.[b] Just as there are, in your soul, the ideal forms of other things, so at that time wisdom in God was like the soul of Christ, containing the ideal forms of all things. *In* Christ *was life* and in him shone the life of other things (John 1).[c]

In God, first was the radiance of Christ. It alone was the first of all things. Then, through it, in it, and because of it, in a secondary **[150]** way, all other dependent things [appeared] in their order. We call this wisdom the ruler and guardian of the world, which God revealed in creation, manifesting the Word visibly to angels and human beings, and creating all things through this manifestation of himself. If God can create a new world through the deity that is now in all things, and through it, appear hypostatically, how

---

[a] Col 2:9. [b] Phil 2:6. [c] John 1:4.

much more [could he do] through the deity of Christ? If, as we noted recently, God took from within himself the shape and substance of all created things, how much more did he take on the shape and substance of Christ? Without any change to himself, God is now able to manifest himself to us visibly and palpably in any form whatsoever, because he contains in himself, as essences, all forms and all bodies.

In accordance with his eternal plan, God first established the form of Christ, *the wellspring of life*,[a] that tremendous mystery, which he revealed both in creation and in his incarnation. What God had in mind was the begetting of the Son. There was not then an actual Son distinct from the Father, but God's inherent knowledge was already shaping and directing life. As a mirror naturally reflects an object set before it, so too God's plan naturally reflects Christ himself and contains his essence. This is the special property of light—not only to express an ideal form in nature, but also to contain a substantial form in essence. If you are able to believe that God begot a human being from himself, then you will also be able to believe that the substance and form of the being who was begotten came out of God from eternity. If you grant that other, secondary [forms] are in God, how can you deny that the primary form [Christ] is in God?

{*The Origins of Natural Things*}

We have not yet sufficiently explained the glory of the essence of Christ and his light, until we can trace the origins of natural things to him, and show that he is the origin of all things.

[*Light, Splendour, and Forms*]

In regard to this, what we have already said needs to be repeated: the Word, in which all things exist, is light.

---

[a] Prov 10:11; 13:14; 14:27; 16:22; see also John 4:14.

Because of the nature of light, all things exist in Christ, <u>by whose power all things are upheld and</u> **[151]** <u>sustained</u> (John 1, Colossians 1, and Hebrews 1).[a] By analogy, what is true of uncreated light is also applicable to created light. By forming light in light, God wanted there to be a form with the power of forming other things. If, therefore, all things exist through light, and if it is light that gives existence to a thing, then light is the form of the thing. Besides, in Genesis 1, <u>earthy</u> matter is called *tohu* and *bohu*,[39] *formless and invisible*,[b] since it had not yet been made to share in the light. Hence you may once again infer that form comes from light. And not only do the forms and existences of beings come from light, but also their souls and spirits. For light is the life of humankind and the life of the spirit. Light is the most beautiful of all things in this world and in the next. Each thing exists in the ideal form of light, in which it shines. Only light forms and transforms heavenly, earthly, spiritual, and corporeal things. From it comes the entire form of the world *and its adornment*.[40] The Creator distributed shining forms to things, lest they continue to exist within <u>that</u> dark and shapeless chaos.

In all generated and corruptible things, the approach of the sun towards us is the cause of generation, while its retreat is the cause of dissolution. A ray of the sun so modifies the elements that a single shining perfection of form can be seen. Nothing would be able to send out a form of light or a natural image from itself, into a mirror or into the eye, unless it contained the light within itself as a form.[41] If you consider it carefully, this is quite a powerful way of thinking. The visible form of all things is light. Everything we can see is light (Ephesians 5).[c] By means of light as a form, light itself transforms everything

---

[a] John 1:4-9; Col 1:17; Heb 1:3. [b] Gen 1:2 (Septuagint).
[c] Eph 5:13: "whatever makes things visible is light" (taken out of context; the verse actually refers to hidden sins being brought to light).

that is seen in various ways: earthy and watery matter into glittering gems, bright pearls, and so forth. Light also forms and transforms our spirit in regeneration, just as light will transform the substance of our bodies at the final resurrection. This reasoning proves the similarity between generation and regeneration, in that both derive their substance from light. Our similarity to Christ also demonstrates this effectively. For the substance of the body of Christ was formed at his begetting and transformed at his resurrection, by the light of the Word of God; <u>just as the transformation of Christ seen on the mountain [that is, the Transfiguration] was done by light</u>.[a]

If Aristotle had known this, then he might have understood [152] that the origin of the forms of natural things is light, and that the divine appears in things as pre-existing archetypes. The origins of all things are in God, in Christ himself, who is *Alpha and Omega*.[b] Thus Aristotle might have been able to understand that light in a spiritual substance is the ενδελεχίαν (*endelecheia*, activity or continuous motion)[42] and vivifying energy of the soul. For light is the life of humankind, the life of our spirit, in generation and in regeneration. The form of fire is light. The form of water is splendour,[43] which is also present in air. The form of the sun's body is light itself, from which other things also receive their forms. The form of the *glorious body* of Christ is divine light, which is to be shared with us as well (Philippians 3).[c] But for Aristotle and all the sophists,[44] to whom the light of the Word and Spirit of God, and the begetting of Christ, were unknown, the way in which other things propagate was unknown as well. For all things are propagated, begotten, and produced according to the pattern of Christ.

---

[a] Matt 17:2. [b] Rev 1:8, 21:6, 22:13; some versions (e.g. Erasmus's New Testament) also include it in Rev 1:11, while others (e.g. the Vulgate) do not. [c] Phil 3:21.

In the seed of Christ were the elements of our own seed, our life, and our spirit. The spirit, life, and form of all things were, and even now are, present in the brightly shining Word of God. All things came into existence through light, and nothing ever existed without light. There is no created thing that does not refer back to the Creator, or in which *the light* of the Creator *does not shine*. Even [one of Job's comforters] knew this (Job 25).[a] And Trismegistus says to his son Tat, "Since it is through God that all things become visible, he himself must, in turn, shine brightly in all things."[b] And after this he says that God, being light, so fashioned all things that we can see him shining in everything.[c] Julian [the Apostate], in his book on the sun, quotes this very ancient doctrine of the Phoenicians: This light is an *endelecheia*[d] and "a pure action, like divine intelligence extending throughout all things,"[e] which manifests deity itself in all things.

Christ wanted his light to be always in full view of our eyes, so that we might see him, shining there in all things. For this light is an extension of the light of the Word of God implanted in him, putting his imprint on things and making them one with [his light]. **[153]** This light, shared with the sun, receives its life-giving power from the primal light. The light of the sun is distributed in various ways, as is the light of Christ. Orpheus and the other ancients called the Word of God φάνητα, *Phanes*, God appearing,[45] who was "the first to appear out of the infinite."[f] This name was later also attributed to the sun.[g] Christ first appeared in the immensity of God, just as the sun appears in the midst of created light.

---

[a] Job 25:3. [b] *Corpus Hermeticum* 5.2. [c] *Corpus Hermeticum* 11.22. [d] See A.R4.42. [e] Ficino, *Interpretatio Prisciani* 17, paraphrasing Julian, Oration 4 (Hymn to King Helios) 134. [f] Lactantius, *Divinae institutiones* 1.5 (PL 6 130A-131A), quoting Orphic Hymn no. 6, "Protogonus" ("First-born"). [g] See Steuco, *De perenni philosophia* 7.10.

Different kinds of forms are mixed together in various ways by light. The divine light and the <u>acquired</u> splendour of the soul make one light, from which come the spiritual forms within us. The light of the sun, and the elements with their innate splendour, make another light, from which come the forms of bodies. Also, the substance of the higher elements,[a] together with the earth itself, makes a single material for things. These are the sources of natural things, the sources of their generation and their dissolution. Heat and cold act on things, but they are derived from light and splendour. I understand solar light to be warming, and watery splendour to be cooling. When it is frozen, as in some heavenly bodies, its power of cooling is increased.

Just as life-giving heat comes from the ordinary light of the sun, moist putrefaction and cold death come variously from the moon, Saturn, and some other heavenly bodies and regions of the sky. And an overpowering fever comes from Mars.[46] The brightness of the sun is one thing, the brightness of the moon is another. One is fire, the other is the splendour of water. Christ, the architect of the world, <u>thus placed these things in light</u>. He himself is the <u>very beginning</u> in which all things are established: heavenly and earthly, bodily and spiritual. He created the matter of the elements, mixed them together, and distributed bright forms to the substances, bringing forth light itself from his storehouses.

[*Light and Creation*]

The first inference from the above is that nothing further can now be created without a subject.[47] Rather, the propagation of things from other things—their formal generation and corruption—comes about by the power

---

[a] The " higher elements" are water, air, and fire. Earth is considered a lower element. See *Restoration*, 159-160.

of light. Form itself, found in a balance of light and elements, is <u>produced</u> as substance by the action of light and elements. And the elements themselves are **[154]** mixed and tempered by the power of heavenly light. Thus all actions and transformations come originally from light, both in bodily and spiritual things, both in Christ and in ourselves. In spiritual things all energy comes from light. Light illuminates all spiritual things, endowing them with essence. And light is the power that chases away demons, who, being creatures of darkness, love darkness and hate light. Pimander says that light was "the first form prevailing in the infinite realm in the divine mind."[a]

[*Forms and Qualities*]

Light is also the substantial form of all corporeal things. That is, it is the source of forms, acting directly in all things. It produces heat, which is very effective and active, and dryness, which is very retentive and passive. Coldness and wetness also come from light; that is, from the created splendour of water, which is also shared by heavenly bodies.[b]

In this lower world colours come from light. This is shown by the light in a rainbow. We see things washed in water becoming white. We also sometimes see whiteness in a cold body. In snow and hail we see the splendour of water increased by freezing. We sometimes see whiteness caused by heat, as in the white residue of fire that comes from complete combustion, such as quicklime or ashes. Blackness, as in soot, charcoal, and pitch, is produced by quenching or smothering light. Thus, when light is blotted out, whether by sin or by the devil himself, blackness or darkness results. Other <u>colours</u> can be looked at in a similar way. They are all contained in the substance of a

---

[a] *Corpus Hermeticum* 1.8.   [b] See A.R4.43.

thing, as is the form of light itself. Colours are a particular part of a form, although they can change, just as parts and elements are subject to change, both in the soul and in the body. Hot and cold, wet and dry, are the [qualities of] substances according to Hippocrates.[48] They are part of the composition of the whole. [The qualities of] substances are part of the form, as are the colours, <u>even if</u>, when they occur, they are called accidents.[49] They pertain to matter and, together with the ideal form, they constitute a single form.

[*Creation Ex Nihilo*]

Secondly, it follows from this that *in the beginning God created*—truly out of nothing and without preexisting matter[50]— a twofold heaven,[51] **[155]** one earth, and light, as described in the book of Genesis.[a] Later, it is said, all other things were created (Colossians 1 and Revelation 10),[b] because these things were truly brought from non-being to being. However, they were not created in the first creation, out of nothing and without preexisting matter. In truth, only water was created at that time. The heavens are actually made of water; and air is produced from water by evaporation. Finally, fire itself, which is also nourished by air, is concocted from airy matter and light. Indeed a flame is air on fire.

On the fourth day God did not "create" the [heavenly] lights; rather he "made" them[c] from the solidified matter of heaven. For the [Hebrew] word for "make" is עשה (*asah*), which, to the Hebrews, does not mean to make from nothing, but to adapt and form from pre-existing matter, as is taught by Rabbi Salomon[d] and Rabbi Abraham [Ibn

---

[a] Gen 1:1-10.   [b] Col. 1:16; Rev 10:6.   [c] Gen 1:16: "Then God made two great lights." The word "make" is עשה (*asah*). This is contrasted with the word "create," ברא (*bara*) in Gen 1:1.   [d] Rabbi Shlomo Yitzhaqi, known by the acronym Rashi.

Ezra], and all the rest [of the medieval Jewish commentators].[52] In the same way, as the Psalmist says, the heavens were made, that is, distinctions were made among the celestial spheres.[a] As it says in Job chapter 37: *spread out the skies, which are as strong as a mirror cast from molten metal*.[b] Apart from the starry heavens, there are seven planetary spheres,[c] which are the seven rulers of the corporeal world, whose disposition some falsely call fate. But Moses makes no mention of this, lest uneducated people fall into an idolatry of these [planetary] rulers, or believe in the inevitability of fate.[d]

[*Everything Comes from Water*]

Thirdly, it follows that Thales of Miletus, who got to know the teachings of Moses and Trismegistus in Syria and Egypt, and was the first among the Greeks to teach about nature, was not wrong when he said that everything came from water.[e] For earth by itself is not suited [to be the primary source], because the form of earth comes from water.[f] Peter very clearly teaches, following Moses's account, that the heavens were formed of water. He said, *by the word of God the heavens and the earth came forth long ago from water and by means of water* (2 Peter 3).[g] The watery splendour which is communicated to the moon and the rest of the heavenly bodies proves this, as does the etymology of the Hebrew word [for the heavens]. For in Hebrew the heavens are called שמים (*shamayim*), which means "the same as water."[53] To the Hebrews there was

---

[a] Ps 8:3; 136:7-9.   [b] Job 37:18.   [c] The five known planets (Mercury, Venus, Mars, Jupiter, Saturn) plus the sun and the moon.   [d] On the difference between natural and judicial astrology, see A.R4.46.   [e] Steuco, *De perenni philosophia* 7.12. Similar information is found in Eusebius, *Praeparatio evangelica* 1.8, 7.12, 14.14 (PG 21 55C-D, 542B, 1226B); Clement of Alexandria, *Stromata* 1.11, 2.4 (PG 8 751A, 913D-916A); Simplicius, *De physica* 1, 3; and other ancient sources.   [f] Gen 1:9-10 (God separates the dry land from the waters).   [g] 2 Pet 3:5, referring to Gen 1:6-8.

no doubt that the firmament [of heaven] was made from water. From water evaporated by the spirit, **[156]** God made something extensive and airy.

As David says in Psalm 103, God made *heaven, stretching it out [like a curtain]*.[a] He made it from water, and its foundation is water. From that foundation, the whole extent of heaven was <u>brought forth,</u> and placed on [that foundation]. Therefore the foundations of the heavens are described as shaken when a tumultuous event occurs (2 Samuel 22 and Job 26).[b] God made *the heavens by stretching them out* (Isaiah 40 and Jeremiah 50).[c] The Hebrew word רקיע (*raqiya*) means expansion or extension.[54] For, by expansion or extension, air is made from water. *God called* that airy expanse *heaven,* commanding [*the firmament*] to *divide the waters from the waters,*[d] the rain waters from the waters lying next to the dry land. <u>The waters above the heavens are vaporous, in the clouds suspended over the mountains, as the psalmist teaches in Psalm 103.</u>[e] <u>Thus, even though</u> water is like a form with respect to earth, it does, nevertheless, supply the higher elements with matter, and receives from them, in turn, formative power.

[Earth Was Created before Heaven]

<u>Fourth, it has already been established that the earth was created before heaven. Moses puts heaven first because of its status (Genesis 1).</u>[f] <u>But in another passage he gives priority to the earth, saying,</u> *when God made the earth and the heavens* <u>(Genesis 2).</u>[g] It is established in Genesis 1 that

---

[a] Ps 104:2. [b] 2 Sam 22:8; Job 26:11. [c] Isa 40:22, Jer 10:12, and Jer 51:15 mention stretching out the heavens, but Jer 50 does not.
[d] Gen 1:6-8. [e] Ps 104:6. [f] Gen 1:1. [g] Gen 2:4 mentions earth and heaven twice: first as "the heavens and the earth," and then as "the earth and the heavens." However, in the Vulgate and Pagnini's Old Testament, "heaven and earth" is used in both places. Servetus was probably familiar with this passage in the original Hebrew.

the firmament, which is heaven itself, was made after the earth.[a] In nature the centre precedes the circumference. The Hebrews teach that God first *laid the foundation of the earth*,[b] just as you draw a circle, in which, having established the centre, the circumference is then measured out, as Solomon says in Proverbs 8.[c] Similarly, David says to God in Psalm 101: *First you laid the foundation of the earth, and the heavens are the work of your hands.*[d] In Proverbs 3 Solomon says: *The Lord by wisdom has founded the earth and by understanding has established the heavens.*[e] In Isaiah chapter 48, God says, *My hand has laid the foundation of the earth and my right hand has measured out the heavens.*[f] [In these passages] earth and the laying of its foundation are always mentioned first. If heaven is made from water, then it follows that water is prior to heaven. And likewise earth, which was created at the same time as water [is prior to heaven].[g]

[Fire and the Third Heaven]

[157] Fifth, there follows a proof of this: Paul says that there is a third, divine heaven.[h] Created heaven is twofold, but the third heaven is uncreated. *In the beginning God created* two heavens, as indicated by the noun שמים (*shamayim*, the heavens), which is dual in number.[i] In a literal sense, we accept that there are two heavens: one formed from air, the other from water.[55] Moses describes these two perceptible heavens, the airy firmament and the watery region.[j] Here he says nothing about angels.

---

[a] The earth is already in existence when creation begins (Gen 1:1). The firmament is created on the second day (Gen 1:6-8). [b] Job 38:4; Ps 102:25; 104:5; Isa 48:13; 51:13. [c] Prov 8:27. [d] Ps 102:25. [e] Prov 3:19. [f] Isa 48:13. [g] Water and earth both exist at the beginning of creation (Gen 1:2). [h] 2 Cor 12:2. [i] See A.R4.51. [j] Gen 1:6-7 (waters above the firmament); Gen 1:20 (birds fly across the face of the firmament).

Book 4

However, since the creation of angels must be contained in this passage [Genesis 1], heaven can, in some way, be called the heaven of the angels, or the choir of angels, who are of a heavenly or ethereal substance. Here are the throne of God, his dwelling-place, and the cherubim and seraphim. It is in this way that Peter describes the second heaven to Clement, calling what we can see, the airy and watery regions, the first heaven.[a] Likewise, Christ teaches that [the upper] *heaven will be opened when the angels*, who are called the heavenly host, *descend*.[b] With the coming of Christ peace was made in this heaven, and from there *Satan fell like lightning*.[c] Therefore, whether you call heaven the entire visible firmament above, or the assembly of angels, [know that] both together form a multifold heaven.

All created things, even angels, are included in the names [of the things] in the heavens and on the earth, since all created things are either celestial or terrestrial. The [Hebrew] article את, to which the demonstrative letter *hey* is added, also indicates this.[56] For [א and ת] — like α and ω [in Greek] — are the first and last letters [of the alphabet], making את an article comprehensive of a whole. It is as if [Moses] had said: *In the beginning God created* all *the heavens and* all of *the earth and everything that is* included *in them*. This is the way God himself explains the creation of all things in Exodus 20.[d] Hence in chapter 2 of Genesis the angelic hosts are included in the creation of the two heavens.[e] And so it is in Psalm 32: *The heavens were made by the word of the Lord, and all their host by the breath of his mouth*.[f] Truly two heavens are indicated in these passages, in addition to the angels who

---

[a] [Clement], *Recognitiones* 1.27 (PG 1 1222). Here the firmament is envisioned as a solid partition separating the sky (the first heaven) from the dwelling place of angels (the second heaven). [b] John 1:51. [c] Luke 10:18. [d] Gen 1:1, Ex 20:11. [e] Gen 2:1. [f] Ps 33:6.

are the *adornments of heaven*, as Job calls them in chapter 26.ª Since the angels are truly the heavenly hosts and the *adornments of heaven*, they take the name of heaven. Also, [they take the name of heaven] because they are a kind of substance like the air of heaven, and **[158]** created at the same time by the breath of God, as can be gathered from the passages cited above.

But beyond all these things there is a third heaven of divinity, which is called the *heaven of heavens*,[b] where the Father *dwells in inaccessible light*.[c] It was to *this third heaven* that Paul *was caught up*.[d] Christ dwells in this heaven, and from him the angels, who are far inferior, receive their splendour. They see only as much as is given to them through Christ. This luminous and fiery heaven is the brightness of the Word, the universal pattern of all things. Deity itself is made accessible through Christ. In the same way, though invisible himself, God is made visible even to the angels (1 Timothy 3).[e] The angels saw God behind a veil, as Isaiah teaches in chapter 6.[f] Yet to come, after the final resurrection, is another absolutely perfect way of seeing, when we will see God as he is, in that most hidden light. This has never yet been seen by anyone, neither by angels nor by blessed spirits, but by Christ alone.[g] Until then, as is the case with us, good angels are more to be blessed, just as bad angels are more to be punished.[h]

But since these things are beyond our present condition and all human thought, let us return to those things which have already been made available to us by Christ. Let us reflect on God in the Word and the heaven that is within us.[i] Christ brought this heaven to us, making us

---

[a] Job 26:13. For further discussion of the word "adornment," see A.R4.40. [b] 1 Kg 8:27; 2 Chr 2:6; 6:18; Neh 9:6; Ps 68:33; 148:4. [c] 1 Tim 6:16. [d] 2 Cor 12:2. [e] 1 Tim 3:16. [f] Isa 6:2. [g] John 6:46. [h] On punishment of bad angels, see Isa 24:21-22; 2 Pet 2:4. [i] See Luke 17:21: "The kingdom of God is within you."

kings in it, so that we might reign among the heavenly ones.[a] Thus the *kingdom of heaven* is frequently spoken about [in the Gospels].[b]

The third heaven is truly fiery. The other two are airy and watery, with a small share of fire. In [his account of] creation Moses does not mention the third heaven, nor does he even mention fire, which is a matter of great mystery. Paul, however, when speaking of great secrets, emphasizes the third heaven.[c] Moses does not mention fire in [his account of] creation, not only because the other elements, together with light itself, are enough to produce things; but also because there is a potential for fire wherever [combustible] matter exists together with light. I shall add another explanation later, when we speak of Adam's sin,[d] which was followed by fiery retribution.[e] There is also another explanation: that the Jews living [at that time] did not know of the regeneration of Christ and his righteous fire. But the fire **[159]** that would renew the old world was to be sent to the earth by Christ.[f] Therefore, Moses does not mention the third heaven [because] the third heaven does not have a particular location. It is within us and, like fire, pervades everything. This fire, which, unlike the other elements, does not have a particular location, is a type of the third heaven. [Fire] is located where it has fuel, without which it cannot be sustained. Fire exists among the other elements so that, acting on them by the power of heavenly light in that weightless and airy substance, it might purify them and raise them to heaven above. Fire renews, purifies, and transforms everything. It cannot be contaminated, remaining forever pure.

---

[a] Col 3:1-4; Eph 2:4-7.   [b] Jesus speaks frequently about the kingdom of heaven in the Gospel of Matthew. The other three gospels use the expression "kingdom of God" instead.   [c] 2 Cor 12:2.
[d] *Restoration*, 357-409, "On the Destruction of the World, and its Restoration by Christ."   [e] Gen. 3:24.   [f] Luke 12:49.

[Earth, the Lowest Element]

<u>Sixth</u>, it can be gathered from the above that water, air, and fire possess a kind of heavenly matter distinct from earthy matter. Rabbi Eliezer the Elder long ago taught this among the Hebrews. After him Rabbi Moses [Maimonides] the Egyptian said, "There is a secret of secrets, a mystery of mysteries of the Law, which the greatest of the wise men of Israel made known."[a] I myself will now demonstrate this with many arguments, since it is something unknown to all philosophers, and is related to knowledge of Christ.

1. There is one kind of matter that is heavenly, and another that is earthy. This is proven by [the account of] the creation of the world, and the perpetual separation of heaven <u>from</u> earth.[b] Earthy matter and watery matter were created separately by God, while air and the whole of heaven are made from watery matter.[c]

2. The begetting of Christ clearly proves this, demonstrating the immeasurable distance between the elements. For in Christ the three higher elements are from the substance of the Father.[d] Just as our paternal seed is watery and filled with an airy and fiery spirit, so too [in the case of] Christ, the cloud of the oracle of God, acting as if it were <u>watery</u>, airy, and fiery,[e] containing nothing earthy in itself, was the physical dew of the begetting of Christ. <u>In short</u>, nothing earthy in embryos comes from the father. Rather it comes from the mother, as I will show more fully later.[f]

---

[a] Maimonides, *Guide for the Perplexed* 2.27 (2.26 in modern editions). In this passage Maimonides mentions Rabbi Eliezer.   [b] Gen 1:6-8.
[c] "Air is produced from water by evaporation" and "the heavens were formed of water" (*Restoration*, 155).   [d] See *Restoration*, 73-74 (book 2), 193-194 (book 5).   [e] The Lord appears in a pillar of cloud and fire in Ex 13:21-22, Num 14:14, Neh 9:19, etc.   [f] *Restoration*, 255 (dialogue 2): "Earthy matter is heated in the bowels of the earth, just as Christ was in the internal organs of his mother. Earth is the mother of all things and there is an earthy element in everything, from the mother." See A.R4.38.

3. The force of the Hebrew word שָׁמַיִם (*shamayim*, the heavens) proves this. For the heavens take their name from water [*mayim*].[a] The heavens contain nothing **[160]** terrestrial, and thus neither does water.

4. This is proven by the other passages of scripture cited above, which teach that the substance of heaven is made of water, <u>not of earth</u>.[b]

5. These passages prove the difference between [earth and the higher] elements. We will talk later, in the books on baptism, about heavenly [re]generation from the three [higher] elements.[c] We are born again through our baptism in water, spirit, and fire (Matthew 3, Luke 3, and John 3),[d] since by these we who were formerly terrestrial creatures, born of earth, become heavenly beings.

6. This is proven by what we shall have to say about the soul, in which the three higher elements are found.[e]

7. This is proven by analogy with the three heavens, which, like the three [higher] elements, are always separate from earth.

8. In scripture, the Holy Spirit, like the heavens, is always indicated by the three higher elements,[f] but never by earth, which is <u>always</u> incompatible with heaven and the spirit, just as terrestrial things are opposed to heavenly ones, and carnal things are always opposed to spiritual ones.

9. Pure water is able to be entirely transformed into vapour and airy spirit, vanishing, as if into the heavens above. However, earth <u>never does this, but</u> turns <u>back</u> into ashes, always moving downward. Hence in Isaiah, chapter 51, it says that *heaven will* <u>*dissolve into*</u> *smoke*[g] and earth will become dust. Also Ecclesiasticus, chapter

---

[a] See A.R4.53. [b] 2 Pet 3:5, referring to Gen 1:6-8. [c] *Restoration*, 547-548 (book 3 of "On Heavenly Rebirth and the Kingdom of the Antichrist"). [d] Matt 3:11; Luke 3:16; John 3:5-6. [e] *Restoration*, 169 (book 5). [f] The Holy Spirit is said to be like air (John 3:8); fire (Acts 2:3-4); water (Isa 44:3). [g] Isa 51:6.

40, says that *what is of earth will return to earth and what is of water will return to water.*[a]

10. Water was created with its own splendour, while earth was unformed.[b]

11. Earth is resistant to light, and like a shadowy demon it is incapable of light. But the admixture of other elements transforms the earth and causes it to shine.

12. Unlike the other three elements, earth is incapable of sound and spirit.

13. Only the earth was cursed because of Adam and given to the serpent as its food.[c]

14. From the chemical process of sublimation, it is clearly evident that earthen matter may always be separated out from the other [elements].[57]

15. Experimentation on all the other [elements] proves this: earth has never been seen to turn into water, nor water into earth, however you mix them together. For each of them always reverts to its original form.[d] The Averroists, not understanding this, said that **[161]** all [four] elements retain their integrity when mixed,[58] whereas [actually only] two kinds of matter remain.

[Warming and Cooling Light]

We may now conclude that there are four sources of natural things, two material and two formal. The material sources are the two kinds of matter already mentioned: the earthy and the watery. The formal sources are the light of the sun, which warms and dries, and the splendour of water, which cools and moistens. Therefore there are four qualities that are called primary, and four elements. But the origins and perfections of these qualities are in only two of the elements.

---

[a] Ecclus 40:11. [b] See Gen 1:2. [c] Gen 3:17. [d] See Ecclus 40:11.

The primary qualities of fire are heat and dryness, while those of water are coolness and wetness. In the heavens, the two celestial providers of these qualities are the sun and the moon. The <u>light</u> of fire, like that of the sun, is <u>generally</u> warming and drying. [The <u>light</u> of] water is cooling and moistening, like that of the moon, which has been given a power balancing that of the sun. Power over the day is given to the sun, the power of warming and drying. Power over the night is given to the moon, cooling and moistening in the absence of the sun, by its own innate splendour of water. Added to this are the properties of the stars and of other regions of the sky.

Earth was created, in itself, unmixed [with other elements]. Once uncovered by the waters, it was given form, dried by light, and called *the dry land*.[a] Also, due to its own density, being pressed upon by water, it remains quite cold.[b] Therefore the substance of the earth receives its form from the splendour of water and the light of heaven, as also do <u>all</u> mixed things. Also, air is in itself nearly devoid of qualities. Being from evaporated water, air preserves water's mixture of coldness and wetness. Through respiration air cools our natural warmth. But evaporation can come from heat, by which air is easily warmed and dried, particularly in drying soil, <u>when it is scattered by the northeast wind</u>.[59]

[*All Things Are One in God*]

Lastly, the preceding discussion confirms the ancient idea that all things are one. For all things are one in God, <u>and exist in him alone</u>. Throughout *Asclepius* and [in a discourse addressed] to his son Tat, Trismegistus teaches that everything is one.[c] Melissus said that the universe is

---

[a] Gen 1:9-10. [b] The qualities of coldness and dryness are associated with the element earth. See A.R4.48. [c] For example, *Asclepius* 1, 2; *Corpus Hermeticum* 12.8.

one, unchangeable and infinite.[a] Thus other, changeable things are restored to an unchangeable unity.

[162] Qualities, or accidental forms, together with an ideal form, make one form. What has arisen from light unites with light to form a unity. When heat, colour, or some other form is added to a body made from light, it unites as one with an ideal form — with light itself, which is the mother of forms. Also, ideas acquired by the soul unite in one light with the soul, and in one spirit with the spirit. Each idea unites as one with spirit and light. In God spirit and light are one. Therefore these other things are also one in him, in accordance with a universal plan. The ideal forms of things, in which things themselves exist singly, are one in God. They make other things one in God by [Christ's] mediation, in the shadow of his truth, under which Christ is united hypostatically with God without mediation. It should always be kept in mind that in all things there are analogies to Christ, *who is the head* [of all things].[b]

It should also be remembered that there are various modes and hierarchies of divinity. If looked at in this way, the ideas of Parmenides and Melissus regarding the one source will be [seen to be] true.[c] This is what Xenophanes, the teacher of Parmenides, clearly asserted when he said that the one source is God.[d] Also Anaximander said that there is one infinite source of all things.[e] Democritus and Anaxagoras maintained that there was one substance with a diversity of forms, which formed many sources.[f] All of

---

[a] Steuco, *De perenni philosophia* 3.8, 3.10. See also Aristotle, *Metaphysics* 1.4.   [b] Eph 4:15-16.   [c] Steuco, *De perenni philosophia* 3.6.   [d] Steuco, *De perenni philosophia* 3.10, quoting Simplicius, *De physica* 1, fol.4v. See also Aristotle, *Metaphysics* 1.5 (986b); Reuchlin, *De arte cabalistica*, fol.28r.   [e] Simplicius, *De physica* 1, fol. 5r. See also Eusebius, *Praeparatio evangelica* 1.8, 14.14 (PG 21 55C, 1226C), quoting pseudo-Plutarch, *Stromateis* 2.   [f] Simplicius, *De physica* 3, fol.113r, commenting on Aristotle, *Physics* 3.4 (203a).

Book 4

these [philosophers] knew the teaching of Trismegistus, of which Aristotle was unaware, which is based on divine ideal forms <u>and is very close to the truth</u>.

There is one source, one light of the Word, the omniform light, and the head of all, who is Jesus Christ our Lord, the source of all of God's creations.

Appendix

The Paris Manuscript

The Paris Manuscript

This appendix contains an alternate version of books 3 and 4, taken from the so-called "Paris manuscript." This manuscript, located in the Bibliothèque Nationale in Paris, is a partial draft of the "On the Trinity" section of *The Restoration of Christianity*, consisting of variant versions of books 3, 4, 5, and dialogue 1. The order of the books in the manuscript is different from the order in the printed book: book 5 begins on manuscript page 1, followed by book 4, dialogue 1, and book 3. Whatever the reason was for copying the books in that order, it does not indicate that the material was reorganized between the draft and the final printing. Manuscript page 1 begins, "On the Divine Trinity, book 5..." and all of the other sections are similarly labelled.

The Date and Provenance of the Manuscript

At one time it was believed that this manuscript was a copy of the draft that Servetus sent to Calvin in 1546.[1] However, this is not possible, since the manuscript includes references to a collection

---

[1] Leonard Mackall, "A Manuscript of the 'Christianismi Restitutio' of Servetus, placing the discovery of the pulmonary circulation anterior to 1546," *Proceedings of the Royal Society of Medicine* 17 (1924), 35-38.

of works attributed to Athanasius, which was published in 1548.[2] It has been argued that the draft probably dates from before 1551, since it does not include citations of some works by Clement of Alexandria, which are included in the final printed version of *Restoration*.[3] Clement's works were first printed in Greek in 1550 and then in Latin translation in 1551. Servetus's wording of the quotations from Clement suggests acquaintance with the Latin translation, so these late changes to the text must have occurred in 1551 or 1552. The manuscript appears, therefore, to be a copy of a draft from c.1549-51.

The copy itself must have been made after Servetus's death, possibly long after, because manuscript page 58 contains a reference to "Ephesians 5.13." Verse numbering within chapters of the Bible was first attempted in the earliest edition of the Pagnini Bible (1527-28). But this system was not adopted in any other Bible, not even the second edition of Pagnini's work (the one edited by Servetus). The next system of numbering, the one still used today, was introduced by Robert Estienne in his Greek New Testament (1551), his Hebrew Bible (1553), and finally his Vulgate (1555). Thus Servetus could not have written "Ephesians 5.13"

---

[2] Whenever Servetus mentioned Athanasius in *The Restoration of Christianity*, he was citing a book called *D. Athanasii ... opera omnia, quae hactenus apud Latinorum officinas reperiri potuerunt* (All of the works of Athanasius in Latin, that have been located so far), which was published in Cologne in 1548. Editions containing varying assortments of Athanasius and pseudo-Athanasius works had previously been published in Paris in 1520, in Lyons in 1532, and in Wittenberg, also in 1532. The set of items included in each of these editions is different, and there are also variations in the titles assigned to them. Based on the works that Servetus cited, the titles he used, and his references to the placement of the works within the volume, we can be confident that he was using the 1548 Cologne edition. For additional details about this edition, see A.R1.96 (*On the Trinity and the Bible*, 371-372).

[3] A similar argument was made by Roland Bainton in "The Smaller Circulation: Servetus and Colombo," *Sudhoffs Archiv für Geschichte der Medizin* 24 (1931). In addition to the argument from the references to Clement, Bainton mentioned the late addition of material by Philo of Alexandria. However, the appeal to Philo is not actually relevant, since Servetus's quotations of Philo are all taken from secondary sources, primarily Agostino Steuco's *Perennial Philosophy* and the works of the fourth-century Christian apologist Eusebius.

in a draft of *Restoration*. The verse number must have been added by whoever copied the draft, most likely after 1555, when the numbers were used in Estienne's Vulgate, and possibly well after that time, when verse numbering had become familiar. We can only guess why a verse number was only used in this one place.

Comparison of the Manuscript and the Final Text

In this volume, where the text of the manuscript is different from the final version, the variant text is underlined in both the appendix and the main text. This allows the reader to compare the two versions and see what Servetus added, removed, or changed between the date of the manuscript and the final publication.

Many of the differences between the manuscript and the final printed version are trivial — just the sort of minor editorial changes that an author routinely makes when revising a text. However, there are some significant additions, deletions, and revisions. The following are among the most noteworthy.

Book 3

The opening paragraphs (pp. 92-93) were revised to strengthen and clarify the theological aim of the book. The manuscript says that "the whole aim of our discussion is to investigate the true mode of the manifestation of God." This was changed to, "The whole object and goal set for us here is to investigate the true mode of the manifestation of God, and to make Christ our aim in all things ... the entire mystery of the Word is the glorification of Christ."

No new topics were introduced in book 3, but some passages were extended with new material. The assertion that God's appearance to the Old Testament prophets was "a true display of the substance of God" and not "a falsely created spectre" (pp. 94-95) was made longer and more emphatic. Also expanded was the argument that God can be present in corporeal things without himself being corporeal (pp. 120-121).

And there were some deletions. Two discussions of the Virgin Mary and the begetting of Christ were removed (pp. 107, 122), probably because the subject was not relevant to the point being made in the book as a whole.

Appendix

Book 4

The changes that Servetus made to book 4 are of two kinds: (1) new conclusions about the origins of created things, and (2) the addition of supporting quotations.

The final section of book 4, which Servetus called "The Origins of Natural Things," consists of two subsections. In the first, he sets forth his ideas about the nature of light and the relationships among light, the Word of God, and the forms of all things. In the second subsection, he presents six conclusions that, he argues, follow from these premises. Of the six conclusions, one is completely new, and one is substantially expanded.

The new conclusion is, "Earth was created before heaven" (p. 156). This is only tangentially related to the preceding discussion about light and forms; for the most part, it is argued on biblical grounds, principally the creation story in Genesis 1 and 2.

The expanded conclusion is the last one, which Servetus claims is "unknown to all philosophers," namely, that "water, air, and fire possess a kind of heavenly matter distinct from earthy matter" (pp. 159-161). He does not claim to have discovered this on his own; he credits it to Maimonides and other Jewish sages. His own contributions are the fifteen arguments with which he supports this claim and the conclusion that he draws about the fundamental structure of the material universe (p. 161):

> We may now conclude that there are four sources of natural things, two material and two formal. The material sources are the two kinds of matter already mentioned: the earthy and the watery. The formal sources are the light of the sun, which warms and dries, and the splendour of water, which cools and moistens. Therefore there are four qualities that are called primary, and four elements. But the origins and perfections of these qualities are in only two of the elements.

This conclusion appears in the final version of book 4, but not in the manuscript. It combines the idea that earth is fundamentally different from the other three elements with the idea, which has been developed throughout book 4, that there are two kinds of light: the warm, dry light of the sun and the cool, moist light, or "splendour," of water.

The Paris Manuscript

The second major change in book 4 is the greatly expanded role of supporting quotations, many of them gleaned from secondary sources such as Agostino Steuco's *Perennial Philosophy*. These quotations bolster Servetus's assertions by appealing to authorities. More importantly, however, they demonstrate the reality of the perennial philosophy. The new quotations are drawn from a wide range of sources: classical authors such as Plutarch and Seneca; Church Fathers such as Augustine, Origen, and Clement of Alexandria; Neoplatonists such as Plotinus, Proclus, and Iamblichus; rabbinic commentaries and the Jewish philosopher Philo of Alexandria. By calling attention to similarities between the religious insights of people from widely differing times and cultures, Servetus hoped to demonstrate that there is a core of basic religious truth that is shared by Christians, Jews, and pagans.

First page of book 3 in the Paris manuscript

THE PARIS MANUSCRIPT

On the Divine Trinity

Book 3

Showing the prefiguration of the person of Christ in the Word, our vision of God, and the hypostasis of the Word

[92] <117> Christ Jesus, our Lord and God, whom we have just now revealed in a great many Bible passages, spurs us on and strengthens our spirits, so that we might bring to light the other remaining great mysteries about him. The whole object, the goal set <u>before</u> us here, <u>and the whole aim of our discussion</u>, is to investigate the true mode of the manifestation of God. Therefore, in this third book, in order to attain our vision of God, we shall first examine the person of the Word, showing the person of Christ[a] in the Word itself.

We say that the first chapter of the Gospel of John has this purpose: that all of us might behold *the glory of God in the face of Jesus Christ*, as Paul says in 2 Corinthians 4. This is to be seen *in the face of Jesus Christ*. And John himself says, *the Word became flesh and we beheld his glory*. <u>The Word had already been brought forth and prepared in wisdom from eternity, and was made flesh</u> so that it could be clearly visible. *And we have seen this and bear witness*. We have seen that *glory in the face of Jesus Christ*, which was once [*seated*] *upon the cherubim*, gleaming within *the gloom and clouds, and the darkness did not overwhelm it*. We have seen the glory of Christ which he himself <u>had</u> from eternity in the presence of God (John 17).

In the beginning, the pattern of the future human being, Christ, already existed in *the Word that was with God*. This πρόσωπον (*prosopon*,

---

[a] The manuscript actually says "showing the person of the Word in the Word itself" (*in verbo ipso personam verbi ostendentes*) but this is probably an error rather than a variation.

Appendix

person) — this person, this countenance, this face, this **[93]** representation of humanity in God — lies mystically hidden in all the passages of scripture that speak of image, face, and person. The prophets of old, called seers, only saw God by seeing Christ in God, or God through Christ. As he himself said, *Whoever has seen me, has seen* God. Long ago when prophets saw the countenance of Elohim, they saw in the oracle of God the prototype and model of the future human being [Christ]. For what else could they have seen in God, *face to face*? They saw there <u>not simply a person or shape, but</u> the very substance of Christ, just as we see the substance of God in Christ. The original exemplar of that archetype in heaven above was the human being, Christ Jesus.

Moses speaks about this likeness, shape, and image in God in Deuteronomy 4 and 5 and Numbers 12. And in Exodus 20, the people heard Moses speaking, but they did not see the image of Christ speaking. **<118>** In these passages *temunah* (image or likeness) designates the form, shape, likeness, and image of Jesus Christ that Moses saw. This is borne out by David's use of this word in Psalm 16, which is Psalm 17 in the Hebrew numbering: *I shall see your face, and I shall be satisfied when your image appears*. Balaam saw this image from afar (Numbers 24). *I shall see him*, he says, *but I shall not look at him now, nor from nearby*.

All the prophets desired to see this shining face, <u>just as it is said that Abraham rejoiced to see Christ (John 8)</u>.[a] Desiring this, David says in Psalm 79, *You who sit upon the cherubim, shine forth*, appear in splendour. *Cause your face to shine*, make your countenance resplendent, *and we shall be saved*. Psalms 4 and 43 relate the same thing about this face and countenance. In the same way, in Psalm 88 one observes in God the face and countenance of Christ.

Isaiah saw this countenance *seated upon a lofty throne, but <u>his</u> face was veiled with wings* of fire (Isaiah 6). What face would you say was there, what feet, other than those of Christ? <u>The reason for this is evident: for God himself does not have a face, hands, or feet. Furthermore, at that time these were said to have been seen through veils</u>. The same thing is proved in the vision of Ezekiel (chapters 1 and 10), as well as in the vision of Daniel (chapter 10) and the vision of the seventy elders in Exodus 24. **[94]** Compare all these visions with the vision of John in

---

[a] John 8:56.

the Apocalypse, chapters 1 and 4, and you will say that they all saw the same thing in Christ, the same person and the same face.

This was not just a mask, such as the sophists devised. For God wanted to reveal himself, to the glory of Christ. [The sophists] invented an unworthy thing about God: that the invisible God needed a falsely created spectre, so that he might maintain visibility in some way, as if God were incapable of this by himself, as if he could not have begotten Christ by himself, and as if he could deceive those who saw [Christ] by means of a dishonest trick.

Indeed they say that the spectre that was seen was something other than an angel, because they claim that an angel has no form. But we shall show that [what was seen in these visions] was an angel and Christ. More than an angel, it was the true face of God, as is clearly established in Exodus 33 and Numbers 12. At that time the radiant face of Christ was the face of God. His face, [scripture] says, is like the sun, shining by its own power. And **<119>** besides, it was the same face that shone in an angel, when the angel was clothed in the light of the Word.

Turn your attention to the cloud, because of which the vision [of the divine] in former times was not as clear as it is now. At that time God dwelt in darkness, and concealed Christ to some degree. Daniel saw the image of *the Son of man*, beneath a veil of clouds (Daniel 7). Zechariah beheld the same thing **[95]** in the darkness of night (Zechariah 1). Christ said that formerly *the prophets and kings longed to see* this face, *and could not see it* (Matthew 13 and Luke 10). This longing can be found as well in Psalms 23, 26, 66, 67, 79, and in 2 Chronicles 9. Indeed it is a teaching of the Law that those wishing to bless someone should say, *may the Lord show his face to you* (Numbers 6). The appearance of that face was a sublime thing. In chapter 8, Isaiah waits for this face to appear openly, as does Habakkuk in chapters 2 and 3.

John reports that *these* and other things *were said by Isaiah* and other prophets *when they beheld the glory* of Christ (John 12), the glory that the human [Christ] had with God (John 17). Isaiah plainly speaks about the glory and splendour of Christ, and he proves that Christ himself is *the splendour of glory*, or the gloriousness shining forth in God (chapter 60 and 66), just as Christ is called *the bright reflection of* [God's] *glory* in Hebrews 1. Thus did his splendour radiate (Habakkuk 3). The splendour that Paul saw glittering in the face of Christ *surpassed the splendour of the sun* (Acts 9 and 26). What was formerly called seeing the Lord *face to face* has now been revealed to us in the gospel as the face of Christ. For the gospels and epistles teach that God was seen in Christ. Otherwise, [God] was not seen, and could not have been seen (John 1, 5, and 14, Hebrews 11, 1 John 4, and 1 Timothy 6).

Jacob's vision shows the same thing. He says that he *saw Elohim face to face* (Genesis 32). Moreover, Jacob himself clearly states that it was the face of the human being Christ, in the comparison that he makes when, in the following chapter, he says to his brother Esau, "*I have seen your face, as if I had seen the countenance of Elohim*, which I saw this night." **[96]** Christ himself teaches the same thing by using the verb ["to see"] in the past tense, "*Whoever has seen me has seen the Father*," not a mask, not a fictitious spectre. And John says about Christ that he explained, as if he were saying not only to us, but even to the prophets of old, that the vision and knowledge of God is to be had through Christ. The prophets of old saw the Word of God, as Irenaeus and Tertullian tell us.

God *has revealed his Word at the proper time*. The grace which now has been openly granted to us, was given to us through Christ <**120**> *before the world began*. For, *before the world began*, God contained in himself the pattern of Jesus Christ — his substance, his light, and his spirit — the grace which he was going to give to us through [Christ]. Christ himself, and the Word itself, are made manifest, as Peter and John tell us (1 Peter 1 and 1 John 1). For Christ was previously foreshadowed in the Word, within darkness and clouds. The Word represented Christ, and he who was represented then was the face of God. Paul says that the man Christ was an εικονα (*eikon*, image), the true *likeness of* the invisible *God*, and that *God's glory was known in the face of Jesus Christ* (2 Corinthians 4). [This face] is recognized, I say, because the glorious face of Christ seen on the mountain was the face of the Word itself and was shining forth in God from eternity. Note Paul's words: when the face of Christ is seen, God can be seen in his glory. That very [face] is "*the glory which I had with you before the world came to be*" (John 17).

Note that it is not the deity but the human being who seeks to be glorified according to that glory, which he formerly had with God. This man was then already glorious in God, and desired by all, not an apparition created in God. It was his face that Moses and the other prophets passionately desired to see. *They saw* him in another way *and rejoiced*, as Christ says of Abraham. They saw his back, <u>and</u> not his face (Exodus 33). To see him from behind is like seeing him with his face covered. Terror overwhelmed them when they turned their eyes to this face, and they *feared* that they *were going to die* (Exodus 3 and 20 and Judges 13). Because of Adam's sin the face of God was hidden, and before it stood *a flaming sword* (Genesis 3). He who had previously been visible to Adam afterwards became invisible. Sin caused *the face of God to be hidden, the cloud* of his *anger* having been thrown over it (Isaiah 59 and Lamentations 3).

Under the Law, visions [of God] were terrifying, alarming, **[97]** and frightening, and made Moses and Elijah hide their faces (Exodus 3 and 1 Kings 19). But now that these terrifying visions have been taken away, Christ speaks graciously to us (Hebrews 11). At one time God showed himself to us in anger, but now he is reconciled to us through Christ. The veil of the inner [sanctuary of the divine] oracle, like the veil on the face of Moses, meant **<121>** that the glory of God, and the true pathway of the saints, was not yet revealed (Hebrews 9). But now, the temple curtain having been torn, we are allowed to gaze upon the *unveiled face* of the Holy of Holies, that is, to see the celestial face of Christ, which to [the Hebrews] was veiled (2 Corinthians 3 and 4). For us there is no other covering than the flesh of Christ which contains in substantial form the entire deity of the Father (Hebrews 10 and Colossians 2). That flesh, which was torn like a veil by the Jews in the Passion, has revealed at the resurrection his true divinity and celestial glory. Thus Moses beheld the veiled features of Christ's face, but not his true face.

They longed, said Christ, *to see what you see, and did not see it. The light gleamed in the darkness, and the darkness did not overwhelm it* (John 1). *He made the darkness* around him *his hiding place* (Psalm 17 and 2 Samuel 22). In those days God *dwelt in darkness*[a] (2 Chronicles 5 and 6). For that reason when John says *the darkness did not overwhelm it*,[b] he indicates that they had all been in darkness, since that glorious face, shining in the darkness, was hidden from them. Every human nature who, because of Adam's sin, is deserving of the darkness of hell,

---

[a] The manuscript says, "In those days, God <u>dwells</u> in darkness," which must be an error. [b] The manuscript says, "and the darkness <u>overwhelms</u> it," which must be an error.

Appendix

is included in the word "darkness." In the same vein, Luke 1 says, *to bring light to those [who sit] in darkness*. And Matthew 4: *The people who were sitting in darkness have seen a great light*. Christ himself says in John 12, "*I have come as a light into the world, so that everyone who sees and believes in me, may not remain in darkness.*" The face of God, hidden to [those in darkness], was revealed to us. For it was truly said, *God was manifested in the flesh* (1 Timothy 3). Isaiah says much the same thing, calling God hidden, in chapter 45. For the countenance of Christ lay hidden within the shadow of the Father.

Then Christ *dwelt in the hiding-place of the Most High*, and *in the shadow* **[98]** *of the Almighty* (Psalm 90). *There was the hiding-place of his strength* (Habakkuk 3). And Deuteronomy 33 is in agreement with this. For at the time when the Law was handed down there was a concealment, when the countenance of the one who was speaking was not seen. Nevertheless, he has now been clearly shown to us. For it <u>had been</u> foretold: *the glory of <u>God</u> shall be revealed, and all flesh shall see it*. [*Thus says the Lord God:*] "*It is I who was speaking, here I am.*" And *they shall see eye to eye*. Christ, the God of Israel, was previously hidden, but *afterward was seen upon earth, and lived among human beings* (Baruch 3). <u>Note that here</u> Baruch is speaking <u>literally</u> about the *Wisdom of God*, the visible Word that *appeared on earth, dwelling* <122> *among human beings*, in the days of the patriarchs and Moses. There was a divine light and a human face. This is the light of God's glory, which was the light of the Word. The Word is the shining and now visible splendour of *the face of Christ*, as Paul teaches in 2 Corinthians 3 and 4. David taught the same thing, saying *the light of the countenance of Elohim*, that is, the light of the face of Christ (Psalms 4, 43, 66, 88 and 89). Who could be so <u>shameless</u> as to say, like the sophists, that all of this light was a deceptive mask, a conjurer's trick, and an imposture?

If you wish to <u>see more of</u> the glory of Christ, rise up to the cherubim and seraphim, and contemplate Ezekiel's [vision of] wheels and creatures. For in all of them the image of Jesus Christ, which is itself the glory of God, is represented as a person and shines out in substance. <u>Ezekiel calls Christ, and the vision, a likeness</u> of *the glory of the Lord*. The same creatures were seen, and the same *sound of many waters* [was heard] in Ezekiel as in the Apocalypse of John. The reference to Christ is always shown by these things.

The angels were heralds of the glory of Christ, as shown by their words, repeated in Isaiah 6, Luke 2 and Revelation 4. The angels, with their human faces, <u>foreshadow</u> Christ. When Christ was seen in an angel, the messenger of the Father was shown in advance, **[99]** the *angel of great counsel*. After Adam's sin, God placed the cherubim before the oracle of the face of Christ. In the same way the cherubim seen in heaven hid both the face of the oracle and their own faces. The pattern for [the cherubim] was revealed to Moses for the construction of the tabernacle, and was also shown to Solomon, so that he might make golden cherubim.

A cherub is generally said to be <u>eminent</u>. The figure is understood by its eminence to be human, and wings add further angelic excellence. According to Hebrew etymology, with the first letter [כ] being considered servile, cherubim are said to be like parties to a lawsuit or like the great and illustrious. In the same way a king is called *a mighty cherub*. The cherubim were shown in the heavens, whenever there was strife [on earth], and their fiery countenances demonstrated that God had become angry. The *wrath* of God *blazed like fire*. For this reason the seraphim are also called fiery, aflame, and burning. These cherubim, <123> like the seraphim seen by Isaiah, were a kind of hidden flame in the likeness of a human being, veiling and shadowing their faces with their wings. They did this not only because it was not granted to the angels to behold the divine splendour without Christ, but also to prevent the blazing light of the face of Christ from being seen by the Jews of that time.

Moses saw in God the image and pattern of Christ, as depicted in Exodus 25, Acts 7, and Hebrews 8. For the pattern that he saw there, which is described in Exodus 25 and mentioned in the preceding chapter, is Elohim, that is, Christ. David saw the same image of Christ above the cherubim (2 Samuel 22). He *gave to his son Solomon this pattern* and likeness (1 Chronicles 28). He calls it the pattern and likeness *of all the things which he* had seen *in his spirit*. And [David] says, *he made me understand all the works of that pattern*. And he says, *all these things were written by the hand of God*. But what can more properly be said to be written by the hand of God, than that which was expressed and given a [visible] shape in <u>God</u> himself?

To [the Hebrews of that time], however, [Christ] was a figure behind a veil. *The wings of the cherubim concealed* and *overshadowed the oracle*

Appendix

of Christ himself (Exodus 25 and Hebrews 9). <u>And</u> even though this writing and shadowing **[100]** present a picture of a temple made of stone, nevertheless the true temple is the body of Christ <u>himself</u> (John 2). The comparison of that pattern to Christ is made clear in Hebrews 9. In summary, *all things* that are in the Law *are a foreshadowing of the body of Christ*, as the apostle to the Colossians and the Hebrews teaches. For the Jews every [contact with the divine] took place through angels, and was a foreshadowing of Christ. Christ was prefigured by the angels.

The angels are often called gods by the Jews, although what they call gods are not the invisible <u>crowd in the God</u> of the tritheists, but God and Christ (1 Corinthians 8). The glory of God is seated on the cherubim, which means that Jesus Christ is superior to the angels. For he is *the Lord of glory* and *sits on his glorious throne* (1 Corinthians 2 and Matthew 25). And he *will come with* splendour, *majesty*, and *glory* (Mark 8 and Matthew 16). The glory and majesty of the Lord, which is described in Exodus 40, is the very thing that, departing from the cherub and coming to Christ, is said to have gone up from the cherub to a much loftier place (Ezekiel 9). Set above the heads of the cherubim was the throne, the seat of Christ, encircled [by a rainbow] (Ezekiel 1 and 10). For Christ is far superior to the angels.

In the letter to the Hebrews Christ is compared to the angels so that the Jews, to whom the angels appeared as God, might thereby be able to understand that Christ, who was prefigured in the Law as superior to the angels, is the true God above the angels. The divinity of the angels **<124>** had only a ministerial character, in the shadow <u>of the</u> prefiguration of the true deity of Christ. This is why Paul calls it superstition when anyone, under the pretext of that divinity, introduces a religion of angels (Colossians 2). For that reason, John says that we should avoid all images, even though they might possess some appearance of deity. Christ alone *is the true God* (1 John 5). *There is no other name under heaven by which we are to be saved* (Acts 4). The truth of Christ shining forth for us casts out the shadows. *The glory of the Lord*, which appeared so often by means of angels, in the cherubim and in the cloud, is now *revealed* in the face of Christ (Isaiah 40 and 46).

When we know Christ **[101]**, because we turn our eyes to him, *we all see* in him *the glory of* God *with his face unveiled* (Isaiah 66 and Habakkuk 2). We recognize that *[glory] in the face of Jesus Christ*, which once, among the Jews, was foreshadowed by angels. The Jews saw an angel in God, and God in an angel; we see Christ in God and God in Christ. They saw *an angel ordaining* all things according to the Law, and, throughout the Law, speaking as God (Acts 7, Hebrews 2, and Galatians 3). An angel is called the face of God (Exodus 33). Having seen an angel, Jacob is said to have seen the face of God (Genesis 32). [The place was called] Peniel [the face of El] because the face and person of Christ were foreshadowed there by an angel. In those days, the name of God, whose dwelling place was said to be among the cherubim, dwelt among the angels in the person of Christ. Exodus 23 says that the name of God dwelt in an angel. At that time it dwelt in shadow, but now it dwells in Christ through his body (Colossians 2). The angel prefiguring Christ took on the person of God, and was called God; as *the angel said* to Jacob, *I am the God of Bethel* (Genesis 31). An angel said to Moses, *I am the God of your fathers* (Exodus 3). And an angel in the person of God spoke and appeared to Abraham (Genesis 18 and 22) and to Hagar (Genesis 16 and 21).

Thus Origen says, in his eighth homily on Genesis, based on chapter 22: "I believe that just as Christ appeared among us humans as a human being, so also he appeared among angels as an angel." What Origen said is true, for angelic substance was a sharer in the light of the Word, and in the Word the person of Christ was assumed by an angel. The angel about whom Ezekiel speaks in chapter 43 was also Christ: *A man standing next to me said to me, "The inner court is the place of my throne, the place of the soles of my feet, where I will dwell in the midst of the children of Israel* <125> *forever."* This was a prefiguration of Christ, by which an angel made himself truly both God and a human being, just as Christ is both God and human.

Angels with human faces allowed themselves to be worshipped (Numbers 22 and Joshua 5). Now, however, **[102]** since Christ, whom the angels prefigured, is revealed, they worship him and are our *fellow servants* (Revelation 19 and 22). At one time God was worshipped in the form of an angel, but now he is truly worshipped in Christ alone. When God was worshipped in the form of angels, they were a foreshadowing of Christ. Just as when the Jews heard the voice of an angel, they were hearing the voice of God (Exodus 23), so also for us [Christians], the voice of Christ is the voice of God (Acts 12). For Christ *speaks the words of* the Father (John 3). Just as, when we see [Christ, the father is seen,] so when we hear [Christ], the Father is heard (John 14). The bread of

Appendix

Christ's body is the bread of God (John 6) and his blood is the blood of God (Acts 20). We are *justified through Christ* by God's justice, and are made *the body and members of Christ*. We are the congregation of God.

The prefiguration of the person of Christ in the Word becomes abundantly clear, because humankind is said to be made in *the image and likeness* of God. For in Genesis 1 [God] says *in our image* and *in our likeness*, that is, according to the form and shape of that image, shared by God, the Word, and the angels. God says "our," using the plural and "image," not "images," using the singular. For there was only one image or face, the person of Christ in God, also shared by the angels.

You may remember that I said earlier that it is the property of speech and wisdom to represent something. The Word was the representation of Christ. *The Word*, as a person, *was with God and <u>the Word</u>* was itself *God*, sharing in the light of the Word. Therefore Jesus Christ himself is the true pattern and the original image, or prototype. In the beginning we were created in his image. So also in baptism we are born anew and regenerated. I am speaking of the real, visible image in the inner self, as I shall show later. But for now, our discussion concerns the external image [of God].

Based on scriptural references, the ancient Hebrews <u>claimed that there was</u> a visible image in God. <u>After</u> Philo, this was <u>referred to by</u> Eusebius, Jerome, **[103]** Petrus Alfonsi, Paul of Burgos, and other Jews who converted to Christ <u>in those days, and those who are converted to the light nowadays</u>. The earliest Christians maintained <u>and taught</u> the same thing, as can be seen in Irenaeus and Tertullian, who both say that there was a human form and shape in the Word itself. This was accepted <u>in ancient times</u> even before Moses, and among foreigners, as Job and his companions teach. <u>I will reserve Zoroaster and [Hermes] Trismegistus for later.</u> In the book's final chapter, Job saw the form of God with his mortal eyes: "*I heard of you with the hearing of my ear,* **<126>** *but now my eye <u>has seen</u> you.*"

On the subject [of the image of God], consider what Eusebius Pamphilus says in book 5 of *Proof of the Gospel* and book 7 of *Preparation for the Gospel*. The body of Adam was formed in the image of God before the soul was breathed into him. Therefore it was the image of a body. In terms of appearance a man was first formed in the image of God, then a woman was formed. Paul teaches this in 1 Corinthians 11.

The image and likeness of the first human being, formed in the image of God, contains the image and likeness of both the soul and the body.

Although the soul, in its likeness to God, is a kind of intelligent mind, nevertheless, in [the account of] the formation of humanity, [the Hebrew words] *tselem* (image) and *demuth* (likeness) refer to the image of the whole [human being], even the visible shape. Furthermore, Christ himself, in his entirety, is called the likeness and shape of God. The meaning of *tselem* is <u>clearly</u> shown in the book of Daniel, where it is said of Nebuchadnezzar that the *tselem*, that is, *the form, of his countenance was changed*. Also, Psalm 72 (Psalm 73 according to the Hebrew numbering): *You will despise their tsalmam*, that is, their faces or countenances. This clearly shows that *tselem* refers to external form. *Tselem* is also used of the form and corporeal image of a statue in Numbers 33, 2 Kings 11, and many other places. Ezekiel 1 and 8 and Isaiah 40 show the same thing about [the Hebrew word] *demuth*. The pattern, according to which **[104]** humankind was first formed, is *demuth*, which Ezekiel saw [in his vision]. <u>Its face shone like fire</u>.[a] By means of the true form and shape of Christ, which was in God, humanity was made to resemble God, even in the body; so much so that even a dead body is said to be in the image of God. Using these same words, *tselem* and *demuth*, <u>it is said that</u> Adam fathered children *in his own image and likeness* (Genesis 5), <u>where the</u> similarity of form <u>is clearly imprinted</u>.

Irenaeus and Tertullian <u>clearly</u> teach that the body of Adam was formed in the image of God. After the era of the ancient Hebrews, in the time of the first Christians, Philo taught the same thing in book 1 of *Questions on Genesis*, which Eusebius Pamphilus <u>also</u> cites in book 7 of *Preparation for the Gospel*. "Nothing mortal," <u>Philo</u> says, "can be compared to the supreme Father as his image, but [the image] is conveyed by means of the Word, as if by <u>an intermediary</u>." In his book *On Agriculture*, Philo also says, "The human soul was made and shaped according to the image of the first, archetypal Word." Therefore, in terms of both his soul and his body, Adam was made according to the pattern, form, shape, and image of Christ.

---

[a] Ezek 1:13.

Appendix

<u>And</u> although <127> "let us make" [humankind] and "our" [image] could be understood literally to refer to angels — because, <u>at creation</u>, angels could contain within themselves the ideal form of humanity — nevertheless, in the mystery [of the Word], Christ is always understood to be foreshadowed by angels. [In the Old Testament, angels] are spoken of in the person of Christ, just as more excellent qualities are ascribed to David and Solomon than could reasonably belong to them. Because the mystery is implicitly understood, <u>as we said in the previous book, great</u> things may be said about them that are not actually due to them.

In Exodus 33, "*My face shall go before you,*" in its literal sense, is said about an angel, **[105]** although the true face is Christ, who was the Son, the companion of the Israelites on their journey (1 Corinthians 10). Indeed, he who said, "*Let us make humankind [in our image and likeness]*" was Christ, that is to say, Elohim, <u>who was</u> the person of the Word, who was the person of God. And [Christ] spoke to the angels, just as in numerous places [in the Old Testament], the angels also spoke as gods. To the angels he said, "*Behold Adam who is as one of us.*" And also, "*Let us go down,*" etc. In the Law all things took place through the agency of angels, and these angels were called gods. Hence some have taught that there are other gods, <u>or another, higher god</u>, above the gods of the Old Testament. From this derives the heresy of Simon Magus, Cerdo, Marcion, and others, who denied that the God of the Law is the father of Jesus Christ, because they perversely understood the God of the Law to be an angel.

Others have imagined that God himself is corporeal by nature, since <u>inherent human body parts and</u> inherent corporeal forms are attributed to him throughout the Law. <u>From what follows, you will make allowances for those who have not yet gained an understanding of this mode of the essence of God.</u> In this regard, Onkelos the Chaldean, in his version [of the Torah], and Rabbi Moses [Maimonides] the Egyptian in his *Guide for the Perplexed*, contort themselves in various ways in order to remove these [corporeal] forms from God. But all of these things are accepted by us [Christians]. And all this perplexity is easily removed by Christ. For he himself is the face, image, likeness, and form of God, containing in himself real corporeal forms. He himself is God of gods and God of the angels, <u>who, it is firmly established, was once truly in God</u>. It should be noted that in this regard an artful method has arisen using a variety of ways of interpreting the scriptures. It is something of a mystery that in the Old Testament, unlike the New, <u>holy</u> scripture assigns such [corporeal forms] to God. It is significant that in the Old Testament <u>we</u> often read about God's hands, eyes, face, and feet being seen by corporeal eyes. Nothing of this sort can be found in the New Testament. Indeed the opposite [is found]: *God is spirit.*

The reason for this is <u>clear</u>. [In Old Testament times] the person of Christ was represented as being with God. There was then no real distinction between the Father and the Son. **<128>** These corporeal forms, which are now in the Son, <u>would then have been</u> attributed to God himself. <u>Even then, the person of the Son had appeared.</u> As a result, angels in the form of God and angels in the form of Christ were intermingled in [Old Testament] writings. If this was Cyprian's understanding, he rightly made use of this ancient truth, when he said that **[106]** [in the Old Testament] God, an angel, and Christ were spoken of as the same being. For in book 2 of *Against the Jews* he shows that in many [passages of scripture], the angel who spoke to Abraham and others, and was seen by them, was also God and Christ. All of this <u>is shown in</u> Exodus, chapter 3. For it was Christ who said "*I will be who I will be,*" when the angel appeared and spoke <u>in the person of God</u>, as the voice of God. <u>God himself was speaking there</u>. Paul makes the same observation in Galatians 3: *The Law* was given from God *by angels through the hand of a mediator.* The glory of Jesus Christ is so great that his person was prefigured in God, angels, human beings, a lamb, a serpent, a calf, a tree, a rock, and other things. If these great mysteries of Christ had been understood in former times, no one would ever have claimed that angels created the world and that they were the gods of the Old Testament. For in their ministry they acted as a foreshadowing of Christ: not only at creation, but in other events that followed later.

Others made God and the ideal form two separate principles, although the ideal form itself was the appearance of the Word, as well as the divine form. It is a wonderful concept: the wonder-working Word. God created by means of the Word, and the person of Christ was the one creating. God created through the Word, creating through his very self, that is, through an <u>actual</u> manifestation of himself produced by his utterance. God manifested himself in creation and shared himself with his creatures, so that, prior to sinning, Adam innocently gazed upon the form of God and received a pure spirit. After [the first] sin, the face of God was hidden from humankind behind an embroidered veil, which was not to be opened until the coming of Christ.

Under the Law, Christ did not allow himself to be clearly seen. He was only visible as if *through a latticed window*, <u>as said in</u> Proverbs 7 and Song of Solomon 2. Zechariah chapter 3 teaches that that the embroidery <u>is open</u> for us. For there, God says about Christ, "*I am engraving his inscription; I am uncovering what has been carved.*" The Hebrew verb *patach* literally means to carve, as with a sharp tool, in order to uncover and expose a hidden figure. Thus God uncovered himself by showing us Christ. <u>Hence Irenaeus refers to this uncovering as the utterance of the Word</u>.[a] The Chaldean translator [in his Aramaic rendering] translates *patach* in the same way: to reveal or **[107]** uncover the face of Christ. For the Targum Jonathan has *ha aena gele chezijathah*a, that is, "Behold, I reveal, or **<129>** uncover, a vision of [Christ]."

To briefly summarize, in their narratives and prophecies about Christ, both the Law and the Prophets very often include the words face, image, hidden, concealed, habitation, and shelter. Because all these things were written about him in *the Law and all the Prophets*, the spirit of the Lord artfully carved them in engraved letters, so that, beneath the silver engraving, the golden Word would lie hidden. In God's mysterious plan, all these things were foreshadowed by historical and ritual types as a kind of cover, just as Christ himself was foreshadowed in God. By analogy to the higher mysteries, there was, in the lesser mysteries of the Law, a foreshadowing prefiguring Christ. Therefore the [divine] plan of foreshadowing came from [heaven] above to [the world] below. In God there was a shining Word; it shone, however, in darkness and shadow.

<u>Thus</u> [the Word] was like the shadow of Christ, not only because it prefigured Christ, but also because diminished light is called shadow. It was diminished light because it did not shine for <u>them</u> as it does for us. The patriarchs spoke of the Word as if it were corporeal. For there was a substance shining in the cloud with <u>a certain solidity. The substance was visible, and in Mary it was also made tangible. That cloud of the glory of God, that divine shadow, overshadowed Mary and, condensing</u>

---

[a] Irenaeus, *Adversus haereses* 4.7.3 (PG 7 992A-B).

The Paris Manuscript ~ *Book 3*

into heavenly rain, became the dew of the physical begetting of Christ. You will easily comprehend the mode of divinity in the cloud, as well as in the heavenly dew, when you have learned about the universal and omniform essence of God, in the next book.

If you are able to believe that God could truly beget out of himself a human son, then you will have no difficulty in believing what I have been saying. Thus it is now time for a plain and simple consideration of Jesus Christ in God the Father. In the preaching of Paul and of the other apostles, we hear of nothing but the *one God, who is the Father, and Jesus Christ* his son. You must keep in mind all the distinctions, and the various ways of speaking, to know whether it is the Word or the Son that is being discussed. For these words mean different things. **[108]** If you can point out to me any place [in scripture] showing that the Word was ever called the Son, I will admit defeat. Therefore I will say, along with the scriptures, that what was once the Word is now the Son. And the person of the Son was once in the Word, shining there as a person.

The person of the Son was correctly spoken of by the ancients. However, the sophists, not understanding this, distorted "persons" to mean something different. Thus they have made up metaphysical, incorporeal, invisible [but somehow] real, not fictitious persons — very foolishly calling them persons. But their abuse of words is as nothing compared to their abuse of God himself, whom they divided, mutilated, and tore to pieces. Listen instead to what scripture teaches about persons, so that you might realize [the extent of] their abuse.

The external appearance, face, and presentation of a human being is called a "person" in scripture, as when we say, "this person is beautiful." This is the way "person" is generally understood in Romans 2, Colossians 3, Acts 10, and 1 Peter 1: *God is no respecter of persons*, that is, he has no regard for <130> outward differences, such as whether someone is *male or female, slave or free, Jew or Greek*, rich or poor. This idea is advocated in 1 Samuel 17, Leviticus 19, Deuteronomy 1, and James 2, where we are taught *not to take into consideration the person of the poor or the countenance of the mighty*. See also 2 Corinthians 1, 2, 3, 4, 8, 10, and 11. Outside of scripture, the meaning of the word προσωπον (*prosopon*, person) in Greek, or of *persona* in Latin, is so well known, that some evil demon must have instigated all of the tritheists to foist upon us these [three] invented invisible beings in place of persons. In Hebrew this matter is clear. What we call a person, they

Appendix

call a face. Reader, examine in the original sources what "the person of the Word" meant to the first Christians. <u>Among these, the earliest disciples, Irenaeus and Tertullian, teach very plainly the visible shape and person of the Word.</u>[a]

Likewise the [Hebrew] scriptures have <u>another</u> way of speaking about <u>persons</u>. One being is said to put on the person of another, <u>as</u> the companions of Job, having taken on the role of God, wished to speak and pronounce judgement as if they themselves were gods <u>(Job 13)</u>. Angels speak in the person of God throughout the Law. Pseudo-apostles, <u>as Paul says</u>, once spoke in the person of the apostles, and *Satan* speaks in the person of a good angel when he *transforms himself into an angel of light*. Wisdom itself, an angel, **[109]** David, and other prophets often speak in the person of Christ.

In the same way, we say that the Word, in the person of Christ, was at one time the Son, and that Christ was at one time with the Father in the person of the Word. Christ is the person of the Word and the Word is the person of Christ, but there is only one person and only one face. What shone forth in the Word, and in Wisdom, is Christ himself. Similarly, if you see me face to face, and also see me in a mirror, you see only one person. Given this, the parable of Wisdom in Proverbs 8 can be readily understood. The person of Christ is shown there, saying that he was formed from eternity. [Wisdom] was a prefiguration of Christ, a reflection and an expression [of God]. Wisdom speaks there in the parable, in a figurative manner. For Wisdom takes on the person of Christ, who was formed in God from eternity, and was begotten and created as an expression [of God]. He is said to be created, because he participates in creation. He was begotten as a person, as [God's] personal son. Thus he was formed as a person.

Having understood the person of the Word and the mode in which it is manifested, it will now be easy to say what remains to be said about our vision of God. With Christ as my teacher, I am compelled to present a vision of God, which the world does not understand. Thus I may call them blind, who **<131>** *having sight do not see, and having understanding, do not understand* God. But you, Christian reader, are

---

[a] Irenaeus, *Adversus haereses* 4.7.4 (PG 7 992B). Tertullian, *Adversus Praxean* 14-16 (PL 2 170C-176A).

gaining a true understanding and vision of God, which, you will <u>learn</u>, you can obtain through Christ, and which you will receive entirely from him. For God in himself is completely incomprehensible. He can neither be seen nor understood, unless you consider that within him there is some visible form, as Christ teaches (John 5). This, as has now been revealed, is the face of Christ, and the person of the Word. When [God] willed it, a great and divine majesty appeared in that face — on the mount, in the temple, or in some other place — so that his face alone, with its wondrous power, could arouse those who saw it.

In heaven this [face] is now more glorious, as it was in the vision of Paul, when **[110]** the human [Christ] was glorified *with that glory which* the Word once *possessed with God* (John 17). *The Word*, which *was with God*, and *was God* himself, was the person of Jesus Christ. Through him the God of glory wished to be seen, is seen, and will always be seen. <u>Just as</u> you see the light in the body of the sun, so in the very body of Christ the apostles saw God shining. They saw him with their outward eyes. You see him with inward ones. Those abstract ideas about God, of which the sophists boast when apart from him, are mere nothings, or illusions rather, when in the presence of God.

What Christian of sound mind would make the Turks, Saracens, and other nations equal to us in forming a conception of God? Making a comparison to this matter, Peter, in book 2 of Clement's *Recognitions*, relates ideas which he had formed about Jerusalem and Caesarea, before he had ever seen those cities. Later, after seeing them, he realized that everything he had thought about them was wrong. We, who see God through Christ, can prove beyond a doubt that the imaginings of others about God are false. For how could a human being ever imagine God, before he made himself visible? He is far more hidden than the cities which were the objects of Peter's imaginings.

The mind fails when it thinks about God, because he is incomprehensible. The eye does not see him, because he is invisible. The ear does not hear him, nor has it ever heard him, except when he has spoken in a human voice. The hand does not touch him, because he is incorporeal. The tongue cannot describe him, because he is indescribable. No place can hold him, because he is unbounded. Time does not measure him, because he is immeasurable. <u>The intellect cannot assess his value, because he is invaluable.</u> In fact he transcends everything, surpassing every intellect and mind.

Appendix

Many people tell us that God can be defined only by saying what he is not. For if you contemplate light or any other thing known to us, you will certainly say that God is not light, but is beyond light; nor is he essence, but is beyond essence; **[111]** nor is he spirit, <132> but is beyond spirit. God is beyond anything that can be thought. This approach to knowing God is false, since it does not teach what God is. No one knows God who does not understand the mode in which he chose to be revealed to us. The mode is clearly set forth for us through the holy oracles. The sophists do not believe in [this mode], because they refuse to see God in Christ.

Nevertheless, this is the most certain truth of the teaching of Christ, which is wholly consistent with the vision of God. We are unable to form a true idea of God himself or of any other being, unless we can observe in him a face or some image. No idea can be said to affect the mind by representing something to it, unless a likeness of that thing is presented to the intellect by means of a mental image. Aristotle's saying, "observing mental images is necessary for understanding," is well known. Likewise, Paul teaches, *now we see in a mirror*. Seeing [a mental image] is the same as understanding something by seeing it in a mirror.

Let the sophists now explain in what mirror they see God. Let them say what image [their mirror] reflects, or what likeness that mental image has, which they envision when they form an idea of God. For certainly that mental image, whatever it may be, places before them a perceptible appearance or likeness. If the sophists had allowed themselves to be taught true philosophy, or rather true wisdom, by God himself, they would already be used to calling up the vision of God that is always found in the holy and divine words [of scripture]. There is no idea of God, or angels, or anything else, that is not based on a vision, even what is called an inward vision, which exists only in the mind's eye. And in the prophets this is always called a vision.

Perhaps [the sophists] will object that the philosophers had an idea of God, because Paul says: *The invisible attributes of God,* such as his power, divinity, justice, and other things attributed to God, *can be understood from created things* (Romans 1). There is no need for any other answer, since Paul himself expressly **[112]** teaches that *the invisible attributes of God* can even be comprehended by means of common knowledge. Certainly we know general things about God and have common <u>knowledge</u> based on other things, as <133> Paul himself concludes. From the greatness of a deed we deduce the power of the doer; from conduct, we deduce justice; and similarly for the other [ideas] that we hold. From the things [in this world] that reflect divinity or hidden power, we deduce that there is something more divine, wiser, and more powerful. These are *the invisible attributes of God*, commonly accepted by people of many nations, <u>as Paul says</u>.

By means of syllogisms, we logically conclude from effects that there is one first cause. From motions we conclude that there is a prime mover. Nevertheless, Aristotle never had a specific or abstract idea about this. These [inferences from created things], says Paul, are what can be known about God. However, God himself cannot <u>therefore</u> be known. On the contrary, Aristotle's entire discourse on cause and motion is nothing but a rearrangement of visual mental images in the brain. Because of this [the Greek philosophers] are said to have known about God in some way. This is because they impressed a mental image of motion on him by means of syllogisms.

<u>Furthermore</u>, anyone who has been accustomed to drink water from the divine fountains [of the scriptures] will immediately recognize the truth that flows from them like light. For God wanted to be shown to the world through his Word. *Whoever sees* Christ, *sees the Father*, and no one sees him except in Christ. If Jews, Turks, and other non-Christians now see God as we do, what [special] vision of God did Christ bring us?

Therefore, Christian reader, you must become acquainted with the visible appearance of God and *perceive God's glory in the face of Jesus Christ* (2 Corinthians 4). <u>Now</u> you will come to know God, whom you have never known before and whose appearance you have not yet seen (John 5). **[113]** In this passage [the Greek word] ειδος (*eidos*, form) means the appearance, the form, the shape, and the face of God. We are taught here that we cannot see God, except in the face of Christ. Here the divine teacher is alluding to what is written in Exodus 20 and Deuteronomy 4. For although the people of Israel in ancient times heard voices, and many of them saw the appearance of someone who spoke with Christ's voice, in more recent times those who do not acknowledge Christ, neither hear God's voice nor see his appearance. Similarly, today the sophists do not see or hear anything at all. For the voice of Christ is the voice of God, just as a vision of Christ is a vision of God. God is known and seen by believers in the face of Christ. If only he would show me, without a veil, that visible countenance that Moses saw *face to face*!

If God clearly showed himself to me, I would see the face that [even] Moses did not see: nothing other than the face of Jesus Christ. This is the manifestation of the invisible God by the visible <134> Word. It is said to be the visible image of the invisible God. This is why Christ is called the face of God. Whatever allows a thing to be seen and known is called its face. Therefore we must agree, purely and simply, that God is seen in the face of Christ. As Paul says, God is seen through Christ. *Whoever sees* Christ *sees the Father. And no one has ever seen him, except* through the Son (John 1, 5, 6, 8, 12, and 14).

Note that here we are always speaking about that vision of God which can be granted to mortals in this world. For in the world to come we will see God differently. No intellect can now attain that future vision, nor does it arise in the human heart. [Of course] we are speaking here of an inward vision, not an invisible illusion.

But our adversaries, using an imaginary illusion, say that the first being is now seen by means of the second. How can this be? How can this invisible and unintelligible being, which is more unknown than the Father himself, ever lead us [114] to a true understanding and vision of Christ? They grant that this being, which they themselves invent, is unknown and uncertain. Wretched are those who say that to see is not to see, and to be fooled is to see! They have never understood the intent of the Gospel message, which so often speaks of a vision of God, seen *eye to eye* through Jesus Christ, and never before seen or known. In John 6 it says that no one sees the Father unless Christ reveals him.[a] Therefore, God is seen through Christ in a different way than before. How do we now understand that God was truly revealed in the flesh? What is it that God promised [when he said] that in the future, we would all see him *eye to eye*? Will God be seen on earth? Beware, reader, lest you be led to accept a meaning far from [its true sense] and, with the sophists, misuse the word "to see." But Christ, who was not a sophist, said to the apostles, *now you have seen the Father* (John 14). John said

---

[a] John 14:6 says that no one comes to the Father except through Christ. John 6 says the opposite: that no one comes to Christ unless sent by the Father (John 6:44, 65). John 6:46 says that no one has seen the Father except Christ, but does not mention revealing the Father to others.

the same thing about the rest of the disciples (1 John 2). But what they saw was nothing other than the face of Christ, in which the deity of the Father was reflected. Consider with what incomprehension Thomas and Philip asked Christ for a vision and manifestation of the Father; and Christ's response there to the thinking behind the questions (John 14).

When Christ says that the Father is seen through him, do not suppose that he was speaking frivolously. Call it a mental vision, <135> an idea, a thought, an understanding, or what you will. Allow me to speak in the same way. God was never before seen, as Christ himself says. Otherwise, Christ would have offered nothing new. He would merely have uttered an empty boast [when he said] that the Father is seen through him. And John would have spoken falsely when he said, *we have seen the glory* [of God], whom *no one has ever seen.*

[The disciples] saw nothing there other than the glorious face of Jesus Christ. By means of God's art, this syllogism holds true: Formerly, God was seen by visual examination of the countenance of Elohim; and this [countenance] is now the face of Christ; therefore, God is seen in the face of Christ. Truly and properly, Christ is now in God in substance, just as *the Word was God* himself *and was with God*. Always keep in mind what the sight of [God's] countenance was like under the Law, in comparison to the face of Christ. You must admit that God is now seen more clearly. Take care not to forget this. Hear him now calling out to us from heaven: **[115]** *when you see me you see* God. Lift up your mind's eye and see. If God had the power to place a sign in the world by which the light of God could properly be seen, this certainly was the sign he placed.

But you may say that it profits us little to see this outward face. My reply is that the very essence of eternal blessedness is to see because you believe (John 6 and 17). Just as one look at [Moses's] serpent of bronze [was enough to cure the bite of fiery serpents], one look [at Christ] cures every sting of the devil (John 3). But you are looking at his face in an unworthy manner. However, once you believe, you will never turn your mind's eye away, and you will realize how greatly this benefits you. For only this vision will lift you completely up to him in heaven, where the light of his countenance, illuminating your darkness, will cleanse you completely of error. *They looked upon him and were enlightened* (Psalm 33). *Make your face shine upon your servant* (Psalm

118). *Lift the light of your countenance over us* (Psalm 4). You will see and be enlightened (Isaiah 60). Did not Christ call those eyes blessed which saw him?

Many prophets are said to have seen God himself face to face. If God is not seen in the face of Christ, they must have seen more than the apostles saw. And, consequently, Christ was talking nonsense when he claimed that, for this reason, the apostles were more blessed than the prophets. But the apostles really saw, as we ourselves now see, *the glory of God* revealed *in the face of Christ*. Indeed, the prophets saw [God] behind the veil of an angel, and in shadow. An angel, appearing as God, prefigured Christ for them. It profited some [of the apostles] little to see Christ only with outward eyes, because they did not believe <136> in him, though they saw him. But this is very different from what exists now: to see, with inward eyes, the face of Christ shining in heaven. This cannot happen without faith.

Those who are reborn in him see Christ deep within themselves. As Paul says, this inward vision *gloriously transforms us into* Christ **[116]** (2 Corinthians 3). To the inner self, the light of the face of Christ is eternal glory, and the enjoyment of divine blessedness. The salvation of Christ *is the salvation of* [the psalmist's] *countenance* (Psalm 41) *and the illumination of* [God's] *countenance* (Psalm 43). This vision has great power, if it is followed by illumination of the mind. And the vision itself is enjoyment of the divine. The eternal blessedness to come is full enjoyment of the divine and a vision of divine light, which is union with God. The vision of the face of Christ, which exists in us, now makes us sharers in his eternal blessedness. Examine that face, gloriously transformed on the mountain [of transfiguration]. In this vision, light itself is seen: *God is light*, and Christ *is the light of the world*. This light illuminates the soul of the beholder and gloriously transforms it.

From what has been said, it is evident that Christ is called not only the image of God, but more than an image. For it is an image when there are two things, formed in a similar way, one of which is called the image of the other. But in Christ there is something more. If the angel Gabriel were to come to me, in the form of an eagle in flight, would I say, "This is the image of Gabriel"? Even if it is called an image, it is more than an image. It is a kind of likeness representing, and also containing, the substance [*hypostasis*] itself. In this way the Word, the person, or the countenance of Elohim, was more than an image. It was the very face of God; it was God himself. It was a kind of likeness or form containing the very being of God.

In a similar way, Christ is now more than an image. He is, as the Apostle says, the *likeness of the* [divine] *essence* itself (Hebrews 1). He is the imprint of the hypostasis of God, engraved on the divine essence. In Psalm 16 and Deuteronomy 4, David and Moses call this *temunah* (image or likeness). Pay attention to the meaning of the word "image," when Moses says that they *did not see the image* of [God] when he was speaking. That image is what David later wishes for us. For if you accept the word "image" [in the psalm] as having the same meaning [as it has in Detuteronomy], you will have understood it correctly. That very image was the form of the face [of God]. The image was an ειδος (*eidos*, form), a manifestation of a being by means of a visible form <137> (John 5). [117] In the same sense Christ is called εικον (*eikon*, image), the image of God, the likeness of God (2 Corinthians 4 and Colossians 1).

In the same way, χαρακτηρ (*charakter*, imprint or representation) is a kind of imprint, an engraving, the shape of the [divine] hypostasis; that is, of the existence, essence, or substance of God. For God subsists in [Christ] alone. The vision of God is attested from all of these things: [likeness, image, form, imprint]. For I am said to see God by seeing the imprint of his likeness, just as I would be said to see Gabriel by seeing the eagle. Otherwise, God would not be able to reveal himself to us in visible form. <u>For if it was possible for this to happen</u>, [God] accomplished <u>it</u> through our looking behind the veil of the [divine] oracle and seeing the revealed face of Jesus Christ. Just as the countenance of the sun appears in the midst of boundless and inaccessible light, so too, in the midst of the heights and depths of God, his oracle appeared in the person of Jesus Christ. Here I pass over any mention of the metaphysical images and invisible imprints which the tritheists place among their [divine] beings. For these are ridiculous fantasies, unknown to scripture, which can neither be perceived nor understood.

[The tritheists] object that I offer humanity no idea of God, angels, or souls. My response is that I am offering a clear and understandable vision. In the next book, we will show the true essence of all of the ideas in our soul, declaring it to be the essence of light. That light,

Appendix

which we see in the face of Jesus Christ through the illumination of the Spirit, we declare to be God himself, seen by us through Christ. We say that this [illumination] is a clear idea of God in us, and that God is seen by us in Christ. *God is light*—the same light that we see in the face of Jesus Christ. Is this not the true vision and knowledge of God through Christ? We will also show that the substance of angels and of souls derives from the substance of light, and that it contains the ideal form of a human being. Otherwise how were those disembodied *souls* seen, which John *saw under the altar* in Revelation 6?

[118] Certainly, nothing can be seen, either in this age or in the future, without the benefit of light. [In John's vision] the shape of an entire human being was seen shining in [that person's] soul, since the soul can contain the entire ideal form and shape of a human being, as Irenaeus teaches in book 2, chapters 33, 63, and 64 [of *Against Heresies*]. Philo teaches, in the work cited above, that the soul is formed according to the image and pattern of the Word. And in what follows I will show that the soul can therefore be seen, and <138> angels can be seen, by means of light, just as God can be seen in Christ by means of light.

The sophists, however, see invisible things. Instead of visions they have illusions. Christ has been made unnecessary for them, because they do not see God any differently than before [the incarnation]. But true Christians understand, and will always understand, that the manifestation of God himself was meant to be visible to the eye. We have no doubt that God is seen through Christ. We know that Christ rebuked Thomas and Philip because they were anxious to seek God through other paths, visions, and manifestations. He testified that every path leading to God was in himself, declaring that he himself was *the way* (John 14). Thus, from eternity, God has established and willed that he should be visible in Christ alone. He wants us constantly to look into this mirror, and to be illuminated in the spirit by this, so that our illuminated spirit, containing this light, is transformed to the same glory that Christ possesses, becoming glorious like Christ (2 Corinthians 3 and 4).

This is a true idea of God, which I profess to have through Christ. With this I delight in God and I worship God himself in spirit—not separately from Christ, but with same delight with which I delight in Christ, and the same worship with which I worship Christ. For, as [Christ says], *whoever sees me, sees the Father*, [that is] whoever delights in me, delights in the Father, and whoever worships me, worships the Father. Christ is *the way and the light*. One must approach God on the way that shines through Christ and **[119]** see God, who is the light.

But the tritheists have not entered on this path. Without realizing it, they dream about a three-headed Cerberus in God, a tripartite God. These three beings, enclosed in one being, are like three [geometrical] points contained in a single point. They reduce every divine substance to something like a geometrical point. They claim that God himself is like a point many times repeated on the same plane, and that there are three points in one simple point. Apart from Christ, is this not how the sophists see God? Is this not the idea of God, of which they are so proud?

If the natural splendour of God shines in the face of Christ, and if the substance of deity *dwells bodily* in the flesh of Christ, is not God seen there? How is God — revealed once in the Word and now in the flesh — seen *eye to eye*, then and now? See and believe, reader, or else woe to you!

So that this vision of God might be better established in us, more needs to be said about the hypostasis of the Word. But we have already sufficiently shown **<139>** that it was the visible and substantial Word, substantial light, and the countenance of Elohim. There was a [divine] oracle subsisting and shining in a fiery cloud. It was said to be *the glory of the Lord* and his majesty in the cloud. This was the very oracle that was protected and concealed by angels' wings, the oracle through which God answered Moses. This was the oracle in the concealed [inner court] of the house [of the Lord], just as Christ was hidden in the shadow of the Omnipotent.

The Hebrew word confirms the meaning of "oracle." For from the word *dabar* (word), which is λογος [in Greek], comes *debir* (oracle or Holy of Holies), which is the oracle of the temple (Psalm 27, 1 Kings 6, and 2 Chronicles 3, 4, and 5). Christ is the true oracle through whom we receive answers from God. He is the mercy-seat, through whom and in whom God is graciously disposed toward us. He is the covering which protects us from every evil, and on account of **[120]** which we are blessed and protected from sin. Just as Christ himself is now the oracle, so previously he was in the temple and in the tabernacle. And before that, the person of Christ was the oracle who gave answers to Adam, Abraham, Moses, and others.

Appendix

See how beautifully the entire Law portrays John's [doctrine of the] Word: not only as the oracle in the cloud, but also in the light of the countenance of Elohim, and so on. From the Law, one can deduce that it was the hypostasis of the Word in the cloud that condensed into the seed of the begetting of Christ. The substance of the Word was the substance of the cloud. It was the substantial dew that watered the soil so that Christ would one day sprout forth (Psalm 71, Isaiah 45, 55, 61, Ezekiel 17, Hosea 6). Hence Christ is called the Branch of God (Isaiah 4, Zechariah 3 and 6, and elsewhere).

[The Law] attests to the same hypostasis in the form of a cloud. For throughout the Law, God is said to have appeared and to have gone before the children of Israel in *a pillar of cloud by day and a pillar of fire by night*. [The Latin Bible] uses the word *columna* (pillar) to translate the Hebrew word *ammud*, which means "firmness" and "consistency." It is derived from a Hebrew verb meaning "stood" or "stood firm." [The usual translation] "pillar" is inappropriate in this context, nor is the idea of a pillar relevant there. Rather, God appeared at that time in the consistency, or essence, of a cloud or of fire. The cloud, the fire, and the light were all the same substance.

But you may object that, if such was the hypostasis of the Word, then its substance was corporeal and divisible. My response: God, incorporeal and imperceptible in himself, showed himself to us perceptibly through the Word, and in the Word was the Spirit. **[121]** <140> The corporeal things of the world are connected in some way to the incorporeal God through an intermediate substance. We say that this substance is the very light of the Word, in which all corporeal and spiritual things exist. Things that, in the world, are called spiritual or incorporeal, are corporeal and material if they are brought to God and are able to receive divine forms. The following book will teach that there are visible forms in God, which are indivisible and unchanging.

No one says that light or the substance of the Word is divisible, since what is divisible is perishable. Certainly there is nothing incorporeal, like an imaginary point, in the nature of things. Nor, despite what the natural philosophers teach, can anything be formed from points. The substance of angels is not like a point, nor is the substance of souls. The substance of the spirit of God, from which angels and souls emanate, is not like a point. Rather, it is like the elemental substance, of which it was the elemental <u>or eternal</u> archetype. In the substance of God that was shown to the world, which is the substance of the Word and of the Spirit, there are no parts. Nor can one speak of any division in it, such as is found in created things. Parts and divisions are spoken of in the substance of God, according to the distribution of the [divine] economy.

God divided up the Spirit that was in Moses and gave portions of it to seventy men. Also, at the sending forth of the Holy Spirit [to the apostles], tongues of fire were dispersed, and each received a portion. In the partition of spirit — each portion of which, as scripture says, is God — the division does not destroy the substance of the Holy Spirit. In keeping with its source, the light radiating from the sun is coarser than the light of God, which is much finer. The former can be destroyed, the latter cannot. Compared to the light of the Word and the Spirit, everything in the world is coarse matter, which is divisible and penetrable. The light [of God] *pierces even to the division of soul and spirit,* as Paul bears witness. The light of God penetrates and fills the very substance of an angel or a soul, just as the light of the sun penetrates and fills the air. The light of God also penetrates the light of the sun and sustains it from within. As the form of forms, this light penetrates and sustains all the forms in the world.

[122] We shall say more later about spirit and light. For now, let it suffice to say that the true substance in the Word was <u>made visible and tangible in Mary: just as a thick cloud can be touched, especially when <141> it condenses into water. Later you will easily understand that these are modes of the substance of God. For now, understand that the action of the seed and the begetting drove [the process] by which the body was begotten by God — truly and naturally begotten</u>. This man could not have been said to be *truly the Son of God*, if God had simply created him in Mary, without making use of the normal manner of begetting from the substance of the father. <u>Therefore the substance of God, by which the begotten man is perceptible, was made perceptible to us</u>. God was given a body and made human. He who was once prefigured is now an actual [man].

John the Evangelist <u>says</u> that he *had touched* the substance of *the Word with* his *hands*. Paul teaches that *deity dwells bodily in* Christ. The ancient theologians spoke of the corporeal Word in bodily terms, as something perceptible, tangible, and visible. You will admit that the incarnate Word is tangible and palpable, once you agree that, in [all] other things, what is felt and touched is not pure matter, but rather a tangible form or a palpable shape. Thus, what is felt and touched is the whole thing, [both matter and] form. Let no one be amazed when we say that the Word of God, which was to be formed into a body, previously had a corporeal form, since the evangelists bear witness that *the Holy Spirit* also *descended in bodily form*. This was not impossible for God, who wished to send his Word as fructifying rain, begetting Christ. The way [to understand the appearances of God] is easy, as we will [now] show.

The hypostasis of the Word is proclaimed at the beginning of the Gospel of John. He says that [the Word] "was," and also teaches that it was visible. John saw that, in earlier times, Jesus Christ already existed. Daniel saw him in a vision, *coming with clouds of heaven*. He directed the four wheels in Ezekiel's vision, *rode on a horse among* Zechariah's *myrtle trees*, and *sat on a throne* in Isaiah's vision. **[123]** He presided over every age. And since this was the artistry of a speaking God, he called it λογον (*logos*). It was the spoken Word. It is as if a word breathed from your own mouth were to contain the ideal form of a human being, by which all things come into being.

In earlier times Christ presided over the world. The parable of Solomon introduces Wisdom, presiding in the person of [Christ]. David reveals the very same thing to us by his use of the word *Yah*, bidding us to praise Christ in his name, which is יה (*Yah*), that is, existence, essence, hypostasis. Psalm 67 says: *Exalt him riding through the wilderness, in his name Yah*. And Psalm 101: *a people yet to be created will praise Yah*, the existence who is Christ. Christ himself teaches about the same hypostasis when he says, [*Before Abraham was*] *I am*; from the beginning I am the eternal first being, existing in God.

<142> So that you may understand the various stages in the manifestation of Christ and his grace that have been made for us, you must first consider that God in himself, infinitely surpassing everything, is to us incomprehensible, unimaginable, and incommunicable. Base your idea of [God] on this: None of us can see him, unless he accommodates himself to us and appears in a form that is within our ability to perceive. Similarly, we cannot have communication with him in our spirit, unless he accommodates himself in some way as a spirit like ours, inwardly

perceptible to us. This divine mode, about which we will speak later, is the Holy Spirit within us. For now, we are only seeking the mode of manifestation and vision of God that was prior [to the incarnation of Christ]. He was set before us as a kind of divine appearance, as we have shown in many places, and as Christ himself points out in John 5 and 14 and elsewhere.

Next, <u>consider</u> the mode in which God visibly revealed himself to Adam in a friendly way. But later, having hidden himself because of [Adam's] sin, he entered into the spirits of human beings in various ways, without being seen. He always practiced mercy toward humanity, in whom he had instilled natural law by an inborn breath of deity. At times he also revealed himself through speech, **[124]** just as I might make my voice heard among those who do not see me. In various modes, God <u>came to the aid of</u> unhappy [human] nature, held captive by Satan. In this way, at the time of the giving of the Law [to Moses on Mount Sinai], God was revealed to the entire [Hebrew] people by his audible voice.

From Adam to Abraham, [God] spoke to <u>a number of</u> people in the same way. Another mode of revelation, vision, began with Abraham (Genesis 15). After Adam, God was seen first by Abraham, and by no one else before him. This privilege was given to the first patriarch, and then to his successors, the holy prophets, <u>who because of this are</u> called seers. *God spoke* to them *at various times* through visions: to some in dreams, to some face to face, revealing himself in different ways. However, these visions, in which foreshadowing was presented by an angel, were always veiled.

At last [God] was revealed to us, shining in spite of **<143>** the darkness, and seen with his face unveiled. *The Word was made flesh and we beheld his glory.* We saw *the glory of God in the face of Christ.* We saw Christ, and in him we saw the Father. In him we saw the light, God himself shining. Would that we could remain steadfast in this vision, so that the inward vision, and the glorification that even now makes us sharers in the glory to come, might lead us to that vision of future eternal blessedness, through Jesus Christ our Lord.

First page of book 4 in the Paris manuscript

THE PARIS MANUSCRIPT

On the Divine Trinity

Book 4

Revealing the names of God, his omniform essence, and the origins of all things

[125] <37> Now that we have seen Christ, and seen in his face God the Father, this fourth book offers an opportunity to explain the meanings of the divine names, so that we, who profess Christ to be our God, might more clearly show the divine manifestation that is in him. <u>In the course of this [book] we will reveal the origins of natural things, and philosophers' ideas about God.</u>

The most well-known names for <u>God</u> [in the Hebrew scriptures] are אלהים and יהוה (*Elohim* and *Jehovah*). [The word] *Elohim* is plural in number. God was called by this name first, as it was commonly used [among various peoples]. However, the name Jehovah is applied particularly to the God [of Israel]. The names Jehovah and Elohim both contain, in themselves, the mysteries of Christ. Jehovah is [God] in essence, while Elohim is [God's] visible appearance.

[*The Names of God*]

[*Jehovah*]

Many say that the name Jehovah signifies God's essence, while others say that it refers to [God's role in] generation. Indeed, we say that these meanings are included in the name [Jehovah], or rather in his essence. For it is not simply essence, but essentializing: essence that causes things to exist. God is not like a [geometrical] point. Rather, he is an infinite sea of substance, essentializing all things, making all things exist, and sustaining the essences of all things.

Appendix

We leave the secret knowledge about this name to the Kabbalists, noting only this: that the *yod* [in the tetragrammaton יהוה], with a *shva*, indicates a future, active verb, of the conjugation *pi'el*, from the Hebrew root הוה (*havah*). This, in turn, derives from היה (*haya*) by changing *yod* to *vav*, and the short vowels **[126]** into long ones, as frequently happens. This [change] is happening here, since the middle letter [*vav*] has no *dagesh*, although [the verb] is of the *pi'el* conjugation, in which *vav* cannot be used as a consonant, only as a vowel. Since this *vav* is a vowel, unless there is some elision, each syllable of the name [Jehovah] must have been pronounced by the Hebrews. This name is ineffable to them, and thus cannot be spoken, unless you say it by pronouncing the syllables separately: Ye-ho-wah. But whether you say it in this way, or with a consonantal *vav* as we do, and whether you say Jehovah or Jova, it is certain that many spoke the name aloud.

Indeed, in other [Old Testament passages] the name [Jehovah] often appears in conjunction with another word, as in Genesis 22 and Exodus 17. For one place is called Jehovah *yireh* (Jehovah will be seen), and another is called Jehovah *nissi* (Jehovah is my banner). God is called vision, God is called exaltation. Similarly, in Jeremiah 23 and 33, we have Jehovah *sidqenu* (Jehovah our righteousness), and in Judges 6, Jehovah *shalom* (the peace of Jehovah). God is righteousness, God is peace — all through Christ. Thus, reasoning according to the future tense of a *pi'el* verb, [the name] Jehovah means: he will essentialize, he will cause to be. Not only does God himself cause [things] to be, but he also creates another creator. For the Father caused the all-creating Son to exist, and essentialized the Son who essentializes all things, so that the Son himself would be the fountainhead of essence.

It is clearly shown that this is the true <38> meaning of the word, on the authority of Jehovah himself, who reveals his name to Moses in Exodus 6. In this passage, because [God] was going to accomplish great things, and was going to grant the power of doing these things to a human being [Moses], he says that his name is Jehovah, the name of him who created so much. The Patriarchs did not know this name, although the names *El* and *Shaddai* were known to them. [God] says, "*I was seen by Abraham, Isaac, and Jacob under the name El-Shaddai, but I was unknown to them by my name Jehovah.*" Previously God had appeared to the Patriarchs, and had revealed himself to them under the name El-Shaddai (Genesis 17, 28, 35, and 48), always saying to them, "*I am El-Shaddai.*"

From the meanings of these names in the Exodus passage, much more can be conveyed by the name Jehovah. The word שדי (*Shaddai*) is [127] from the root שדד (*shadad*), which means to destroy, and the noun שד (*shad*), destruction or devastation. Hence God is called Shaddai, the destroyer, or he who has the power to destroy everything. This is clearly demonstrated in Isaiah 13 and Joel 1: כשד משדי (*ke-shod mi-shaddai*), which means "like destruction from the destroyer." Here our translator renders "destroyer" as "Almighty." Similarly [God] is called *El*, that is, powerful. Thus we have *El Shaddai*, a powerful destroyer. It was under this name that God appeared to Abraham, saying, "*I am El-Shaddai*" (Genesis 17). Because of this, Abraham had the courage not to fear others, and walked blamelessly with God, considering himself to be always in the presence of God Almighty. When Abraham was angered by his enemies, God comforted and supported him, saying, "*Walk with me, and be blameless.*"

Indeed God says to Moses, in chapter 6 [of Exodus], "Although I appeared to your forefathers under the name El-Shaddai, and although they knew that I had destroyed Sodom and Gomorrah, nevertheless I did not reveal to them that I was Jehovah. They did not yet fully know me as the essence-maker, or the one who causes things to exist through another, who gives the power of performing miracles to others, as I now do for you, Moses, against the Egyptians." No one before Moses had been given the power to perform miracles, and so the significance of the name [Jehovah], conveying all this about God, had been known to no one, even though the name had been heard by the Patriarchs. The Patriarchs did not fully know whether Christ was Jehovah, with such great power of essentializing all things, or Jehovah was Christ, and was thus the power that was to essentialize.

<39> Furthermore, the perfect name for the essentializer or creator was demonstrated from the creation of the world, from the first passage in which that word [Jehovah] begins to be uttered by the Holy Spirit. For during the six days of the work [of creation] God was not called by that name — just as Christ was not while he was active on earth — but only when he rested in heaven. Once creation had been completed, God rested and gave the power of essentializing, creating, and gener-

ating to those whom he created. **[128]** Jehovah was then said to create or essentialize through another (Genesis 2). There God is said to be essentializing essences, so that those can, in turn, essentialize others. [God] himself is the source of all essence, the source of light, *the source of life, the father of* <u>all</u> *spirits*, and *the father of lights*. He essentializes the heavenly spirits. From him flow the essential rays of divinity and the essential angels, who, in turn, pour essence into other beings. God himself is in them, and the light of his Word shines in them.

Thus the Father assigned to Christ all the power of essentializing, so that he could essentialize all things. *All things are* and *are held together through* Christ *and in him*, as Paul teaches. [Christ] bears, carries, and *upholds all things by the word of his power* (Hebrews 1). *All things are held together*, both *in heaven and on earth* (Colossians 1). The angels were made sharers in Christ's deity, and this is written about in the Law. Through angels God sends out his light, and this light is God himself. And Christ himself, whom the angels serve, is the dispenser of God's light, sending it out from his substance. He sends out the Spirit by means of angels, and this spirit is God himself. The <u>very</u> essence of God, the very spirit of God, divinity itself, the very light of God, always shines there. For this reason he is called Jehovah <u>God</u> Zebaoth (Lord <u>God</u> of Hosts), that is, he who creates his own armies, or the essence of warfare. Jehovah endows all the heavenly hosts and armies with the splendour of his essence. Although [scripture] says that there are innumerable thousands of infinities and myriads of myriads [of angels], Jehovah <u>himself</u> is in all of them (Psalm 67 and Daniel 7). This is why the name <u>of God</u> is always in the names of angels: because [God's] essence is in them.

[*The Omniform Essence of God*]

The essence of God essentializes human beings and all other things. His spirit was implanted in us from the beginning, and afterwards more abundantly poured into us. God therefore has within himself the essences of infinite thousands, **<40>** and the natures of infinite thousands. These are distinguished from each other, not metaphysically, but in an ineffable way. <u>The sea of substance is infinite</u>. From this we draw a conclusion opposite to what the trinitarians sophistically teach. For they **[129]** set up three invisible metaphysical beings in one essence and nature <u>of God</u>, like three [geometrical] points in a single point.

The Paris Manuscript ❧ Book 4

We, on the contrary, say that there is one [divine] being only, which contains the essences of infinite thousands and the natures of infinite thousands. Not only is God infinite in terms of the number of beings to whom he communicates <u>deity</u>, but also in terms of the modes of his deity. The divine modes are ineffable. However, we will now explain <u>them</u>, at least as far as human frailty will permit.

There is a single primary divine mode, which is the source of the others. This is the mode of the fullness of substance, the divine mode without measure, present only in the body and spirit of Jesus Christ. It is a mode of manifestation in the Word, and a mode of communication in the Spirit—a <u>twofold mode</u>, corporeal and spiritual. Both of these are modes of substance, essentializing other beings in body and spirit: the source of all life, all light, and all spirit. <u>From this spring all other modes</u>, like branches from a trunk, sprouts from a root, or shoots from a vine.

<u>Thus</u> there is another <u>manifold</u> divine mode of spirit given according to measure: one [measure] to us, and another to the angels. Further, one spirit is innate, and another, over and above, is given by grace. Each of these is manifold, in accordance with a distribution made by Christ. The final [divine] mode is in each and every thing, according to its own specific and individual ideal form. This is the lowest [mode] of all. Nevertheless, there is some divinity in all things. These are the modes of divinity that are in us, in our present state. There will be more and loftier [modes] after resurrection, which we will not touch upon here.

For the moment, regarding this final mode, in individual things, and speaking simply of the essence of God, we say that the essence of all things is God himself. God encompasses and contains all things. <u>He</u> **[130]** *upholds* and *carries* us (Isaiah 46 and 63). He *gives life to all things* (1 Timothy 6). *In him we live, move, and have our being* (Acts 17). *All things are held together in him* (Colossians 1). <u>Thus</u>, all things are in <u>God</u>. He <41> gives existence to things, and he is the formal [pattern] of all individual forms. Because he contains in his essence the ideal forms of all things, he may be considered the formal part of all things. And, by a special dispensation applicable to ourselves alone, we are said to be sharers in the divine nature. He is <u>a</u> portion, and a portion of our spirit. This is not like earthly possession of land, but is a possession which is heavenly and divine, so that we may rightfully say, *the Lord is my portion* and *my share* (Psalm 15 and 72). Through Christ, a share of the divine spirit is distributed to us and we all receive this share from his fullness, just as, long ago, it was said that a share of the spirit of Moses was distributed to others.

God is said to be in all other created things, not by means of <u>such</u> a gift of the spirit, but in another, more general way. Thus he sustains the essence of all things, so that any created thing whatsoever, left without this sustenance, reverts to nothingness, just as it came from nothing. The ancient Hebrews and <u>all the ancient</u> philosophers taught this very thing. Among the Hebrews, Rabbi Moses [Maimonides] the Egyptian says in book 1, chapter 68 of his *Guide for the Perplexed*: "In the Creator is everything that is," and he himself is in all things, to help and sustain them, "by that mode which is called splendour" or secondary light. [Abraham] Ibn Ezra teaches the same thing in [his commentary on] Genesis, as do all the other [Jewish commentators], and the prophets themselves. All of the ancient philosophers agree with this. It is now the proper time to hear what they have to say.

In *Parmenides*, *Cratylus*, and *Phaedo*, Plato asserts, based on Pythagoras, Anaxagoras, and other more ancient [philosophers], and on the wise Zoroaster and [Hermes] Trismegistus, that there is One, that is the prime being, and that all things are contained and held together in the One. Only the One is beautiful and good in itself. Other things are not called beautiful and good, except by participation in the One. And they are more beautiful the closer they come to it. The One is **[131]** the sole ψύχωσιν (*psychosin*, animator) of the world <u>itself</u>. It is a kind of νοῦν (*nous*, mind), ἔχουσαν (*echousan*, containing) in itself all of the natures of the world. For in it all things are held together and διακοσμουσαν (*diakosmousan*, set in order). Hence the world is called κοσμος (*kosmos*, the universe). In *Cratylus* Socrates calls God φυσέχην (*physichin*, natural), the essence of nature, because God ὀχει (*ochei*, carries) and ἔχει (*echei*, contains) φύσιν (*physis*, nature) itself. In the natural order, all motions lead back to one prime mover, all natures to one nature, and all lives to one primary life, through which and in which all other things live and move.

God himself, all the ancient theologians say, shed light on everything coming out of chaos. And by drawing out disordered matter from [chaos], he introduced <42> bright and visible forms, in the likeness of his own beauty. Being himself beautiful and good, he first made the light, beautiful and good like himself, and then all the other things, beautiful and good, as described in Genesis. For <u>there</u> the Hebrew word טוב (*tov*) means beautiful and good. Iamblichus, Macrobius, and Philo, citing very ancient [philosophers], say that the mind is the mother of the forms of all things, and contains in itself the ideal forms of things, putting on things the stamp of its own deity: that is, spirit and light. For within itself it contains the light which forms all things, and the spirit which it breathes into things. Zoroaster <u>himself</u> teaches the same thing in *The Oracles of Wisdom*, which [in Greek] is called μαγικά λογια (*Magika Logia, The Magical Oracles*).

The oracle of Apollo, cited by Porphyry in book 10 of *On the Praise of Philosophy*, clearly says that God himself is the form, the soul, and the spirit of all things. **[132]** In his sacred discourse in *Pimander*, [Hermes] Trismegistus, the father of ancient philosophy, <u>says</u>: "God is the nature of all things, the glory and the source of all things," and "he in whom all nature is held together." To [his son] Tat, he says, "All things are one God," and "he is, so to speak, many-bodied, since there is nothing in bodies that he is not." And later he says, "God originates, encompasses, and contains all things." In effect, he is all things. And this idea is in [Hermes'] book *The Beautiful and the Good Are in God Alone*. "All things," he says, "are in God and depend on him." In the same book he says, "God is all things," and "God, who creates all things, makes all things similar to himself," just as "every agent produces something similar to itself." <u>And</u> in *Asclepius*, he says, "God is everything in all things and the omniform varieties [of all things]." He says that the Word of God is the archetypal world, "the archetypal light, and the archetype of the soul." And "In <u>everything</u>, there shines some image of God." Hence he sings in the hymn in *Pimander*, "Holy is God, whose image is all of nature." To his son Tat, he says, "There is nothing in the nature of things that does not display some likeness of divinity." All around us we observe with our own eyes, the image of God, which is the image of light, presenting itself and imprinting itself on us.

In Acts 17 Paul quotes [the poet] Aratus: "We are the offspring of the Divine," and of the race of God, as Pythagoras says. For we have in us the seeds of deity. In the same chapter [of Acts], <u>Paul</u> says that in

God himself *we live, move, and have our being*. Our life and our breath are <u>from</u> him. For this reason early philosophers said that Jove is air or is [to be found] in the air in which we live, since in the air there is <43> divine, life-giving breath. Aratus, whom Paul cites speaking of Jove, also said, **[133]** "Everything is full of Jove." And "Whatever you see is Jupiter; wherever you go is Jupiter."

[The ancient Romans] spoke of [God] as Jove, which follows the tradition of the ancient Hebrews, who called God *Jova*. [The Hebrew] *Jova*, which is indeclinable, is turned, by means of an inflection, into *Jovem* [the accusative case of the name of the Roman god *Jovis*]. Jova, however, is the way Jehovah is pronounced, since the *shva* is silent at the beginning <u>of a word</u>, and the pronunciation of the aspirate is omitted, which happens not infrequently in that language.

[Hermes] Trismegistus, speaking about the Spirit to Asclepius, says, "The spirit of God fills all things and gives life to all things," and "The world feeds bodies, while the spirit feeds and sustains souls." In the third discourse [Hermes] says that the spirit, which gives life to all things, proceeds from a sacred source. He says that the soul maintains its connection with, and its dependency on, its origin, just as light and heat depend on their source. David expresses this same thought in Psalm 103: when God withdraws his spirit, souls die. Likewise, all the Platonists affirm that God is the soul of the world and that the spirit of the universe sustains all things and gives them life. I shall soon say more about this universal essence and the ideal forms of all things. But first I will say something about Elohim.

[*Elohim*]

[*What Exists from Eternity*]

So that we may <u>better explain</u> the name Elohim, we must look into what has been said about God, as the name Elohim must be consistent with that.

According to the *Bereshit Rabbah*, or *Great Genesis*, the ancient Hebrews teach that these things have existed from the beginning of the world: the Messiah, the throne of God's glory, the city of Jerusalem, the garden of Paradise, the souls of the just, the Law, and Israel. Truly, the throne of deity, the seat of glorious majesty seen by Isaiah, has existed from the beginning, with the Messiah himself (Isaiah 6). This is <u>clearly demonstrated</u> in Deuteronomy 33, Jeremiah 17, Psalm 92, and Psalm 102, all of which speak of the throne and the seat of God, from the beginning [of the world]. This is *our holy place*, prepared *from the beginning*, as Jeremiah says. It is the garden of celestial paradise and *the heavenly city of Jerusalem*, <u>which existed from the beginning</u>. And Christ says that *a kingdom has been prepared for us from the beginning*, as well as the [*eternal*] *fire* **[134]** of retribution with which the wicked are to be punished (Matthew 20 and 25 <44> and Isaiah 30). <u>Note here</u> the sense in which the Hebrews <u>granted</u> that the Messiah existed from the beginning—not in the manner proposed by the trinitarian sophists, but because <u>the</u> person and visible form <u>of the Messiah himself</u> was <u>at that time already manifested</u> in God <u>on the throne, as has been adequately shown in the preceding book</u>.[a] The Hebrews prove, from <u>the book of</u> Deuteronomy, chapter 33, that from the beginning, the Law was in the right hand of God. And because the Law is said to have been *written with the finger of God* in God's book, [they say] that it was brought down to earth from heaven. They also assert that Israel existed from the beginning, because it is said that *the people of old*, that is, the eternal people, *were established* from the beginning (Isaiah 44) and *engraved on* [*the hands of*] *God* (Isaiah 49). Likewise they demonstrate that the earthly Jerusalem was founded in the beginning (2 Kings 19, Isaiah 37 and 49, and Psalm 86).

But since these were foreshadowings of a very different truth, [and] since we [Christians] are implanted substantially in Christ by the eternal spirit, we can more truly claim to be, in a special way, sharers in Christ from eternity. The spirits of those reborn in Christ are in Christ in substance, <u>specially</u> recorded in the book of glory. They possess eternity, that is, they have a share in Christ's eternal spirit. For they possess a <u>certain</u> portion of the substance of his spirit or substantial breath. Thus it is fitting that the kingly throne of Christ is adorned and attended upon by those chosen for all eternity. This extends to what Christ says to the apostles <u>themselves</u>: *You have been with me from the beginning; your names are written in heaven. You are the people of old, engraved in God.* [God's] *throne has been from the beginning.* There could never have been talk of a heavenly city at that time, unless there were citizens in that city.

---

[a] References to Christ on the throne in *Restoration*: 93, 100, 122 (book 3).

Appendix

Behold how great is the power of the eternity of Christ, and how much of his eternal deity is shared with us according to special forms and spirits. Indeed, not only the spirits of the just, but also those of other human beings, and **[135]** the luminous forms of all things exist from eternity in God, as we will soon say about ideal forms. This applies especially to the elect, predestined in Christ himself, who are in number twelve times one hundred and forty-four thousand thousands of thousands (Revelation 21). For these there are <45> many homes prepared from eternity, and a spirit prepared for each of them in God.

Also existing in God from the beginning, and seen around the throne of majesty, are cherubim and seraphim, and heavenly powers, principalities, and authorities, having various duties, together with their thrones, as Paul says. There are also, as Daniel says, countless myriads of legions of <u>other</u> attendant spirits and ministering angels. Ezekiel saw [many] beings in God in chapters 1 and 10, where he says that he *saw visions of gods.* In the last chapter of 1 Kings, Michaiah saw similar visions, as did David in 2 Samuel 22. Ezekiel attests that *the sound of the words* of God *was like the sound of an army,* and Daniel attests in chapter 10 that [God's] voice is *like the sound of a multitude.* Such great majesty was seen and heard in the multitude, in which shone the splendours of the faces of Christ, or, as the Hebrews have it, the splendours of the faces exhibited by the angels, and the various faces of the cherubim and seraphim, with so many flashing eyes and so many forms of deity.

[*The Plurality in God*]

So many things seen and heard in heaven by Adam, Abraham, and others, could not be called anything else than Elohim, gods; Adonim, lords; or Adonai, my lords. Jacob saw and recorded this plurality in God, saying that gods were revealed to him (Genesis 35). And Abraham said, "gods made me a wanderer" (Genesis 20). From these passages it is clear that Elohim contained many things in himself. In fact, Elohim was God. The form [of Elohim] was Christ, together with a multitudinous ministry of angels. In summary, Elohim contains divinities, or splendid forms: blessed gods, or the faces of gods. The name [Elohim] was first applied to God, and then to other beings who displayed illustrious forms. **[136]** When angels were sent on a ministry, they assumed a divine persona, <u>still</u> under the person of Christ, and were therefore called gods.

Concerning this name [Elohim] **<46>** the trinitarians are wildly incoherent. For they assert that the word "gods" is predicated of the three beings [of the Trinity], as if these were three gods, which they themselves deny. <u>Do they tell us who these gods were who</u> caused Abraham to become a wanderer? <u>What gods</u> appeared to Jacob? Besides, the Jews would never concede that these three beings exist in God. So that they <u>can</u> avoid the idea of a plurality in God, they <u>attribute</u> the use of a plural noun to linguistic tradition, claiming that there is nothing mysterious about it. But if they were to acknowledge the true Messiah, they would recognize that the mystery of God, Christ, and the angels was made clear in the word Elohim, which is sanctioned throughout the Law. The customary use of the plural [in Hebrew] did not happen by chance, nor could it have arisen in the sacred language without an element of mystery.

What is more, in addition [to the passages] where gods [Elohim] caused <u>Abraham</u> to become a wanderer <u>in Genesis 20</u>, and gods [Elohim] appeared <u>to Jacob in Genesis 35</u>, plural words are used in several other places [in the Hebrew scriptures]. [Elohim] are called *holy gods* in Joshua 24, <u>living gods</u> in Jeremiah 10 and 23, and *gods who judge* in Psalm 57. In 2 Samuel 7, gods, that is, the heavenly powers—God, Christ, and the angels—*went to redeem* [*the Jews*]. Indeed, now that Christ alone contains, in himself, all that is *his and the Father's*, along with the majesty *of the angels*, as Jesus himself attests in chapter 9 of Luke, he <u>alone</u> is rightly called Elohim, possessing divinity in all of its forms.

It is open to question whether the name Jehovah should be assigned to Christ. However, there is no doubt that in the Law an angel is called Jehovah. Therefore, Christ is far more worthy [of that name], especially since that name is <u>undoubtedly</u> given to the angel [who appears] in the form of Christ. Just as, in the beginning, Elohim and Jehovah were the same — because God was the Word — so too are they now, since Christ has been raised to his original glory. Nevertheless, when Christ was active on earth, the name [Jehovah] was not assigned to him by the prophets, and **[137]** Christ claimed for himself [at most] the deity of Elohim. But now he is the true Jehovah, who causes all things to be and sustains them, and grants the power of **<47>** performing miracles. He is the source of the light which forms all things, and pours the ideal forms of things into our minds; <u>especially since</u> the ideal forms were previously in the Wisdom of God, which is Christ himself.

[*The Ideas or Forms of All Things Are in God*]

We have several times come upon the term "ideal forms." Since an understanding of these produces a deeper knowledge of Christ and of the essence of God and a revelation of his names, we must now speak about them.

[*Ideal Forms*]

The images, or representations, of all things were in God from eternity — in the wisdom <u>of God</u> itself, in the Word itself — as they were shining in the world of archetypes. For God saw all things in himself, by his own light. He saw the ideal forms of all things within himself, as though they were shining in a mirror. From the beginning of the world this was the accepted teaching about the wisdom of God, recorded in sacred literature. This doctrine, handed down from their ancestors, was taught to the Greeks by the Chaldeans and the Egyptians. This is what Job, Moses, David, Solomon, and others taught in holy scripture. The same thing was taught to all the Greeks, from Orpheus to Plato, by Zoroaster and [Hermes] Trismegistus — <u>especially</u> by Trismegistus. In both *Pimander* and *Asclepius* he teaches that, in the first patterns of the world, the shining forms of all things were contained in the Word of God; and that the first <u>archetype</u> of the world possessed a kind of innate wisdom, filled with the ideal forms and origins of all things.

[*Wisdom: The Maker and Form of All Things*]

These words are written about the wisdom in God himself: God *observes every single thing, sees all things under heaven*, and regulates each thing, <u>according to</u> Job 28. For more about this wisdom, describing how everything existed from the beginning with God, see the Proverbs of Solomon, chapter 8. It is spoken of in the same way in Baruch, chapter 3, and more extensively in Ecclesiasticus and in the book of Wisdom. There Wisdom is called *a unique and manifold spirit*, containing all things. We are taught that *Wisdom is the maker of all things*, like an architect who contains in himself an idea of a future **[138]** house. In chapter 8 [of Proverbs], Wisdom itself says, *In God's presence I was a* *multitude, and I was daily his delight;* that is, a multitude of <u>all things</u>, with their **<48>** <u>various</u> delights, producing every single thing.

Wisdom itself was the λογος (*logos*): the miraculous design, in which <u>every single thing</u> shone visibly. The Word of God is God's wisdom. The light of Christ's face is for us the light of understanding, and the ideal form of all things. It is the visible and audible word of God, both in terms of sense perception and intellectual understanding. From the words we speak, the sense of hearing perceives this or that idea, just as the eye perceives by vision. But the Word of God contains at once all things that are seen, heard, and understood, indeed all that is perceived by the other senses as well.

[*The Omniform World*]

The Word of God was called by the ancients omniform: the archetypal world, the intellectual world. Trismegistus, after the sermons to Asclepius and to his son Tat, is taught by Mind that there is an omniform world in God, that this lower world was created in its likeness, and that in God <u>himself</u> there exists the ideal form of the world, which expresses the forms by means of individual bodies. <u>For</u> all things exist and are contained in God. Orpheus said that God's essence is omniform. This is <u>clearly demonstrated</u> in this way <u>only</u>: he sustains <u>in essence</u> the forms of all things. And to sustain them, he sees them in himself, as they appear in his own light. We call these appearances ideal forms.

<u>This is also the reason that</u> human beings conceive the likenesses of things according to divine images: because God himself places the likenesses and the ideal forms in their minds. This is what Mind teaches Trismegistus in the passage cited above, speaking to him as to a friend: "Consider how many things you know. Then contemplate God, who possesses all knowledge in himself. Thus, unless you <u>have made</u> yourself like God, you cannot understand God. For like is understood by like." Therefore, the likenesses and ideal forms of things are in God. If they are in us, we too become like God.

[139] But let us seek no further for confirmation of this. For all these things are amply proven in holy scripture, once we come to understand, <u>especially</u> through Christ, the special character of the light of God, which makes all things visible and bright. The ideal forms of the things to be created were in the mind of God before the things themselves were created. God knew all kinds of things and viewed

Appendix

them in his own light, saying, *Let the earth bring forth living creatures according to their kinds.*

In the same way, when we are planning to build a house, a city, or any other thing, <49> we form ideas in our minds, which are from the light of God, <u>and</u> are like the light of God. This reasoning powerfully inspired Timaeus of Locris, Archytas, and Plato. We think about things that are communicated to us by divine wisdom, which, as Philo says, are *an emanation of the glory of God, a radiance of eternal light, and a spotless mirror,* reflecting all things in us as *his image* (Wisdom 7). Also, Jesus the son of Sirach, having studied *the books of his forefathers*, in which, he says, *was no small or contemptible teaching*, teaches that there is a wisdom in God, in which God himself, as if by his own light, *saw and numbered* all created things, every *drop of rain* and all *the sands of the sea.* This same *wisdom, poured* into us, gives us a clear understanding of things.

[*Ideal Forms in God's Book*]

This tradition of the Hebrews is plain to see. In *On the Allegorical Interpretation of the Laws*, which is based on the teachings of the Torah, Philo proves the existence of ideal forms, explaining the words of Moses, *Blot me out of your book.* Here Philo says, "Moses calls the word of God a book, in which the existences of all things are written down and engraved." Psalm 138 (in the Hebrew Bible, Psalm 139) renders this beautifully. The prophet David says to God, *In your book all things were written down,* <u>which were formed in the days</u> *when none of them as yet existed.* And in Psalm 55: *You have numbered my wanderings; all things are in your book.* In Psalm 49 God says, **[140]** *I know that all [the birds] and all [the beasts] of the field are with me.* One of the ancients, Plato, writes to Dionysius [Dionysius II, tyrant of Syracuse], "all things are always present to the king of the universe."

[*Ideal Forms in the Church Fathers*]

Irenaeus, <u>a disciple of apostolic truth, clearly teaches</u> in book 2, chapters 3 and 21, that there were "preformations of all things in God." He said that God preformed all things in himself, and "took the pattern and form of all things from within himself." And in book 4, chapter 37, he says that God "took from himself the substance of created things, the patterns of the things he made, and the forms of the adornments in the world." Also, in *Against Praxeas*, Tertullian says that before the creation of the world everything existed in the wisdom of God, arranged and made according to his plan. "The only thing lacking was that these things could not be openly perceived or grasped in material form." Similarly, in *Against Hermogenes*, Tertullian says that wisdom contains the likenesses of all things.

Origen, in his **[141]** third homily on the Song of Songs, says that the patterns of all things were in the heavens, so that just as God made humankind in his own image, he also made other creatures according to other celestial images. Behold the true teaching, which was accepted by the first Christians, just as it was by the ancient Hebrews and the most eminent philosophers.

[*Ideal Forms in Ezekiel's Vision*]

<50> Ezekiel's vision, in chapters 1 and 10, confirms that this is the way ideal forms function in God. For in that vision there are wheels full of living and seeing eyes, just like those shining in the other animals, and the various faces there. Even though the prophet saw, in this mysterious way, only four faces, nevertheless all other things always shine out in God. God himself is full of eyes with which he contemplates, present in himself, all things that are, and were, and will be. There are infinite eyes and infinite fountains in the one essence of God. For according to the Hebrew way of speaking, the eyes of God [may be called] living fountains which pour into everything, in which all things are seen reflected *as in a mirror* and in which all things exist. Here is the book of God's writing, which contains the essences of all things, even, as Christ says, *the hairs of your head.*

Now let us explain the vision of Ezekiel, since until now it has been poorly understood.

In [the vision] there is a fiery chariot coming *out of the north*, to incinerate the city and drive the Jews swiftly into exile in Babylon. This chariot was sent by God through Christ, as explained in chapters 10 and 43. God in his anger declares that [the Jews] must be compelled to go to Babylon by violence and suffering inflicted by fiery wheels, urged on by [creatures who are] partly humans, partly oxen, partly lions, and partly eagles. [The Jews] are shown that they will bear various afflictions, **[142]** and be tormented by human beings, by beasts of burden, by wild animals, and by birds [of prey]. The wheels, called deprivations or removals, are sent to carry the people [into captivity]. All [the wheels] were full of eyes, watching attentively lest any captive escape. They emitted a brilliant light, to prevent King Zedekiah or any of his [attendants and soldiers] from escaping by fleeing in the night. The wheels, together with the creatures, moved quickly in every direction, lest anyone escape by any path.

This was a terrifying vision of the wrath of God, aimed at the impious, similar to the vision in Revelation 4, in which <u>Christ</u> showed his anger to the followers of the Antichrist. However, with the others, who give glory to him, he is pleased, and carries them up to heaven in an angelic chariot. There, too, are *creatures full of eyes*, who carefully watch over <u>the</u> elect, lest any of them perish. These creatures also guard us from all harm from human beings, beasts, birds, and wild animals. All those eyes are always on Christ — <u>those</u> eyes in which all things are reflected, but especially the elect, who are recorded in a special *book of life*, and reign in a special kingdom.

[*Patterns and Reflections in the Light of God*]

The way to think about a pattern in God can be demonstrated by thinking about [patterns in] other things. For if God made a microcosm [for example, a human being] according to the image of <u>another</u> pattern, that pattern was already in God. <51> Everything in the entire universe is contained in this microcosm. Therefore, the pattern of the universe was in God. Indeed, this single pattern of a human being contained all things in itself, just as all things exist in Christ, and just as in a single soul there are patterns of many things. Also, when God commanded certain things to be made, he <u>visibly</u> displayed, in himself, their clearly defined forms (Exodus 25, Numbers 8, Ezekiel 40, and 1 Chronicles 28). All of these [patterns] were seen shining in the light of God when God opened himself or <u>presented</u> himself in some way. This is not difficult [to understand], for it is natural and appropriate for God. By means of <u>his</u> light he brought all things to life.

[143] These [patterns], and everything else, were formed in the light of the Word of God for the glory of Christ. For there are no other ideas in God or in Christ himself. Here I would gladly ask <u>the sophists</u> whether they believe that the ideas that they call qualities are now present in the soul of Christ. In the afterlife, in blessedness, <u>by its very nature</u>, there will be for us no qualities or ideas other than

God's love, which brings things to life in their own individual forms. For this is a special property of [God's] light. It is an effective way of knowing, if you think about it carefully and understand well how angels can see the future in God, with no masks interposed between God and themselves.

Samuel, *who was called a seer*, saw in God what Saul was searching for in the past and what would happen to him in the future (1 Samuel 9 and 10). Micaiah saw in God what would happen in the coming battle: *Israel was to be scattered* and Ahab was to be killed (last chapter of 1 Kings). While he was in Babylon, Ezekiel saw in visions of God, in the Spirit, and in God himself, everything that was happening in Jerusalem (Ezekiel 8). In a vision of God Balaam saw what was going to happen in the future, *in much later times* (Numbers 24). And similar things in Jeremiah 1, Ezekiel 1, Amos 1, and in many other passages. For the prophets were called seers because they saw — within themselves, in the Spirit, <u>and</u> in God—the future appearing visibly in his light. Sometimes this was by means of an internal vision. At other times it was an external one, as God himself says (Numbers 12). This light is so widely diffused that ideas themselves, which we <u>now</u> grasp with our intellect, are like sparks of light and radiant images, illuminating the mind itself and presenting likenesses of <u>every single thing</u> to us in the divine light. For without light nothing whatsoever can be given form, depicted, seen, or <u>truly understood</u>.

Now consider further evidence based upon the eye, which proves these ideas about light in the clearest way. The visible likenesses <52> brought before a mirror and then reflected back to the eye from any object, are like sparks of light, which display the precise form and image of the object **[144]** seen in the mirror. Thus, by the magnificent artistry of God, something that is not corporeal contains within itself the bright image, form, and likeness of every corporeal thing, as it truly exists in the incorporeal light of God, in which all things in the world shine out. In God there are no bodily parts, but [God is] like rays of light reflecting the bodily forms of all things, as if they were reflected in a mirror. Thus, without any actual partitioning or division of God, there are, in his boundless light, infinite rays shining out in an infinity of ways. Indeed all of these rays, and their mirror-like way of representing things, have a heavenly origin.

Moreover, in order to perceive, by means of a parallel drawn from everyday life, how it is possible to see things to come in God himself, you should consider the following analogy. If, after you have formed an idea of something, you inwardly reflect upon this idea, as if in the mirror of your mind, you might say that you can see this thing, even though it be absent, and even dead. This is because the light of your mind contains in itself the physical image of the thing, like the appearance of light reflected in a mirror. I use the terms "physical image" and "natural kinship" so that you will understand [what I am telling you] based on the physical and substantial form of things themselves. The light of the divine Word, *in* whose *light we see light*, as the Prophet [David] says, contains the images and ideal forms of things. The light of the Word is quite properly said by Trismegistus to be "the archetypal light," and "the archetype of the soul." For there could not be in our soul any light containing images of things, unless that light was like the original light from which souls emanated, possessing the ideal forms of the bodies they were going to shape. Indeed, not only souls themselves but even the substantial forms of other things contain the ideal form of the whole, which they send to [be reflected in] a mirror, imitating the original primal light, in which all things have been shining and continue to shine.

If it were granted to anyone to see clearly the very essence of God, or the entire splendour of Christ, that individual would behold, in [God], everything that is, was, and will be, all things shining in God as forms. **[145]** But this is not given even to angels, except in part, and in the form of reflected knowledge, which is directly known only by Christ. In this way an angel can see <53> more things in God than another being, and is able to instruct others about things to come, as is clear from the visions of Daniel and John [of Patmos].

[*Substantial Forms*]

It follows from all this that, in both divine and human ideal forms, there are not only patterns but also substantial forms. For in ideal forms there is a system of reference and correspondence to nature, as well as a natural kinship with substantial forms. Not only are all things shown by light, but the existence of all things depends on light. And the Word, *in which all things exist*, is light (John 1 and Colossians 1). God, who sees all things in himself, sustains all things. And he sustains them by means of the ideal form of each one. Plato teaches this, following Anaxagoras and Trismegistus. After him, Plotinus and Proclus, the interpreters of Plato, taught that in divine ideal forms there are not only patterns but also essential forms, from which all created things derive.

[*Seedbeds of Light*]

The vital powers of things originate in the light of God, and are then found in created light and in the elements. This created light is like an offshoot of the primal light. It acts as a seedbed, containing the formative properties of things, and the vital forces implanted in the substantial forms themselves. In the soul there is also a seedbed of imprints of light. By reason of that same light and an ideal form, any seed contains the formative property of the thing that will grow from it; just as the Word of God, which <u>is</u> the seed of Christ, contained in itself <u>all vital powers</u>. [The Word] itself is the primal element, the primal seed, from which power is disseminated to all elements and seeds. Hence in *Pimander* Trismegistus says, "The will of God, containing the Word and contemplating in itself the beautiful world according to the pattern of the elements of nature, adorned everything else with its own elements and the seeds of life."

Such excellent plants and animals, with their own forms, could not have been produced so precisely from such tiny seeds, unless there was **[146]** preexisting in them a divine ideal form and formative plan. The soul could not have generated the truth on its own, by turning to itself <u>alone</u>, unless it had an innate seedbed of divine truth. Therefore, both in the soul and in other things, there is a seedbed of light that comes from the substantial seed of the Word, in which was the light and life of all things. Like a seed tossed upon the earth, the Word of God, which was the seed of the begetting of Christ, generates all things by an imprint of itself, <54> and causes them to grow, bringing everything to life with spirit and light. This is a marvelous analogy. Just as all generative things first conceive a seed in themselves and transfer it to an embryo outside themselves, so, too, the seed of the Word was in God before his Son was conceived in Mary. What makes this argument so potent is that the begetting of Christ is the model and prototype of all other generation.

Appendix

The primal cause worked *a priori*, from cause to effect. We ourselves, however, reverse the process of deduction, moving backward from perceptible objects. We reason *a posteriori*, from effect to cause. This is the *a priori* deduction: just as in God there was first a generative seed, which became the real Son of God, so, in other generation, the Creator wanted to preserve the same order. The substantial seed of Christ was truly in God—<u>that is to say, from the very light of God</u>—and in it were the vital plans and model forms of all things.

[*The Natural Kinship of Light*]

The substantial forms of things are made from created light, and they possess the formative imprint of uncreated light, <u>as will soon appear. For now we conclude that</u>, just as all things, corporeal and spiritual, take their existence from light, so all things are seen outwardly in light, and all things are conceived of inwardly in the light of the intellect. What is true [of uncreated light] is also true of created light, by analogy and by the second type of reasoning [*a posteriori*]. Hence, as Plato said beautifully in *Timaeus*: "Ideas themselves, that is, intellectual concepts, have a natural kinship with the things they express." There is truly a kinship of light, which teaches that the forms of things are made from light. This is the **[147]** meaning of "natural kinship" and "natural image."

The forms of things are made from light. From this light, images which appear in a mirror enter the eye and are transmitted all the way to the soul. These are rays of the same formative light sent to the intellect, which is also light. Thus, penetrating a luminous medium, they imprint upon it the luminous image of an external object. This image naturally refers to the thing itself, because of the natural and formative imprint, kinship, and participation of light. **<55>** The light of your mind, with which you picture me within yourself, has a <u>direct relationship</u> to my form as it is seen by you. <u>For</u> my form has imprinted its mark on your soul. It is light, containing all things in itself, which links spiritual and corporeal things and makes them clearly visible to our eyes. The images in our souls are naturally luminous, there being a natural kinship of this light with external forms, with external light, and with the essential light of the soul itself. The essential light of the soul contains the original seedbed of the images. This is formed by the imprint of deity and the light of the Word, in which is the original pattern of all things. Hence the images that are located in the soul naturally manifest themselves to the soul itself, whenever it reflects upon them. Nor is there is any need for another new idea. Rather, from the soul's own light and from the light that enters it from outside, a single light is composed. For light often unites with light.

[*Transformation and Truth*]

Separation [of lights] can also occur; or one may be destroyed while the other remains, as when the form of a thing is destroyed while the matter remains. Although the images **that enter the soul may change, yet the mind**, that is, the primary substance of the soul, **remains the same.**[a]

"Temporal things," as Parmenides says, "participate in the eternal ideal forms" to which they are related and to which they belong. However, when these things change, the divine mind does not change. This is no more difficult than [understanding] that Christ's human nature underwent transformation, while his divine nature remains forever the same. In this world the transformation of forms and bodies is so fluid that they never remain the same. Therefore, [148] as Timaeus concludes, there must be other things, which remain whole and pure, above those that are defective or imperfect in their parts. Imperfect things must be judged in relation to those that are perfect. Hence this Platonic paradox: Bodies do not truly exist, and in corporeal things there is no truth. For if you say, "This is Socrates," before you finish speaking, the man you just now pointed to has already ceased to exist. Therefore, he does not exist when you present him as Socrates. There is no truth in bodies; otherwise, [truth] would change when bodies change. Therefore truth exists only as an idea in the mind, and God alone is truth. This statement of Timaeus also follows: "The intelligible world <56> has always existed and never began to be, while the sensible world is always coming into being and never exists."

There is no time given [to us] in which we can say, "This is the world." For even before you finish speaking the world has changed. Therefore, this world is the *vanity of vanities*, something that does not exist [in its own right], but arises out of something else. It is the likeness and shadow of the intelligible world. However, there is no truth in a

---

[a] The text shown here in bold is missing from the manuscript. Since the remaining text does not form a complete sentence, these words were probably omitted in error.

thing that does not exist. Therefore, there is no truth in this world, and anyone possessing truth is *not of this world*. If somehow there appears to be truth in these things, it is but a likeness and *a passing shadow* of the truth. For truth is the unchanging and spotless purity of any nature. Truth is the eternal Word of God, which contains eternal patterns and the true plans of all things.

From this it also follows that there is an ideal form within an ideal form, *like a wheel within a wheel*, an eye within an eye, or a light within a light. In God, one ideal form of a human being contains an infinite number of ideal forms, just as one ray of light contains an infinite number of points of light, in which God eternally contemplates everything that belongs to this human: *sitting down, standing up, lying down*, all movements and all the parts of the body, even *the hairs* **[149]** *of your head*. In Psalm 138, David, contemplating all things that are thus contained in God, says that [God's] watching over these things is wonderful and beyond human comprehension. Nevertheless this is not difficult for God, as the following reasoning shows. If in our soul there are potentially—and at times actually—separate ideal forms of the parts, changes, and actions of a human being, why would we not say that all of these always exist, [not just potentially, but] actually, in God? Furthermore, there are not distinct things in God. Rather, all beings shine in his light, as an infinite number of appearances in an infinite number of ways. And every single being exists in the ideal form of light, in which they all shine, all of them present to God and contained in him.

[*Christ Is the Substantial Form of Deity*]

I have discussed patterns at some length so that you may understand that, without any change in God, the first pattern has been shining in him from eternity. This is the pattern of Christ, the head and originator of all things, the living pattern and the source of all life. He was the first and he was in God in a different way — a very different way from other beings. He was the first and greatest substantial mode of divinity: understanding, living, and pouring life into things. <57> All things that are now in God were naturally arranged in order by him before creation. He alone is the first, the Son and the heir. He alone is begotten by God. Not only was Christ first in rank in God, but from eternity

God revealed Christ alone in substance. God manifested himself in Christ alone. In accordance with the [divine] plan, he generated Christ from himself, with all the *fullness of deity* flowing out from Christ to others. In every way that you can conceive, the entire *fullness of deity was in the body* of Christ.

You must consider [Christ's] <u>fullness [of deity]</u> separately during the time that he was living in the form of a human being, and say that he was Jesus Christ, who was at that time *in the form of God.* <u>Consider that your soul has the ideal form of a human being, and that in it are</u> the ideal forms of other things. So, at that time wisdom in God was like the <u>likeness of the</u> soul of Christ, containing the ideal forms of all things.

In God, first was the radiance of Christ. It alone was the first of all things. <u>And</u> then, through it, in it, and because of it, in a secondary **[150]** way, all other dependent things [appeared] in their order. We call this wisdom the ruler and guardian of the world, which God revealed in creation, manifesting the Word visibly to angels and human beings, and creating all things through this manifestation of himself. <u>The utterance of the Word in creation was the substantial manifestation and revelation of Christ. Here, reader, you must exert all your effort and your powers of reasoning</u>. Without any change to himself, God is now able to manifest himself visibly and palpably in any form whatsoever, because he contains in himself, as essences, all forms and all bodies.

In accordance with his eternal plan, God first established the form of Christ, *the wellspring of life*, that tremendous mystery, which he revealed both in creation and in his incarnation. What God had in mind was the begetting of the Son. There was not then an actual Son distinct from the Father, but God's inherent knowledge was already shaping and directing life. As a mirror naturally reflects an object set before it, so too God's plan naturally reflects Christ himself and contains his essence. This is the special property of light—not only to express an ideal form in nature, but also to contain a substantial form in essence. If you are able to believe that God begot a human being from himself, then you will also be able to believe that the substance and form of the being who was begotten came out of God from eternity. If you grant that other, secondary <u>forms</u> are in God, how can you deny **<58>** that the <u>first</u> form [Christ] is in God?

Appendix

[*The Origins of Natural Things*]

We have not yet sufficiently explained the glory of the essence of Christ and his light, until we can trace the origins of natural things to him, and show that he is the origin of all things.

[*Light, Splendour, and Forms*]

In regard to this, what we have already said needs to be repeated: the Word, in which all things exist, is light. And because of the nature of light, all things exist in Christ **[151]** (John 1, Colossians 1, and Hebrews 1). By analogy, what is true of uncreated light is also applicable to created light. By forming light in light, God wanted there to be a form with the power of forming other things. If, therefore, all things exist through light, and if it is light that gives existence to a thing, then light is the form of the thing. Besides, in Genesis 1, airy matter is called *tohu* and *bohu, formless and invisible,* since it had not yet been made to share in the light. Hence you may once again infer that form comes from light. And not only do the forms and existences of beings come from light, but also their souls and spirits. For light is the life of humankind and the life of the spirit. Light is the most beautiful of all things in this world and in the next. Each thing exists in the ideal form of light, in which it shines. Only light forms and transforms heavenly, earthly, spiritual, and corporeal things. From it comes the entire form of the world *and its adornment.* The Creator distributed shining forms to things, lest they continue to exist within a dark and shapeless chaos.

In all generated and corruptible things, the approach of the sun towards us is the cause of generation, while its retreat is the cause of dissolution. A ray of the sun so modifies the elements that a single shining perfection of form can be seen. Nothing would be able to send out a form of light or a natural image from itself, into a mirror or into the eye, unless it contained the light within itself as a form. If you consider it carefully, this is quite a powerful way of thinking. The visible form of all things is light. Everything we can see is light (Ephesians 5.13).[a] By means of light as a form, light itself transforms everything

---

[a] Here the copyist of the manuscript supplied the verse number, Ephesians 5:13. This suggests a late date for the copying of the manuscript. See introduction to this appendix.

that is seen in various ways: earthy and watery matter into glittering gems and bright pearls, and so forth. Light also forms and transforms our spirit in regeneration, just as light will transform the substance of our bodies at the final resurrection. This reasoning <59> proves the similarity between generation and regeneration, in that both derive their substance from light. Our similarity to Christ also demonstrates this effectively. For the substance of the body of Christ was formed at his begetting and transformed at his resurrection, by the light of the Word of God.

If Aristotle had known this, then he might have understood [152] that the origin of the forms of natural things is light, and that the divine appears in things as pre-existing archetypes. The origins of all things are in God, in Christ himself, who is *Alpha* and *Omega*. Thus Aristotle might have been able to understand that light in a spiritual substance is the ενδελεχίαν (*endelecheia*, activity or continuous motion) and vivifying energy of the soul. For light is the life of humankind, the life of our spirit, in generation and in regeneration. The form of fire is light. The form of water is splendour, which is also present in air. The form of the sun's body is light itself, from which other things also receive their forms. The form of the *glorious body* of Christ is divine light, which is to be shared with us as well. But for Aristotle and all the sophists, to whom the light of the Word and Spirit of God, and the begetting of Christ, were unknown, the way in which other things propagate was unknown as well. For all things are propagated, begotten, and produced according to the pattern of Christ.

In the seed of Christ were the elements of our own seed, our life, and our spirit. The spirit, life, and form of all things were, and even now are, present in the brightly shining Word of God. All things came into existence through light, and nothing ever existed without light. There is no created thing that does not refer back to the Creator, or in which *the light* of the Creator *does not shine*. Even [one of Job's comforters] knew this (Job 25). And Trismegistus says to his son Tat, "Since it is through God that all things become visible, he himself must, in turn, shine brightly in all things." And after this he says that God, being light, so fashioned all things that we can see him shining in everything. Julian [the Apostate], in his book on the sun, quotes this very ancient doctrine of the Phoenicians: This light is an *endelecheia* and "a pure action, like divine intelligence extending throughout all things," which manifests deity itself in all things.

Christ wanted his light to be always in full view of our eyes, so that we might see him, shining there in all things. For this <60> is an extension of the light of the Word of God implanted in him, putting his imprint on things and making them one with [his light]. [153] This light, shared with the sun, receives its life-giving power from the primal light. The light of the sun is in turn distributed in various ways, as is also the light of Christ. Orpheus and the other ancients said that the Word of God was φάνητα, *Phanes*, God appearing, who was "the first to appear out of the infinite." This name was also attributed to the sun. Christ first appeared in the immensity of the light of God, just as the sun appears in the midst of created light.

Different kinds of forms are mixed together in various ways by light. The divine light and the splendour of our soul make one light, from which come the spiritual forms within us. The light of the sun, and the elements with their innate splendour, make another light, from which come the forms of bodies. Also, the substance of the higher elements, together with the earth itself, makes a single material for things. These are the sources of natural things, the sources of their generation and their dissolution. Heat and cold act on things, but they are derived from light and splendour. I understand solar light to be warming, and watery splendour to be cooling. When it is frozen, as in some heavenly bodies, its power of cooling is increased.

Just as life-giving heat comes from the ordinary light of the sun, moist putrefaction and cold death come from the moon, Saturn, and some other heavenly bodies and regions of the sky. And an overpowering fever comes from Mars. The brightness of the sun is one thing, the brightness of the moon is another. One is fire, the other is the splendour of water. Christ, the great architect of the world, is himself the firm foundation on which all things are established: heavenly and earthly, bodily and spiritual. He created the matter of the elements, mixed them together, and distributed bright forms to the substances, bringing forth light itself from his storehouses.

[*Light and Creation*]

The first inference from the above is that nothing further can now be created without a subject. Rather, the propagation of things from other things — their formal generation and corruption — comes about by the power of light. Form itself, found in a balance of light and elements, is <u>dissolved</u> as substance by <u>one</u> action of light and elements, <u>and produced as substance in another form</u>. And the elements themselves are **[154]** mixed and tempered by the power of heavenly light. Thus all actions and transformations come originally from light, both in bodily and spiritual things, **<61>** both in Christ and in ourselves. In spiritual things all energy comes from light. Light illuminates all spiritual things, endowing them with essence. And light is the power that chases away demons, who, being creatures of darkness, love darkness and hate light. Pimander says that light was "the first form prevailing in the infinite realm in the divine mind."

[*Forms and Qualities*]

Light is also the substantial form of all corporeal things. That is, it is the source of forms, acting directly in all things. It produces heat, which is very effective and active, and dryness, which is very retentive and passive. Coldness and wetness also come from light; that is, from the created splendour of water, which is also shared by heavenly bodies.

In this lower world colours come from light. This is shown by the light in a rainbow. We see things washed in water becoming white. We also sometimes see whiteness in a cold body. In snow and hail we see the splendour of water increased by freezing. We sometimes see whiteness caused by heat, as in the white residue of fire that comes from complete combustion, such as quicklime or ashes. Blackness, as in soot, charcoal, and pitch, is produced by quenching or smothering light. Thus, when light is blotted out, whether by sin or by the devil himself, blackness or darkness results. Other [colours] can be looked at in a similar way. They are all contained in the substance of a thing, as is the form of light itself. Colours are a particular part of a form, although they can change, just as parts and elements are subject to change, both in the soul and in the body. Hot and cold, wet and dry, are the [qualities of] substances according to Hippocrates. They are part of the composition of the whole. [The qualities of] substances are part of the form, as are the colours, <u>although</u>, when they occur, they are called accidents. They pertain to matter and, together with the ideal form, they constitute a single form.

Appendix

[*Creation Ex Nihilo*]

Secondly, it follows from this that *in the beginning God created* — truly out of nothing and without preexisting matter — a twofold heaven, **[155]** one earth, and light, as described in the book of Genesis. Later, it is said, all other things were created (Colossians 1 and Revelation 10), because these things were truly brought from non-being to being. However, they were not created in the first creation, out of nothing and without preexisting matter. In truth, only water was created at that time. The heavens are actually made of water; and air is produced from water by evaporation. Finally, fire itself, which is also nourished by air, is concocted from airy matter and light. <62> Indeed a flame is air on fire.

On the fourth day God did not "create" the [heavenly] lights; rather he "made" them from the solidified matter of heaven. For the [Hebrew] word for "make" is עשה (*asah*), which, to the Hebrews, does not mean to make from nothing, but to adapt and form from pre-existing matter, as is taught by Rabbi Salomon and Rabbi Abraham [Ibn Ezra], and all the rest [of the medieval Jewish commentators]. In the same way, as the Psalmist says, the heavens were made, that is, distinctions were made among the celestial spheres. As it says in Job chapter 37: *spread out the skies, which are as strong as a mirror cast from molten metal*. Apart from the starry heavens, there are seven planetary spheres, which are the seven rulers of the corporeal world, whose disposition some falsely call fate. But Moses makes no mention of this, lest uneducated people fall into an idolatry of these [planetary] rulers, or believe in the inevitability of fate.

[*Everything Comes from Water*]

Thirdly it follows that Thales of Miletus, who got to know the teachings of Moses and Trismegistus in Syria and Egypt, and was the first among the Greeks to teach about nature, was not wrong when he said that everything came from water. For earth by itself is not suited [to be the primary source], because the form of earth comes from water. Peter very clearly teaches, following Moses's account, that the heavens and earth were formed of water. He said, *by the word of God the heavens and the earth came forth long ago from water and by means of water* (2 Peter 3). The watery splendour which is communicated to the moon and the rest of the heavenly bodies proves this, as does the etymology of the Hebrew word [for the heavens]. For in Hebrew the heavens are called שמים (*shamayim*), which means "the same as water." To the Hebrews there was no doubt that the firmament [of heaven] was made from water. From water evaporated by the spirit, **[156]** God made something extensive and airy.

As David says in Psalm 103, God made *heaven, stretching it out [like a curtain]*. He made it from water, and its foundation is water. From that foundation, the whole extent of heaven was <u>drawn forth</u>, and placed on [that foundation]. Therefore the foundations of the heavens are described as shaken when a tumultuous event occurs (2 Samuel 22 and Job 26). God made *the heavens* by *stretching them out* (Isaiah 40 and Jeremiah 50). The Hebrew word רקיע (*raqiya*) means expansion or extension. For, by expansion or extension, air is made from water. *God called* that airy expanse *heaven*, commanding [*the firmament*] *to divide* <63> *the waters from the waters*, the rain waters from the waters lying next to the dry land. <u>However, although</u> water is like a form with respect to earth, it does, nevertheless, supply the higher elements with matter, and receives from them, in turn, formative power.

[*Fire and the Third Heaven*]

[157] <u>Fourth, from the above</u>, there follows a proof of this: Paul says that there is a third, divine heaven. Created heaven is twofold, but the third heaven is uncreated. *In the beginning God created* two heavens, as indicated by the noun שמים (*shamayim*, the heavens), which is dual in number. In a literal sense, we accept that <u>the entire expanse above is</u> two heavens: one formed from air, the other from water. Moses <u>described this, saying, *In the beginning God created*</u> these two perceptible heavens, the airy firmament and the watery region. Here he says nothing about angels. However, since the creation of angels must also be contained in this passage [Genesis 1], heaven can, in some way, be called the heaven of the angels, or the choir of angels, who are of a heavenly or ethereal substance. Here are the throne of God, his dwelling-place, and the cherubim and seraphim. It is in this way that Peter describes the second heaven to Clement, calling what we can see, the airy and watery regions, the first heaven. Likewise, Christ teaches that [the upper] *heaven will be opened when the angels*, who are called the heavenly host, *descend*. With the coming of Christ peace was made in this heaven, and from there *Satan fell like lightning*. Therefore, whether you call heaven the

Appendix

entire visible <u>expanse</u> above, or the assembly of angels, [know that] both together form a multifold heaven.

All created things, even angels, are included in the names [of the things] in the heavens and on the earth, since all created things <u>must be</u> either celestial or terrestrial. The <u>Hebrew</u> article את, to which the demonstrative letter *hey* is added, also indicates this. For [א and ת] — like α and ω [in Greek] — are the first and last letters [of the alphabet], making את an article comprehensive <u>and demonstrative</u> of a whole. It is as if [Moses] had said: *In the beginning God created* all *the heavens and* all of *the earth and everything that is* <u>contained</u> *in them*. Hence in chapter 2 of Genesis the angelic hosts are included in the creation of the two heavens. And so it is in Psalm 32: *The heavens were made by the word of the Lord, and all their host by the breath of his mouth.* <u>However</u>, two heavens are <u>always</u> indicated in these passages, in addition to the angels who are the *adornments of <u>the heavens</u>*, as Job calls them in chapter 26. <**64**> <u>Therefore</u>, since the angels are the hosts <u>of heaven</u> and the *adornments of heaven*, they take the name of heaven. Also, [they take the name of heaven] because they are <u>from</u> a substance like the air of heaven, and **[158]** created at the same time by the breath of God, as can be gathered from the passages cited above.

But beyond all these things there is a third heaven of divinity, which is called the *heaven of heavens*, where the Father *dwells in inaccessible light*. It was *to this third heaven* that Paul *was caught up*. Christ dwells in this heaven, and from him the angels, who are far inferior, receive their splendour. They see only as much as is given to them through Christ. This luminous and fiery heaven is the brightness of the Word, the universal pattern of all things. Deity itself is made accessible through Christ. In the same way, though invisible himself, God is made visible even to the angels (1 Timothy 3). The angels saw God behind a veil, as Isaiah teaches in chapter 6. Yet to come, after the final resurrection, is another absolutely perfect way of seeing, when we will see God as he is, in that most hidden light. This has never yet been seen by anyone, neither by angels nor by blessed spirits, but by Christ alone. Until then, as is the case with us, good angels are more to be blessed, just as bad angels are more to be punished, <u>as Christ teaches</u>.

But since these things are beyond our present condition and all human thought, let us return to those things which have already been made available to us by Christ. Let us reflect on God in the Word and the heaven that is within us. Christ brought this heaven to us, making us kings in it, so that we might reign among the heavenly ones. Thus the *kingdom of heaven* is frequently spoken about [in the Gospels].

The third heaven is truly fiery. The other two are airy and watery, with a small share of fire. In [his account of] creation Moses does not mention the third heaven, nor does he mention fire, which is a matter of great mystery. Paul, however, when speaking of great secrets, emphasizes the third heaven. Moses does not mention fire in [his account of] creation, not only because the other elements, together with light itself, are enough to produce things; but also because there is a potential for fire wherever [combustible] matter exists together with light. I shall add another explanation later, when we deal with the sin of humanity, which was followed by fiery retribution. There is yet another explanation of the mystery: that the Jews living [at that time] did not know of <65> the regeneration of Christ and his righteous fire. But the fire [159] to renew the old world was to be sent to the earth by Christ. And he would endow us with a new spirit of fire. Therefore, Moses mentions neither fire nor the third heaven, because it was reserved for us in the future, and now it is within us. This third heaven, in which Christ reigns, does not have a particular location, but is within us, just as *the kingdom of heaven is within* us, as [Christ] himself says.[a] It is within us and, like fire, pervades everything. This fire, which, unlike the other two elements [water and air], does not have a particular location, is a type of the third heaven. [Fire] is located where it has fuel, without which it cannot be sustained, just as the kingdom of God cannot be sustained in us, nor can the our inner self live, unless nourishment is provided. Fire exists among the other elements so that, acting on them, it might purify them and raise them to heaven above. Fire renews, purifies, and transforms everything. It cannot be contaminated in us, remaining forever pure.

[*Earth, the Lowest Element*]

Fifth, it can be gathered from the above that water, air, and fire possess a kind of heavenly matter distinct from earthy matter. Rabbi Eliezer the Elder long ago taught this among the Hebrews. After him Rabbi Moses [Maimonides] the Egyptian said, "There is a secret of secrets,

---

[a] Luke 17:21.

Appendix

<u>and</u> a mystery of mysteries of the Law, which the greatest of the wise men of Israel made known." I myself will now demonstrate this with many arguments, since it is something unknown to all philosophers, and is related to knowledge of Christ.

1. There is one kind of matter that is heavenly, and another that is earthy. This is proven by [the account of] the creation of the world, and the perpetual separation of heaven <u>and</u> earth. Earthy matter and watery matter were created separately by God, while air and the whole of heaven are made from watery matter.

2. The begetting of Christ clearly proves this, demonstrating the immeasurable distance between the elements. For in Christ the three higher elements are from the substance of the Father. Just as our paternal seed is watery and filled with an airy and fiery spirit, so too [in the case of] Christ, the cloud of the oracle of God, acting as if it were airy and fiery, containing nothing earthy in itself, <u>condensing into water and overshadowing Mary</u>,[a] was the physical dew of the begetting of Christ. Nothing <**66**> earthy in embryos comes from the father. Rather it comes from the mother, as I will show more fully later.

3. The force of the Hebrew word *shamayim* (the heavens) proves this. For the heavens take their name from water [*mayim*]. The heavens contain nothing **[160]** terrestrial, and thus neither does water.

4. This is proven by the other passages of scripture cited above, which teach that the substance of heaven is made of water.

5. These passages prove the difference between [earth and the higher] elements. We will talk later, in the books on baptism, about heavenly [re]generation from the three [higher] elements. We are born again through our baptism in water, spirit, and fire (Matthew 3, Luke 3, and John 3), since by these we who were formerly terrestrial creatures, born of earth, become heavenly beings.

6. This is proven by what we shall have to say about <u>the essence of</u> the soul, in which the three higher elements are found.

7. This is proven by analogy with the three heavens, which, like the three [higher] elements, are always separate from earth.

8. In scripture, the Holy Spirit, like the heavens, is always indicated by the three higher elements, but never by earth, which is incompat-

---

[a] Luke 1:35.

ible with heaven and the spirit, just as terrestrial things are opposed to heavenly ones, and carnal things are always opposed to spiritual ones.

9. Pure water is able to be entirely transformed into vapour and airy spirit, vanishing, as if into the heavens above. However, earth turns into ashes, always moving downward. Hence in Isaiah, chapter 51, it says that *heaven will* be reduced to *smoke* and earth will become dust. Also Ecclesiasticus, chapter 40, says *what is of earth will return to earth and what is of water will return to water.*

10. Water was created with its own splendour, while earth was unformed.

11. Earth is resistant to light, and like a shadowy demon it is incapable of light. But the admixture of other elements transforms the earth and causes it to retain [light].

12. Unlike the other three elements, [earth is incapable of] sound and spirit.

13. Only the earth was cursed because of Adam and given to the serpent as its food.

14. From the chemical process of sublimation, it is clearly evident that earthen matter may always be separated out from the other [elements].

15. Experimentation on all the other [elements] proves this: earth has never **<67>** been seen to turn into water, nor water into earth, however you mix them together. For each of them always reverts to its original form. The Averroists, not understanding this, said that **[161]** all [four] elements are distinct and integral when mixed, whereas there are [actually only] two always distinct kinds of matter.

[*Warming and Cooling Light*]

Elements are also distinguished in various ways by their formal qualities. The primary qualities of fire are heat and dryness, while those of water are coolness and wetness. In the heavens, the two celestial providers of these qualities are the sun and the moon. The splendour of fire, like that of the sun, is warming and drying. [The splendour of] water is cooling and moistening, like that of the moon, which has been given a power balancing that of the sun. Power over the day is given to the sun itself, the power of warming and drying. Power over the night is given to the moon, cooling and moistening in the absence of the sun, by its own innate splendour of water. Added to this are the properties of the stars and of other regions of the sky.

Earth was created, in itself, unmixed [with other elements]. Once uncovered by the waters, it was given form, dried by light, and called *the dry land*. Also, due to its own density, being pressed upon by water, it remains quite cold. Therefore the substance of the earth receives its form from the splendour of water and the light of heaven, as also do other mixed things. Also, air is in itself nearly devoid of qualities. Being from evaporated water, air preserves water's mixture of coldness and wetness. Through respiration air cools our natural warmth. But evaporation can come from heat, by which air is easily warmed and dried, particularly in drying soil.

[*All Things Are One in God*]

Lastly, the preceding discussion confirms the ancient idea that all things are one. For all things are one in God, in whom all things exist. Throughout *Asclepius* and [in a discourse addressed] to his son Tat, Trismegistus teaches that everything is one. Melissus said that the universe is one, unchangeable and infinite. Other, changeable things are restored to an unchangeable unity.

[162] Qualities, or accidental forms, together with an ideal form, make one form. What has arisen from light unites with light to form a unity. When heat or <68> some other form is added to a body made from light, it unites as one with an ideal form — with light itself, which is the mother of forms. Also ideas acquired by the soul unite in one light with the soul, and in one spirit with the spirit. Each idea unites as one with spirit and light. In God spirit and light are one. Therefore these other things are also one in him, in accordance with a universal plan. The ideal forms of things, in which things themselves exist singly, are one in God. They make other things one in God by [Christ's] mediation, in the shadow of his truth, under which Christ is first united hypostatically with God. It should always be kept in mind that in all things there are always analogies to Christ, *who is the head* [*of all things*].

It should also be remembered that there are various modes and hierarchies of divinity. If looked at in this way, the ideas of Parmenides and Melissus regarding the one source will be [seen to be] true. This is what Xenophanes, the teacher of Parmenides, clearly asserted when he said that the one source is God. Also Anaximander said that there is one infinite source of all things. Democritus and Anaxagoras maintained that there was one substance with a diversity of forms, which formed <u>innumerable</u> sources. All of these [philosophers] knew the teaching of Trismegistus, of which Aristotle was unaware, which is based on divine ideal forms.

There is one <u>sure</u> source, one light of the Word, the omniform light, <u>universal wisdom</u>, and the head of all, who is Jesus Christ our Lord, the source of all of God's creations.

ANNOTATIONS

Annotations

Book 3

1. The phrase "angel of great counsel" is the Septuagint translation of פלא יועץ (wonderful counselor) in Isaiah 9:6. This verse, often translated as "unto us a child is born … and his name will be called Wonderful, Counselor, Mighty God…" is a messianic prophecy. For this reason there is a long tradition among Christians of interpreting "angel of great counsel" as a title of Christ.[1]

2. Following Moses Maimonides,[2] Servetus equated the visions of Isaiah and Ezekiel, and thus equated the cherubim seen by Ezekiel (Ezek 1:5-25; 10:1-22) with the seraphim seen by Isaiah (Isa 6:2, 6), who cover their faces with their wings.

3. The Hebrew word *kerub* is similar to words used for minor deities in other ancient Near Eastern cultures, such as the Akkadian *karibu*.[3]

---

[1] For example: Tertullian, *De carne Christi* 14; Augustine, *De Trinitate* 2.13. See Christiaan Keppes, "The Angel of Great Counsel and the Angel-Redeemer," in *Studies in Eastern Christian Liturgies* vol. 1 (Münster: Aschendorff Verlag, 2020).

[2] Maimonides, *Guide for the Perplexed* 3.6.

[3] E. A. Speiser, *Anchor Bible: Genesis* (Garden City, NY: Doubleday, 1964), 24.

Annotations & Book 3

4. The Hebrew alphabet is divided into 11 "radical letters," which are used only to form root words, and 11 "servile letters," which may form root words but are also used to indicate number, person, gender, etc. or as auxiliary particles. From Pagnini's *Thesaurus*, Servetus picked up the idea that *kaf* (כ), the first letter of the Hebrew word *kerub* (כרוב), is a servile letter that can carry the meaning "like."[4] Servetus might then have interpreted *kerub* as meaning "like" a dispute or quarrel or "like" something vast, numerous, or mighty: two Hebrew words with the same root as *kerub*. This etymology is no longer considered correct.

5. The word translated as "tritheists" here is *tritoitae* ("tritoites"). Servetus appears to have found this word in Isidore's *Etymologies*.[5] A few manuscripts of *Etymologies*, including some early ones, used the word "tritoite," while the majority used "tritheist" in the same location. The print editions available to Servetus (1499, 1500, 1509, and 1520) all use "tritoite." Modern critical editions of *Etymologies* opt for "tritheist," as do the English translations based upon them.

6. In Exodus 33:11 "the Lord spoke to Moses face to face, as a man speaks to his friend." But later in the same chapter, in Exodus 33:20, the Lord tells Moses, "You cannot see my face; for no one shall see me and live." Therefore, Servetus reasons, it must have been an angel who spoke to Moses face to face. See A.R3.8 for a different solution.

7. In Genesis 18:1-15, Abraham receives a prophecy of the birth of Isaac. Throughout this story it is thoroughly unclear whether Abraham is being visited by the Lord, or by "three men" (generally understood to be angels, though the word "angel" is not used), or both. The passage is sometimes considered a trinitarian proof-text, because Abraham's heavenly visitor(s) appear to be both three and one. "Abraham saw three, but worshipped only

---

[4] Pagnini, *Thesaurus*, 1068-1069. Pagnini cites David Kimhi, *Book of Roots* as the source of his information.

[5] Isidore, *Etymologiae* 8.5.68 (PL 82 304C).

one" is an ancient trinitarian formula, used by, among others, Ambrose and Augustine.[6]

8. In his "Apology to Melanchthon," included in *Restoration*, Servetus identified the passages from Jerome that he had in mind:

> Jacob, Job, and Isaiah saw this face, which was also seen, face to face, by others, not as a mental image, but with their bodily eyes. The Hebrews believed this to be a vision of the divine face, as Jerome, following Philo and Eusebius, cites in the first of his letters [to Paulinus] and in another letter, to Damasus.[7]

In these two letters,[8] Jerome was making a point that was important to Servetus: that human beings can see the face of God, but only when and to the extent that God reveals himself in a form that humans can comprehend. To Paulinus, Jerome wrote, "A revelation is needed to enable us ... when God uncovers his face, to behold his glory."[9] In the letter to Damasus, Jerome discussed the question of how it was possible for God to speak to Moses face to face (Ex 33:11) when in the same chapter God says, "You cannot see my face; for no one shall see me and live" (Ex 33:20). The explanation, according to Jerome, is that "God was seen [by Moses], not as he is, but as he wished to be seen, according to human possibility."[10]

Servetus says that, in these letters, Jerome was following Eusebius and Philo. Since Servetus mentioned Jacob, Job, and

---

[6] Ambrose, *De fide* 1.13.80 (PL 16 547B 570A). Augustine, *Contra Maximinum* 2.26.7 (PL 42 809).

[7] *Restoration*, 692.

[8] The two letters are Jerome's letter 53 to Paulinus (PL 22 540-549) and letter 18 to Pope Damasus (PL 22 361-376). The letter that Servetus describes as "the first of [Jerome's] letters" is number 53 in modern editions. However, it is called "Jerome's first epistle to Paulinus," and in Jerome's *Opera omnia* edited by Erasmus, it is the first letter in volume 3. It also has priority in another way: as a recommendation to read the Bible and a survey of its contents, it was sometimes used as an introduction to early Bibles, including the famous Gutenberg printing.

[9] Jerome, *Epistolae* 53.4 (PL 22 543).

[10] Jerome, *Epistolae* 18.13 (PL 22 369-370).

Isaiah, he may have been thinking of a text such as book 5 of *Proof of the Gospel*, where Eusebius describes the appearances of God to various Old Testament figures, including those three.[11] Here and elsewhere in *Preparation for the Gospel* and *Proof of the Gospel*, Eusebius argued that the Jewish philosopher Philo of Alexandria had a concept of the Logos that made him a kind of proto-Christian. This was important for Eusebius's larger project, which was to position the Christians as the legitimate heirs of the Hebrew tradition, and justify the inclusion of the Hebrew scriptures in the Christian canon.

Following Philo, Eusebius wrote that the patriarchs and prophets did not actually see God, but instead encountered God's Logos or Wisdom, an aspect or emanation of God that was able to appear in human form.[12] This is not the same as the Christian concept of the Word made flesh, nor is it the same as Jerome's idea of God accommodating his self-revelation to the limitations of the human mind; but it is similar enough to both to explain why Servetus might have thought that Jerome was following Eusebius and Philo.

9. "Women Should Not Behave Shamelessly" is not a book, but a heading found in some manuscripts of Philo's *Special Laws*.[13] Servetus, having no direct access to Philo's works, copied the citation from Agostino Steuco's *The Perennial Philosophy*.[14]

---

[11] Eusebius, *Demonstratio evangelica* 5 (PG 22 333-410). See especially 5.4 (Isaiah), 5.10-11 (Jacob), and 5.20 (Job).

[12] See Ronald Williamson, "Philo's Logos Doctrine," in *Jews in the Hellenistic World* (Cambridge University Press, 1989), 103-143.

[13] The relevant passage is Philo, *Special Laws* 3.34.189-194. In manuscript *Parisinus Graecus 433*, located in the Bibliothèque Nationale in Paris, the heading is in the margin of folio 87v. The heading is incorporated in C. D. Yonge's English translation in *The Works of Philo* (1855; reprint, Hendrickson Publishers Inc., 1993), 611. It also appears in the critical edition of the Greek text, *Philonis Alexandrini Opera quae supersunt*, ed. Leopold Cohn and Paul Wendland (Berlin, 1906), 5:197.

[14] Steuco, *De perenni philosophia* 1.26 (p. 65).

10. *On the World* (*De mundo*) is a collections of extracts from works attributed to Philo of Alexandria. The attribution to Philo was considered doubtful even in ancient times, though it was accepted as genuine during the Middle Ages. *De mundo* was translated from Greek to Latin by the French humanist Guillaume Budé, and in 1526 it was published, together with Budé's translation of another work with the same title, this one attributed to Aristotle.[15] These two pieces were reprinted, along with various other works, in Basel in 1533 and in Paris in 1541. By that time the attribution of *De mundo* to Philo was once again being questioned; in his introduction to the work, Budé referred to the author "whoever he was."[16]

The "old saying" that Servetus cites here is not found in the pseudo-Philo *De mundo*. However, a very similar idea (preceded, as in Servetus, by the phrase "There is an old saying that…") does appear in the pseudo-Aristotle *De mundo* in the same volume.[17] Servetus may have mistakenly attributed the sentiment to Philo, despite the running header "ARISTOTELES" on the facing page.

11. The word for God in Genesis 1:26 is *Elohim*. The word *Elohim*, which is grammatically plural, has a wide variety of meanings in the scriptures: God or gods, but also angels, demons, and powerful humans.[18] For Servetus, *Elohim* had the additional meanings of Christ and the Word.

Servetus was fascinated by the dense web of interconnected meanings implicit in the word *Elohim* (see *Errors*, 13v-15v; *Restoration*, 80-81, 135-137). Regardless of which meaning is most relevant in a given passage, he understood the full range of meanings to be present. So in Genesis 1:26, when Elohim says "Let us make humankind in our image," Elohim is simultaneously

---

[15] *Aristotelis philosophi nobilissimi de Mundo libellus Gulielmo Budaeo interprete. Philonis Iudei itidem De Mundo libellus ad eodem traductus* (Paris, 1526).

[16] See Eric J. Demeuse, "Nostre Philon: Philo after Trent," *Studia Philonica Annual* 29 (2017), 89.

[17] [Aristotle], *De mundo* (Basel, 1533), 21; or (Paris, 1541), fol. 15v.

[18] See Ps 8:5 (angels), Deut 32:17 (demons), Ex 21:6; 22:8-9 (human judges).

understood to be God, in whose image human beings were made; angels, as implied by the use of the plural words "let us make" and "our"; and Christ, through whom, as Servetus often reminds us, all things were created.[19]

12. Among the Gnostic heresies catalogued by Irenaeus in *Against Heresies* is that of Simon the Magician (*Magus* in Latin). Like other Gnostics, Simon believed that the universe was created, not by the supreme God, but by a lesser deity in a chain of subordinate divine and semi-divine beings. According to Irenaeus, Simon claimed that he himself was the supreme God, and his partner Helena was his first creation. Helena created angels, who in turn created the world, and then rebelled and trapped their creator in a human body. She was reincarnated many times (including as Helen of Troy) until the Father—that is, Simon—took on human form in order to free her. Simon taught that those who believed in him would likewise be freed from the thrall of the evil angels, and from the moral law that they had created.[20]

Irenaeus identified Simon Magus with Simon the Samaritan sorcerer in Acts 8:9-24, who offers to pay the apostles to teach him how to bestow the Holy Spirit on people. When Peter rebukes him for imagining that the gifts of God could be bought, Simon accepts the reproof meekly, asking Peter to pray for him—a picture that is hard to reconcile with the arch-heretic described in *Against Heresies*.

Irenaeus identified Cerdo as a Simonian, or follower of Simon Magus. Little is recorded of him except that he believed that the God of the Old Testament and the God of the New were two distinct deities. He left no writings and did not found a sect, though he was an influence on Marcion and the Marcionites.

Marcion was not a Gnostic, although he shared their belief that the God of the Old Testament and God the Father of Jesus Christ were two entirely different beings. Marcion's writings are

---

[19] Biblical texts that Servetus cited in this regard include 1 Cor 8:6; Eph 3:9; Col 1:16; Heb 1:2, 2:10. See *Restoration*, 85.

[20] Irenaeus, *Adversus haereses* 1.23.1-4 (PG 7a 670B-673A).

no longer extant, but much of his doctrine can be reconstructed from Tertullian's arguments in *Against Marcion*. He dismissed the Old Testament God as a lesser being, lacking in power, wisdom, and goodness. He rejected the Old Testament and most of the New Testament, keeping only his own version of Luke's Gospel and ten letters of Paul. Marcion was successful in attracting followers and Marcionism was a serious challenge to the emerging Catholic church.

13. This is an allusion to Johannes Reuchlin's 1494 book *The Wonder-Working Word* (*De verbo mirifico*). Reuchlin was interested in the mystical or magical use of language, especially the power of sacred names. One such powerful name is the tetragrammaton (יהוה), the sacred name of the God of Israel, transliterated as YHWH (Yahweh) or IHVH (Jehovah).[21] In *The Wonder-Working Word*, Reuchlin taught that, just as the tetragrammaton was the sign of God's covenant with the Jews, so the pentagrammaton YHSWH (pronounced Yeshua, the Hebrew name of Jesus) was the sign of God's new covenant with the Christians. It was the sacred name of Jesus Christ, a word of magic and mystery — in short, a wonder-working word.[22]

14. A curtain or veil, with an embroidered or woven design of cherubim, surrounded the Holy of Holies, first in the tabernacle (Ex 36:8) and then in the temple built by Solomon (2 Chr 3:14). There was also a veil in the second temple built by Herod, but no decoration of this veil is described in the Bible. At the death of Christ the veil of the temple was torn in two (Matt 27:51; Mark 15:38; Luke 23:45).

15. Zechariah 3 describes the installation of the High Priest, Joshua, as part of the re-establishment of temple worship in Jerusalem following the Jews' return from exile. Zechariah 3:9

---

[21] See A.R4.1.
[22] Charles Zika, "Reuchlin's *De verbo mirifico* and the Magic Debate of the Late Fifteenth Century," *Journal of the Warburg and Courtauld Institutes* 39 (1976), 104-138.

describes a ritual involving a carved or engraved stone, but there is no mention of a veil. The carving of a stone and the embroidering of a veil are connected through the Latin verb *caelo*, which covers a range of decorative techniques including carving, engraving, embossing, and embroidering. Following Pagnini, Servetus used this verb in his quotation of Zechariah 3:9, "I am engraving an inscription." A few sentences earlier, he used a form of the same verb to describe the embroidered veil surrounding the Holy of Holies (see A.R3.14). This connection exists only in Latin; in Hebrew, different words are used for engraving and embroidering.

16. Servetus could have found a Latin translation of the Targum (Aramaic) version of Zechariah 3:8-9 in Santes Pagnini's *Isagoge* or in Pietro Galatino's *On the Mysteries of Catholic Truth*.[23] The Aramaic quoted by Servetus is from Galatino; the transliteration is probably Servetus's own. The passage from the Targum reads:

> Behold, I bring forth my servant, the Messiah, and he will be revealed. For behold the stone that I have given in the presence of Joshua. On one stone are seven eyes. Behold, I reveal its visions, said the Lord of Hosts.[24]

The most distinctive feature of Zechariah 3:8-9 in the Targum is the explicit mention of the Messiah, where the standard Hebrew text says, "Behold, I bring forth my servant, the Branch." Servetus would in any case have understood the Branch as a messianic prophecy,[25] but the Targum provides powerful confirmation of this interpretation.

In verse 9, speaking of the stone, the Lord says, "I reveal its visions" — in Pagnini's Latin, *ego revelo visiones eius*. Since *eius*

---

[23] Pagnini, *Isagoge* 9.15. Galatino, *De acanis* 3.19.

[24] Servetus quotes Pagnini's Latin; Galatino's translation is slightly different. Instead of "on one stone are seven eyes," Galatino has "on the stone are seven visions."

[25] For example, Jeremiah 23:5, where the Lord says: "Behold, days are coming when I will raise up for David a Branch of righteousness, and he shall reign as king and will prosper and bring righteousness and justice to the land." Similar prophesies are found in Isa 4:2; Isa 11:1; Jer 33:15; and Zech 6:12.

can mean "his" or "of him" as well as "its," Servetus may have interpreted the sentence as referring to Christ rather than to the stone. This would be consistent with the promise in verse 8 that the Messiah will be revealed, and may explain why Servetus changed the word "vision" from plural to singular. We have therefore translated Servetus's rendering of the phrase from the Targum as "I reveal a vision of [Christ]."

17. The text quoted, or rather incorporated, in this paragraph is taken from the most popular theological handbook of the late Middle Ages, *Compendium of Theological Truth* (*Compendium Theologicae veritatis*). The *Compendium,* valued by clergy and laypersons alike for its theological depth and simple language, originated in the thirteenth century and was still widely used four centuries later. This text is found in many works of Servetus's time, often without any attribution, as though it were a scripture passage that anyone should know.

At various times the *Compendium* was attributed to Albertus Magnus, Thomas Aquinas, Bonaventure, and others. The introduction to the 1551 edition begins, "The authorship of this compendium is not easy to establish with any certainty." Modern scholars assign the work to the Dominican theologian Hugh Ripelin of Strasbourg (c.1205-c.1270).

In the Paris manuscript, this text is prefaced with a Latin abbreviation meaning "he says." Looking back at the previous paragraph, one might suppose that Servetus thought that the speaker is Peter, as portrayed in pseudo-Clement's *Recognitions.* However, it is more likely that the copyist who produced the Paris manuscript added the abbreviation to indicate that the text is a quotation.

18. Here Servetus wishes to explain that Christ is more than an image of God; he is "a kind of likeness or form containing the very being of God." In order to make this clear to the reader, he offers an analogy: if he were to see the angel Gabriel in the form of an eagle, he would know that it was not merely an image, but a kind of likeness containing the very being of the angel. This

suggests that he thought his readers would readily understand the idea that the eagle contained the essence of the archangel, and could use this to help them understand the nature of Christ.

The connection between Gabriel and the eagle is based on a set of correspondences involving the four creatures in Ezekiel's vision: the lion, man, ox or bull, and eagle.[26] In Jewish lore, these creatures were associated various things, such as the tribes of Israel, gemstones, colours, and natural features.[27] In Christianity, there is a strong tradition associating the four creatures with the four evangelists. Less well known is their association with the four archangels: Michael (the lion), Raphael (the man), Uriel (the bull) and Gabriel (the eagle). An early version of this tradition is recorded around 250 CE in Origen's *Against Celsus*, where Gabriel is called "eagle-like" and said to have "the form of an eagle."[28]

19. The word translated as "substance" here is *hypostasis*. Like the Latin word *substantia*, the Greek word *hypostasis* is formed from roots meaning "under" and "stand," and means something that stands under or underlies. But the word *hypostasis* has come to have a specialized meaning when applied to the Trinity. The trinitarian formula is three *hypostases* (persons) in one *ousia* (substance or essence). Servetus rejected the formula of three persons in one

---

[26] The four creatures of Ezekiel's vision are described in Ezek 1:5-11 (also Ezek 10:14, with a cherub instead of the ox or bull). The lion, man, ox, and eagle are traditionally referred to as the four creatures of Ezekiel's vision, but this is an oversimplification. What the passage actually describes is a vision of four creatures, each of which has four wings and four faces. "As for the likeness of their faces, each had the face of a man; each of the four had the face of a lion on the right side, each of the four had the face of an ox on the left side, and each of the four had the face of an eagle" (Ezek 1:10).

[27] For example, according to one version, the eagle was associated with the tribe of Dan, the sapphire, the colour blue, and the ocean. Barbara Maria Stafford, *Symbol and Myth* (University of Delaware Press, 1979), 71.

[28] Origen, *Contra Celsum* 6.30 (PG 11 1339A-1342A). Origen's argument against the pagan philosopher Celsus includes a long description of a diagram that apparently represented the beliefs of a Christian Gnostic sect called the Ophites. According to Origen, the diagram shows seven demons, of which four correspond to the four archangels: "Michael the lion-like," "Suriel the bull-like," "Raphael the serpent-like," and "Gabriel, the eagle-like."

essence — this was, in his view, the principal "error of the Trinity." According to him there is just one hypostasis, God, and Christ is its presentation to humankind. In God, he wrote, "there is only one person, and only one face."[29]

20. In Acts 17:22-31, Paul preaches to the Athenians, noting that they have an altar with the inscription, "To the Unknown God." For Paul, this was a hopeful sign that the Athenians were ready to hear the Good News of the coming of Christ: "Therefore, I proclaim to you the One God, whom you worship without knowing." Servetus, however, was addressing Christians. When he said that they worshipped an "unknown god," he was likening them to pagans who needed to be instructed and converted.

21. In four places in *Restoration*, Servetus compared his opponents' depiction of the Trinity to Cerberus, the great three-headed dog that, in ancient Greek mythology, guarded the gate to Hades.[30] This featured prominently in the Genevan verdict against Servetus. He was accused of saying "that to make such a distinction in the essence of God" is to make a Cerberus. This was taken as a great insult to Calvin and his theology.[31] However, Servetus was not on trial for mere disrespect. (If insult had been a crime, few would have been more deserving of punishment than Calvin himself, for he used harsh language more often than most of his peers.[32] Interestingly, "dog" was Calvin's most common epithet for Servetus. Not just dog, but "dirty dog," "filthy dog," and "detestable dog." Or "Spanish dog," a term which combined the canine insult with an ethnic slur.[33])

Calvin advised the prosecutors to focus on the charge of blasphemy, which, according to some legal codes, was subject

---

[29] *Restoration*, 109.

[30] *Restoration*, 119, 406, 675, 700.

[31] This was charge no. 7 against Servetus. See *Calvini opera* 8:728.

[32] Ross William Collins, *Calvin and the Libertines of Geneva* (Toronto: Clarke, Irwin & Co. Ltd., 1968), 109-110.

[33] Calvin, *Defensio*, 59. *Institutes* (1559) 2:14.5, 14.8. *Commentariorum in Acta Apostolorum* 20:28.

to capital punishment. According to the Caroline Code, which was the law in the Holy Roman Empire, blasphemy was defined as "attributing to God what does not belong to him," "saying things that deprive God of attributes that do belong to him," or generally insulting God.[34] If Servetus had said that God was a three-headed dog, that would have fallen under the definition of blasphemy. But he did not say that; on the contrary, he claimed that it was his theological opponents who portrayed God as a Cerberus.

22. For example, Anselm used the analogy of a geometrical point to show how God could be three while still remaining one. Just as "a point superimposed on a point is only one point," so, since God is infinite, "God in God does not add plurality to God."[35] One reason that Servetus disliked the three-point analogy for God is that it reduces the image of God to a dimensionless point, in effect nothing. The equation $P + P + P = P$ implies that $P = 0$. (Servetus would not have put it that way, since the symbol "0," the idea of zero, and its contribution to mathematics, was just beginning to be established in his time.) As Anselm points out, the equation also applies if P is infinite. But a further difficulty with the analogy is that, if P is zero or infinite, then the sum of any number of P's is zero or infinite, thus opening the argument that God could be a quaternity or have any number of persons, even an infinity of them. Servetus probably also disliked the idea of God as a point—or even as infinity—because of its abstraction. His idea of God revolved around Christ, the human face of God.

23. The Hebrew word דבר (*dabar*) means "word." Like the Greek λογος (*logos*), it is a word that calls things into being. For this reason it also means "thing," since it is the word that creates a thing.

The word דביר (*debir*) occurs fifteen times in 1 Kings and 2 Chronicles, where it refers to the Holy of Holies, the innermost

---

[34] *Constitutio Criminalis Carolina* (1532) 106.
[35] Anselm, *De fide trinitatis* 9 (PL 158 283).

sanctuary of the Temple.³⁶ Other than that, it is used only once in the Bible, in Psalm 28:2 (where it means simply "sanctuary"). It may be derived from *dabar*, as Servetus says; for this reason it is translated in the Vulgate as *oraculum*, or utterance of God. It is also possible that it is derived from a word meaning "behind."³⁷ Both meanings would be appropriate for the Holy of Holies: the place behind the curtain, and the place where God speaks.

24. By "natural philosophers" who believe that things can be formed from "points," Servetus may have been referring to ancient Greek atomists such as Leucippus, Democritus, and Epicurus—although atoms, though small, are not infinitely small like geometrical points.

In this context it is tempting to read the phrase "in the nature of things" as a reference to the epic poem *On the Nature of Things* (*De rerum natura*) by the Roman poet and Epicurean philosopher Lucretius, who believed that all things are composed of tiny indivisible particles. It is, however, not likely that Servetus intended a reference to Lucretius's poem. Lucretius did not use the word "points" (*puncta*) to mean small particles, reserving the word to indicate precise instants in time. Moreover, Servetus used the expression *rerum natura* in two other places where it is clear that no allusion to Lucretius is intended.³⁸

25. The word translated here as "divine economy" is *dispensatio*. This is the word that Tertullian selected to render the Greek word οἰκονομία (*oikonomia*, economy) into Latin.

In Christian theology, the word "economy" refers to one of the two main ways of presenting the Trinity: the metaphysical and the economic. The metaphysical approach looks into the interior of the Godhead and tries to deduce how the persons of the Trinity relate to, and interact with, each other. Servetus favoured the other approach: the "economic Trinity" or "economy

---

[36] 1 Kg 6:5, 16, 19-23, 31; 7:49; 8:6-8; 2 Chr 3:16; 4:20; 5:7-9.
[37] Mordechai Cogan, *Anchor Bible: 1 Kings* (Yale University Press, 2001), 241-242.
[38] *Restoration*, 132, 164.

of God." The "economic" approach sees God from the outside, from the point of view of a finite creature, and does not attempt an internal or structural description of God.

26. To Aristotle the form of forms was the intellect, or mind. For the Jewish philosopher Moses Maimonides and some Christian thinkers (e.g. Marsilio Ficino and Agostino Steuco) the form of forms is the ultimate form, which is God.[39]

27. The term "ancient theologians" (*prisci theologi*) refers to a group of historical and legendary prophets and philosophers who were thought to have inherited revelations from God to Adam and to have been given divine illumination, parallel to the Torah that was given to Moses. Among these were Orpheus, Pythagoras, Plato, Hermes Trismegistus, Zoroaster, and the Sibyls. Renaissance thinkers such as Marsilio Ficino and Giovanni Pico della Mirandola saw these ancient traditions as ancestors of Christianity: they believed that ancient Egyptian and Middle Eastern theology was carried to Greece, and that subsequently Greek philosophy, notably that of Plato, combined with Hebrew religion to give birth to Christianity. This use of the term *prisci theologi* was given currency by Ficino.[40]

28. Here Servetus is referring to the Aristotelian idea that every object is an inseparable compound of matter and form. Matter is the underlying substrate that creates the potential for objects to exist, but an object only comes into existence when matter is organized into the form of the object. Servetus's source for this simplified version of Aristotle's metaphysical speculation was probably *Authoritative Passages from Aristotle*.[41]

---

[39] Aristotle, *On the Soul* 3.8 (432a). Maimonides, *Guide for the Perplexed* 1.68 (1.69 in modern editions). Ficino, *Theologia Platonica* 10.3.1. Steuco, *De perenni philosophia* 1.23.

[40] Ficino, *De Christiana religione* 22; *Theologia Platonica* 10.7.2, 12.1.14, 18.4.4.

[41] *Auctoritates Aristotelis*, "Metaphysica" no. 160-217, based on *Metaphysics* book 7 and 8.

29. *Yah* (יה) is a short form of *Yahweh* (יהוה). It is used about fifty times in the Hebrew Bible, mostly in Psalms.

30. Psalm 68 is a notoriously difficult text; it exists in several different forms in Hebrew, and contains words whose meaning is uncertain because they are found nowhere else in the Bible. It may not be a single poem at all, but a collection of fragments of other poems.[42]

The text quoted by Servetus, "Exalt him riding through the wilderness," is one of many possible interpretations of Psalm 68:4.[43] Among the versions available in Latin in Servetus's time were:

Make way for him who rises beyond the sunset (Vulgate)

Prepare a road ascending through the wilderness (Jerome, translation from Hebrew)

Build a road for him who rides through the highest heaven (Estienne)

Exalt him who rises above the heavens (Pagnini)

Exalt him who sits astride the spheres of the heavens as if on horseback (Münster)

Lift up the one who sits upon the seat of glory in the ninth heaven (Septuagint)

Servetus did not use any of these. Even when he used images that appear in one or more of them, he did not use the same vocabulary. This may be his own translation from Hebrew.

---

[42] The twentieth-century Hebrew scholar W. F. Albright believed Psalm 68 to be a list of the first lines of thirty or so different poems. "A Catalogue of Early Hebrew Lyric Poems," *Hebrew Union College Annual* (January 1, 1950).

[43] Or 68:5. There is some confusion about the versification of this psalm, over and above the usual problem of the different ways of numbering the psalms.

Book 4

1. The tetragrammaton יהוה (conventionally transliterated as YHWH) is the name of the God of Israel, revealed to Moses in Exodus 6:3. Observant Jews do not pronounce the name, but substitute another word such as אדני (*Adonai*, Lord) or אלהים (*Elohim*, God).

No one really knows how יהוה was pronounced in Old Testament times, but most scholars agree that it was probably something like *Yahweh*. However, the three-syllable version, derived by combining the consonants of the tetragrammaton with the vowel sounds from *Adonai*, has a long history, going back at least to the Middle Ages.[1] The tetragrammaton was rendered in Latin as *Iehova* or *Iehovah* (Servetus used both forms). Until the nineteenth century, the standard form in English was *Jehovah*, based on the Latin. Beginning in the nineteenth century, the use of *Yahweh* by Christians became more common. In this book, we translate Servetus's *Iehova* as *Jehovah*. This may not be the most accurate transliteration of the tetragrammaton, but it accurately reflects Servetus's sixteenth-century Latin.

2. Both *Adonai* and *Elohim* are plural forms and may be used as such when referring to humans, angels, or the gods of other nations, but are treated as singular when used to refer to the God of Israel. See A.R3.11.

3. *El* is a common word for "god" across a wide range of Semitic languages. *Elohim* is a Hebrew word meaning "god" or "gods," and often used in the Hebrew scriptures as a name for the God of Israel. It is usually assumed that *Elohim* is related to *El*, but this has not been definitively established.[2]

4. In the early modern period, the word *generatio* was a general term for bringing into being something that did not previously exist. In book 4 of *Restoration*, Servetus used it for phenomena as varied

---

[1] D. N. Freedman and M. P. O'Connor, "Yahweh," in *TDOT*, 5:500-501.
[2] Helmer Ringgren, "Elohim," in *TDOT*, 1: 272-273.

Annotations & Book 4

as the creation of the world, the begetting of Christ, the production of blackness by excluding light, and the experience of being born again.[3] Here he seems to be using it in its broadest sense, encompassing everything pertaining to God's role as the Creator.

5. Here Servetus is discussing the meaning and pronunciation of the tetragrammaton (יהוה). In this discussion he uses a number of technical terms related to Hebrew spelling and grammar, particularly vowel marks. The Hebrew alphabet does not include vowels (but see the discussion of *vav* below). In the Middle Ages, a system of diacritics or "points" was developed: symbols that could be added to a consonant to indicate the associated vowel sound. The following terms are used in this paragraph:

- **Yod** (י) is the first letter of the tetragrammaton.
- **Shva** is a vowel mark, written as two vertical dots below a letter, representing a sound similar to English "short e." Thus a *yod* pointed with a *shva* would be pronounced like "yeh."
- Hebrew has seven "verb stems," which specify the voice (e.g. active, passive) and the type of verb (e.g. simple, static, causative, resultative). The verb stem *Pi'el* indicates that the verb is active and resultative. A resultative verb indicates that something has undergone a change as a result of the action.
- **Haya** (היה) is a Hebrew verb meaning to be, become, or happen. It is the verb used in Exodus 3:14 when God identifies himself to Moses as "I am who I am" or "I will be who I will be."
- **Vav** (ו) is the third letter of the tetragrammaton. It is one of four Hebrew letters that, although technically considered consonants, are sometimes used as vowels. As a consonant, *vav* is pronounced like V or W. When combined with the diacritic *holam* (a dot above the upper left corner of the letter), it is pronounced like O or U.

---

[3] *Restoration*, 127 (creation of the world); 146 (begetting of Christ); 154 (production of blackness); 159 (born again).

- **Dagesh** is another type of diacritic, written as a dot within the letter. It is not a vowel mark, but modifies the sound of the consonant. For example, the letter *beit* (ב) without the *dagesh* is pronounced like V, but with the *dagesh* it is pronounced like B.

6. The final printed version of this sentence says that the letter *vav* is pointed with *dagesh* (see A.R4.5). The Paris manuscript says that it is not (using *dagesh* as a verb — the letter is not "dageshed"). Either way, this is a puzzling statement, because *dagesh* is used with only six letters, and *vav* is not one of them. Servetus may have been thinking of a different diacritic, *holam*, which changes the sound of *vav* to O or U.

7. There are many possible ways to pronounce יהוה (see A.R4.1). Here Servetus points out two possible variations:
    (1) It may have two syllables (like *Yahweh*) or three (like *Jehovah*).
    (2) The letter *vav* may be pronounced as V (the "consonantal *vav*") or W. Incidentally, when Servetus says that "we" use the consonantal *vav*, this is an indication that in the Latin of his day, the letter V was pronounced as it is in English, and not like W, as it was in classical Latin.

8. Beginning late in the Second Temple period (probably in the second or third century BCE), it became taboo to pronounce the Name of God in worship or other public settings. However, it was still used in informal private conversation.[4] Prior to this time, of course, many must have spoken the name aloud.

9. The derivation of the name *Shaddai* from a word meaning "to destroy" is possible, but by no means certain. Among the many meanings that have been proposed are: destroyer, mountain, tent-dweller, spirit, breast, and strength. Modern scholars consider the meaning and derivation of the name unknown.[5]

---

[4] D. N. Freedman and M. P. O'Connor, "Yahweh," in *TDOT*, 5:500.
[5] William H. C. Propp, *The Anchor Bible: Exodus 19-40* (New York: Doubleday, 2006), 759-761.

10. Pagnini's Old Testament uses "Almighty" (*omnipotens*) in Isaiah 13:6 and Joel 1:15. The Vulgate uses "The Lord" (*Dominus*) in Isaiah and "mighty" (*potens*) in Joel. In English Bibles, *Shaddai* is traditionally rendered as "the Almighty."

11. *El* is the common Semitic word for "god" (see A.R4.3). The word may be derived from a verb that means "to be strong." It carries connotations of strength, power, force, and might.[6]

12. "I appeared to your forefathers under the name El-Shaddai ... I did not reveal to them that I was Jehovah" is a paraphrase of Exodus 6:3. The rest of the speech is not scriptural. Servetus may have mentioned the destruction of Sodom and Gomorrah to support the interpretation of *El-Shaddai* as "the destroyer."

13. The name *Yahweh Zebaoth* (also spelled Sabaoth, Tsebaoth, etc.), or *Yahweh Elohim Zebaoth*, occurs more than 250 times in the prophetic, historical, and wisdom books of the Hebrew scriptures (though not in the Torah). Usually translated as "Lord of Hosts" or "Lord God of Hosts," this name portrays God as attended by a large number of angels or celestial beings — the "heavenly host"— especially when these are pictured as being arranged in orderly ranks, like an army.

14. The word "myriad" was used in Servetus's day, as in ours, to mean "a very large number." More precisely, it means a unit of 10,000. "Myriads of myriads" echoes Daniel 7:10 and Revelation 5:11, where the throne of God is said to be surrounded by "ten thousand times ten thousand" (identified as angels in Revelation, though not in Daniel).

Servetus's ideas about angels may have been influenced by the author known as pseudo-Dionysius the Areopagite, a Christian theologian and Neoplatonic philosopher who wrote in the sixth century under the name of St. Paul's convert, Dionysius the Areopagite (Acts 17:34). In his influential work *The Celestial Hierarchy*, Dionysius suggested that numbers such as "ten thousand times

---

[6] Wolfgang Herrmann, *Dictionary of Deities and Demons in the Bible* (Brill, 1999), 274. F. M. Cross, "El," in *TDOT*, 244.

ten thousand" should not be taken literally: "These numbers ... accumulate and multiply themselves so as to show clearly that the ranks of heavenly beings cannot be counted by us. For the multitude of the blessed armies beyond this world completely exceeds the weak and restricted reckoning of our material numbers."[7]

15. The Bible, including the Apocrypha, mentions three angels by name: Michael, Gabriel, and Raphael.[8] Isidore adds an additional one, Uriel.[9] All of these names contain the syllable *el* (from the divine name El; see A.R4.3). Johannes Reuchlin's *The Art of the Kabbalah* includes a list of 72 angels. All have names that end with either *el* or *iah* (from the divine name Yah; see A.R3.29).[10]

16. In the 1520 Latin translation of Maimonides's *Guide for the Perplexed* (*Dux neutrorum seu dubiorum*), the word *splendor* is used to translate the Hebrew[11] word *shefa*, a richly evocative word meaning "flow" or "emanation." The primary meanings of the Latin word *splendor* are brightness, brilliance, magnificence, and grandeur, making it a somewhat odd choice as a translation for *shefa*.

The word *splendor*, however, may have been what drew Servetus's attention to this passage of Maimonides. Over the course of book 4, Servetus will develop his idea of *splendor*, eventually revealing it as a kind of light and one of the four sources of all created things.[12] His addition of "or secondary light" to the Maimonides quotation is the first step in this process.

17. Ibn Ezra's biblical commentaries take the form of a detailed verse-by-verse analysis, often focusing on fine points of grammar.

---

[7] [Dionysius the Areopagite], *De coelesti hierarchia* 14.1 (PG 3 321).

[8] Dan 10:13; 10:21; 12:13; Jude 1:9; Rev 12:7 (Michael); Dan 9:21; Luke 1:19, 26 (Gabriel); Tobit 12:11-15 (Raphael).

[9] Isidore, *Etymologiae* 7.5.10-15 (PL 92 272C-273A). Isidore specifies the meanings of these angels' names: Michael, "who is like God"; Gabriel, "strength of God"; Raphael, "God's remedy" (or healing); Uriel, "fire of God."

[10] Reuchlin, *De arte cabalistica*, 58v.

[11] *Guide for the Perplexed* was originally written in Arabic, but the Hebrew version was prepared during Maimonides' lifetime and in consultation with him.

[12] *Restoration*, 152-154, 161.

There is very little discussion of overall themes or theological interpretation. One exception is his comment on Genesis 1:26, "Let us make humankind in our image." Here Ibn Ezra offers what seems like a personal statement of faith: "God is one. He is the creator of all. He is all. I cannot explain further."[13]

18. Servetus claims that Plato's theology may be summarized as "There is One, that is the prime being, and all things are contained and held together in the One," and that this agrees with the Jewish and Christian idea of God. In this he was influenced by Ficino's interpretation of Plato, which emphasized the similarities between Plato's thought and Christian doctrine. However, Servetus overstates the case more than Ficino did, because, unlike Ficino, he does not distinguish between the remote and ineffable One and the subordinate omniform deity that participates in creation.

19. The passage under discussion, *Cratylus* (400b), concerns the etymology of the word "soul" (*psyche*), not God. Socrates proposes that, since the soul carries and holds (*ochei* and *echei*) the nature (*physis*) of the body, a good name for it would be "nature-carrier," or *phys-echei*. He explains the word *psyche* as a contraction or "more elegant" way of pronouncing *phys-echei*. Being a play on words in Greek, the passage is difficult to translate, hence the awkwardness of Servetus's rendering with its profusion of Greek words.

There is good reason to believe that Plato did not intend this etymology to be taken seriously. In the dialogue, it is one of two etymologies for *psyche* that Socrates suggests, "off the top of my head," offering this one because his previous attempt failed to impress his interlocutor; moreover, after explaining this etymology, Socrates says, "I cannot help laughing, if I am to suppose that this was the true meaning of the name."[14] The entire etymological section of *Cratylus* is often interpreted as ironic or

---

[13] Ibn Ezra, *Commentary on Genesis*. Translated by H. N. Strickman and A. M. Silver. Menorah Publishing Company, 1988-2004. https://www.sefaria.org/Ibn_Ezra_on_Genesis

[14] Plato, *Cratylus* (400b). Translated by B. Jowett (1892).

satirical, though some scholars disagree.[15] Even if Plato believed the etymology to be accurate, his larger point is that etymology is not a valid form of philosophical inquiry; the nature of a thing cannot be understood by knowing the history of its name. Thus, in taking this short passage out of context, Servetus appears to have misunderstood the point that Plato (or his character Socrates) was making.

20. *On the Praise of Philosophy* is an alternate title for Porphyry's *On Philosophy from the Oracles*. The work is no longer extant except in quotations in other ancient works such as Eusebius, *Preparation for the Gospel*; Augustine, *City of God*; and Lactantius, *Divine Institutions*.

21. This is a variant of a scholastic maxim, "Every agent causes something similar to itself." It is found, with slight variations in wording, in Aquinas, Duns Scotus, Ibn Rushd (Averroes), Pierre d'Ailly, Gianfrancesco Pico della Mirandola, and others, all loosely based on statements of Aristotle such as "for any living thing ... the most natural act is the production of another like itself"[16] and "each substance comes into being from something of the same name."[17]

22. The connection of Aratus and Pythagoras with Paul's sermon (Acts 17:22-31) comes from Steuco, who wrote:
> Wise people everywhere agree that humans are of the divine race. For this reason Pythagoras proclaimed to all, "Take courage, for we have a divine origin." And Aratus said, "Therefore we are of the same race as God." When it suited St. Paul, he called attention to these words.[18]

Aratus (c.310-240 BCE), who is generally assumed to be the poet referred to by Paul in Acts 17:28, wrote, "Always we all have

---

[15] See, for example, David Sedley, "The Etymologies in Plato's Cratylus," *Journal of Hellenic Studies* 118 (1998), 140-154, https://www.jstor.org/stable/632235.
[16] Aristotle, *On the Soul* 2.4 (415a). Translated by J. A. Smith.
[17] Aristotle, *Metaphysics* 12.3 (1070a-b). Translated by W. D. Ross.
[18] Steuco, *De perenni philosophia* 9.21. See also Reuchlin, *De verbo mirifico* 2, fol Ii v.

Annotations ⁊ Book 4

need of Zeus. For we are also his offspring."[19] The reference to Pythagoras is to an anonymous list of moral precepts or proverbs called *The Golden Verses of Pythagoras*. It is not by Pythagoras, who left no writings, but the authorship and date of composition are unknown. Verse 63 is, "But take courage; the race of humans is divine."

23. This view was credited primarily to Anaximenes of Miletus (c.585-c.528 BCE). It was adopted by other philosophers such as Diogenes of Apollonia (5th century BCE) and Cleanthes of Assos (c.330-c.230 BCE). By "air" Anaximenes meant, in particular, aether, the air that was believed to extend beyond the earthly atmosphere infinitely, throughout the celestial realm.

24. It is now known that Latin, an Indo-European language, and Hebrew, a Semitic language, belong to different language groups and do not share a common ancestor, so any resemblance between the Hebrew and Roman names of God is coincidental. The idea that they were related would have seemed more plausible in the sixteenth century, because of the widespread belief that Hebrew was the original language of humankind and thus the ancestor of every other language.

25. To support the claim of a relationship between the Hebrew and Roman names of God, Servetus returns to the discussion of the pronunciation of the tetragrammaton (יהוה). As he pointed out earlier (see A.R4.5), the first letter of the tetragrammaton, *yod*, is pointed with a *shva*, a vowel mark representing a sound similar to English "short e." If the *shva* is silent, and the aspirate (the H sound at the beginning of the syllable *ho*) is omitted, then the pronunciation would change from *Je-ho-va* to *J-o-va*.

26. Psalm 104 is full of images of animals: beasts of the field and of the forest, birds, wild goats, young lions. In this context, verse 29 is usually translated in a way that can apply to any air-breathing creature: "when you take away their breath, they die and return to

---

[19] Aratus, *Phenomena*, line 4-5. Translated by G. R. Mair, in *Callimachus, Lycophron, Aratus* (Loeb's Classical Library, 1921).

the dust." Servetus interpreted it in a more spiritual sense: when God withdraws his spirit, souls die. This is a plausible interpretation, since the Latin word *spiritus*, like the Greek *pneuma* and the Hebrew *ruach*, means both breath and spirit. For Servetus the air that a human being breathes physically contains the Holy Spirit. In book 5 he describes how the Spirit is taken into the lungs, where it enriches the blood, and is then sent via the heart to the brain, where it maintains the soul.[20]

27. Interestingly, Calvin, like Servetus, thought of Plato in connection with Psalm 104:29. In his commentary on this verse, after declaring that "we stand or fall by God's command," he went on, "even Plato saw this, who very often teaches that, strictly speaking, there is one God, and that all things subsist only in him."[21]

28. The Jewish tradition includes several different lists of things that have existed from the beginning of the world. *Bereshit Rabbah*, a rabbinic commentary on the Book of Genesis compiled between the third and fifth century CE, lists two things that God created before he created the world (the Torah and the Throne of Glory) and four more that he contemplated creating (the patriarchs, Israel, the Temple, and the name of the Messiah).[22] The Babylonian Talmud lists seven things: the Torah, Gehinnom (hell), the Garden of Eden, the Throne of Glory, the Temple, repentance, and the name of the Messiah.[23] Servetus's list does not exactly match either of these. It is likely that he obtained it from a secondary source that cited *Bereshit Rabbah*.

29. Here Servetus uses terminology usually associated with the theology of Calvin: "the elect, predestined in Christ himself." For Calvin, predestination means that salvation is offered to some and

---

[20] *Restoration*, 170-171.

[21] Calvin, *Commentarii in librum Psalmorum* 104:29. Calvin's summary of Plato's theology is similar to Servetus's. See A.R4.18.

[22] *Bereshit Rabbah* 1. https://www.sefaria.org/Bereshit_Rabbah.1

[23] *Pirkei De Rabbi Eliezer* 3:3. https://www.sefaria.org/Pirkei_DeRabbi_Eliezer.3.3

not others. In his system there is no place for free will. Without God's saving grace, the will is in bondage to sin; in the elect, the will is effaced and created anew by God.[24] Servetus's view is just the reverse: Christ's forgiveness is available to all, but it must be freely accepted, either in this life or the next. Eternal torment is reserved for those who choose to reject the offer of salvation: those who "have resisted, out of willful wickedness, the good spirit acting in them" and "conscious of their sin, choose not to repent."[25] By using the language of predestination and election, Servetus implicitly invites the reader to contrast his view of salvation with Calvin's — even though the full extent of the contrast will emerge only as we read on in *The Restoration of Christianity*. Here he only hints at the difference by asserting that the number of the redeemed is enormous (see A.R4.30).

30. The question of how many souls will be saved is addressed several times in the book of Revelation. The famous number 144,000 is mentioned in two places, but it is not claimed that this is the total number of the saved. Revelation 7:1-8 says that 144,000 (12,000 for each of the twelve tribes of Israel) will be "sealed," but the next verse, Revelation 7:9, describes "a great multitude which no one could number, of all nations, tribes, peoples, and tongues, standing before the throne and before the Lamb." In Revelation 14:1-4, the Lamb of God has 144,000 specially chosen attendants, described as the "firstfruits" of the (presumably much more numerous) redeemed.

Servetus's citation of Revelation 21 here is somewhat puzzling, because this chapter does not mention the number of the saved. It says that the New Jerusalem will be open to "the nations of those who are saved ... those who are written in the Lamb's Book of Life," but closed to "anything that defiles, or causes an abomination or a lie" (Rev 21:24, 27). It lists specific classes of sinners — including cowards, unbelievers, murderers, fornicators, sorcerers, idolaters, and liars — who will be damned (Rev 21:8).

---

[24] Calvin, *Institutes*, 5th ed. (1559) 2.3.8.
[25] *Restoration*, 243 (dialogue 1).

Servetus refers indirectly to chapters 7 and 14 through the use of the numbers 12 and 144,000. The number of the saved, by Servetus's reckoning, is over 1.7 trillion, far more than the number of people who have ever lived on earth—or ever would, since Servetus believed that the end times were imminent. By placing this huge number in the context of Revelation 21, he implies that few if any human souls will ultimately be excluded from salvation because of sin.

31. The book of Ezekiel opens with the words, "In my thirtieth year, in the fourth month on the fifth day, while I was among the exiles by the Kebar River, the heavens were opened and I saw visions of Elohim." The word *Elohim* is grammatically plural (see A.R3.11). However, when used as a name for the God of Israel, *Elohim* is generally treated as singular. Accordingly, Ezekiel 1:1 is normally translated as, "…I saw visions of God." Here Servetus translates it as "I saw visions of gods." There will be several other similar instances in the following paragraphs. Servetus is not arguing that the word *Elohim* in these passages really refers to many gods. Rather, he is calling attention to the multitudes that exist *within* God. Elohim is a God big enough to contain the creatures, the wheels, and the throne that Ezekiel saw in his visions, and much else besides. Elohim, Servetus will tell us, "contains divinities." No mere singular noun could do justice to such a multifarious deity.

32. In the Gospels, Jesus never claimed to be Elohim (or any of the other names of God), and rarely even identified himself as the Son of God. His favourite title for himself was Son of Man. The place where he comes closest to identifying himself as Elohim is in John 10:34-36, where he is defending himself against the charge that "you, a man, make yourself God." Jesus replies:

> Is it not written in your law, "I said, You are gods"? If he called them gods, to whom the word of God came (and the Scripture cannot be broken), do you say of him whom the Father sanctified and sent into the world, "You are blaspheming," because I said, "I am the Son of God"?

Annotations ॐ Book 4

In this complicated series of nested quotations, "I said, You are gods" is a quotation of Psalm 82:6. In Hebrew, the word translated here as "gods" is *elohim*. In the context of the psalm, the word does not appear to be intended as a name of God, and Jesus's point is that it can be applied to human beings as well as gods (see A.R3.11). Nevertheless, in this passage he does seem to be saying, not that he calls himself Elohim, but that it would not be blasphemy if he did.

33. The meaning of the Hebrew word אמון (*amon*) in Proverbs 8:30, translated here as "multitude," is "one of the great puzzles in the Hebrew Bible."[26] It has been variously translated as (1) artisan, master craftsman, architect; (2) nursing child; (3) nurse, guardian, teacher; (4) binding, uniting, fashioning; (5) true, faithful; (6) great; (7) covered or hidden. Each of the possible meanings is attested in ancient sources, referred to by later writers, and reasonably coherent in context,[27] and each has its adherents to this day.[28]

One meaning that is not included in the list of possibilities is the word that Servetus uses, "multitude." He would not have found this in any of the Latin Bibles he usually consulted: the Vulgate uses *cuncta componens* (constructing or ordering everything); Pagnini uses *nutricius* (nurse); and Sebastian Münster uses *educata* (someone being brought up or educated; a child). So where did Servetus get the idea that *amon* means "multitude"? One clue is that a similar-sounding Hebrew word, המון (*hamon*), does mean "multitude." It is possible that Servetus, or someone he consulted, simply read the Hebrew incorrectly. There is also a possibility that he found this interpretation in a rabbinic source. For

---

[26] Michael V. Fox, "'Amon Again," *Journal of Biblical Literature* 115: 4 (Winter 1996), 699.

[27] R. B. Y. Scott, "Wisdom in Creation: The 'āmôn of Proverbs VIII 30," *Vetus Testamentum* 10.2 (Apr 1960), 213-223.

[28] See, for example, Victor Avigdor Hurowitz, "Nursling, Advisor, Architect? אמון and the Role of Wisdom in Proverbs 8, 22-31," *Biblica* 80:3 (1999), 391-400, which argues for nursing child; or Stuart Weeks, "The Context and Meaning of Proverbs 8:30a," *Journal of Biblical Literature* 125:3 (Fall 2006), 433-442, which argues for teacher or advisor.

example, the words *amon* and *hamon* are linked in a commentary by Sa'adia Gaon, the tenth-century rabbi, translator and philosopher.[29]

34. Orphism was a mystery religion imported into Greece from Asia Minor, probably around the sixth century BCE. The mythical founder of Orphism was Orpheus, who descended into the underworld in an unsuccessful attempt to rescue his deceased wife Eurydice. He was later torn to pieces by maenads, female followers of the Orphic god Dionysus, who were ritually reenacting the death (followed by resurrection) of Dionysus himself. Some of the ideas of Orphism — mingled with those of Greek religion and philosophy, including Pythagoreanism and Neoplatonism — were cast into hymns as late as the mid-third century CE.

Servetus's statement, "Orpheus said that God's essence is omniform, having all things in itself" may have been based on Ficino's quotation, in *Platonic Theology*, of a line from an Orphic hymn, "Zeus, the form of all things," combined with Ficino's own conclusion that "God is omniform in essence."[30] Alternatively, Servetus might have been familiar with a text that explicitly states, "Orpheus also knows that God is omniform in form." This statement appears in a commentary on the *Mystical Theology* of pseudo-Dionysius the Areopagite, written by Johann Eck, a German Catholic scholar and opponent of Martin Luther.[31]

35. Here Servetus includes, without comment, a reference to "Plato, who was taught by Moses himself" in a quotation from Clement of Alexandria. The idea that Plato was taught by Moses — or, more broadly, that Greek philosophy was heavily influenced by or

---

[29] In his commentary on Genesis 17:4, Sa'adia Gaon gives four interpretations of the word *hamon*, ranked in order from the most to the least literal. The fourth, most extended, interpretation links this passage with Proverbs 8:30, based on the similarity of sound between *hamon* and *amon*. Robert Brody, *Sa'adyah Gaon* (Liverpool University Press, 2013), 77.

[30] Ficino, *Theologia Platonica* 2.11.1, quoting Orphic Hymn no. 14, "To Zeus."

[31] Eck, *De mystica theologia*. In addition to Eck's commentary, the work includes several translations of pseudo-Dionysius's *Mystical Theology*, including one by Ficino.

dependent on the Hebrew scriptures — has a long history in both Jewish and Christian thought. To Servetus, it probably seemed so familiar and uncontroversial that no comment was necessary. In his time it was a commonplace, especially in the form of a rhetorical question attributed to the late second-century Platonist philosopher Numenius: "What is Plato but Moses speaking Attic Greek?" Servetus could have encountered this quotation in sources ranging from the fourth-century church historian Eusebius to recent writers such as Marsilio Ficino, Johannes Reuchlin, and Agostino Steuco.[32]

In fact, it appears that the idea that Plato was taught by Moses was already a commonplace when Clement was writing around 200 CE. In the passage quoted by Servetus, Clement mentions it in an aside, as if it were already well known and accepted: "there is a region ... which Plato, who was taught by Moses himself, called the region of ideal forms." By the time of Clement, the conversation about the relation between Greek and Jewish culture had been going on for hundreds of years.[33] The assertion that Greek philosophers such as Plato had appropriated ideas from the Hebrews could be used, as Tertullian and Eusebius did, to discredit pagan teachings.[34] Or it could be used as Clement (and Servetus) did, to justify the use of non-Christian authorities in Christian discourse, by placing Jews, pagans, and Christians all in one overarching tradition.

---

[32] Eusebius, *Praeparatio evangelica* 9.6, 11.10. Ficino, *Theologia Platonica* 10.3.5. Steuco, *De perenni philosophia* 7.8. Reuchlin, *De arte cabalistica*, fol. 38r.

[33] An early example is Aristobulus of Alexandria, a Jewish scholar of the second century BCE. Like Numenius, Aristobulus is known only by fragments preserved in the works of others. See Clement, *Stromata* 1.15, 6.3; Eusebius, *Praeparatio evangelica* 8.10, 13.12.

[34] Tertullian famously asked, "What has Athens to do with Jerusalem?" and asserted that anything true in pagan teachings had been appropriated from the Jews (*De praescriptionibus adversus haereses omneis* 7; *Apologeticus adversus gentes* 47). Eusebius argued at length that there is nothing new or original in Greek philosophy; even Plato's theory of ideal forms was learned from Moses and the Hebrew prophets (*Praeparatio evangelica* 11.8-9).

36. When Servetus said that the wheels in Ezekiel's vision were called "deprivations" or "removals," he was probably thinking of Ezekiel 10:13. In this verse, two different Hebrew words for "wheel" are used: "As for the wheels (*ophanim*), they were called 'wheel' (*galgal*) in my hearing." The words *ophan* and *galgal* are synonymous; both simply mean "wheel." However, Servetus may have taken the word *galgal* to mean removal or deprivation, based on its similarity to a different word, *golah*, which means exile.

37. The original statement paraphrased here, "Angels know all things in the Word of God before they happen," comes from Isidore of Seville, *On the Highest Good*, and is quoted by Peter Lombard in book 2 of *Sentences*.[35] (Confusingly, *On the Highest Good* is also known as *Sentences*.) Among the prominent theologians who quote Isidore (or Isidore via Peter Lombard) are Peter Abelard, Albertus Magnus, Thomas Aquinas, Hugh of St. Victor, and Duns Scotus.

38. This is one of two places in book 4 where Servetus describes the begetting of Christ in terms of the creation and development of an ordinary embryo.[36] The other occurs on page 159: "Nothing earthy in embryos comes from the father; rather it comes from the mother." Taken together, these passages suggest that Servetus's ideas about reproduction were broadly in line with those of Aristotle. Aristotle believed that the male seed provides the soul and the form of the offspring, while the mother's role is to provide material and nourishment for the developing embryo. This is in contrast to the ideas of Galen, who believed that offspring are formed from both male and female seed.[37]

39. *Tohu wa-bohu* (תהו ובהו), traditionally translated as "without form and void," is the Hebrew expression used in Genesis 1:2 to

---

[35] Isidore, *De summo bono* 1.12.17, quoted in Peter Lombard, *Sententiae* 2.11.8.

[36] This idea, in almost the same words, also appears in dialogue 2, in the context of an extended discussion of the begetting of Christ as the pattern for the development of "all things born or created."

[37] Aristotle, *On the Generation of Animals* 1.21-22, 2.1-2. Galen, *On the Usefulness of the Parts of the Body* 14.6-7.

describe the condition of the earth immediately after God created the heavens and the earth. The word *tohu* means both formless and empty; it is used in the Bible for a range of meanings such as empty, vain, futile, nothing, wasteland, chaos, and confusion. The word *bohu* never appears on its own, but only in association with *tohu*.

The Septuagint version of Genesis 1:2 uses "formless and invisible" rather than "formless and empty." Servetus probably selected this translation because it emphasizes the importance of light in dispelling the primaeval chaos. The world would remain invisible until God said, "Let there be light."

40. The word translated here as "adornment" is *ornatus*, a Latin word meaning equipped, furnished, decorated, or adorned. It is the word the Vulgate uses in Genesis 2:1 to describe the condition of the world at the end of the six days of creation: "Heaven and earth were completed, and all of their adornments." A more accurate translation of the Hebrew — used in the Septuagint, Pagnini's Old Testament, and most modern Bibles — would be "and all of their hosts" or "all their multitudes."

There is a tradition, dating back to the Middle Ages, of dividing the six days of creation into three stages: first *creatio*, or the creation of the cosmos out of nothing; then *dispositio* (ordering or arrangement); and finally *ornatio* (adornment). During the three days of *dispositio*, God created light, day, night, heaven, earth, the seas, and the dry land. During the three days of *ornatio*, he adorned or furnished the world with the sun, moon, stars, plants, animals, and finally human beings. The use of the word *ornatio*, if not the entire scheme, was suggested by the word *ornatus* in the Vulgate rendering of Genesis 2:1.[38] The scheme remained in use for several centuries because it showed creation unfolding in an orderly way, and provided an answer to the question of why an omnipotent God did not create everything at once.

---

[38] Timothy Bellamah, "Medieval Christian Interpretations of Genesis 1-2," in Greenwood, *Since the Beginning*, 171-174.

41. In the ancient world there were two primary theories about the nature of vision. "Extramission," the theory associated with Pythagoras and Plato, is the idea that the eyes emit some kind of rays or beams, described by Plato as a stream of fire, "not burning, but giving a mild light." Seeing takes place when an object is encountered by this visual stream in the presence of light.[39] The alternative theory, "intromission," held that objects emit forms or images that are detected by the eye. Versions of these two theories continued to be taught and debated until they were finally superseded by advances in optics in the seventeenth century.

Servetus might have been expected to favour extramission, since this was the theory taught by Galen.[40] But he says here that objects "send out a form of light or a natural image ... into a mirror or into the eye," which sounds like intromission. He may have found this model more congenial than Galen's because it is consistent with his belief that light is the form of all things, and that objects are able to emit and transmit light because their very nature is light.

42. The Greek word *endelecheia* means activity or continuous motion. Aristotle used a similar word, *entelecheia* (related to *telos*, or final cause), to mean something that is stable and complete.[41]

There is a long history of confusion between the words *endelecheia* and *entelecheia*. In *Tusculan Disputations* Cicero read Aristotle's word as *endelecheia* instead of *entelecheia*, thus transforming stability into restless, uninterrupted motion.[42] Cicero, who may have possessed a defective copy of Aristotle, was criticized for this error by the fifteenth-century Greek translator John Argyropoulous. But the humanist scholar Angelo Poliziano defended Cicero (and the honour of Latin philology), arguing that both words could be applied to the soul, and that Cicero's version is actually a more nuanced and subtle conception of the soul than

---

[39] Plato, *Timaeus* (45a-b).
[40] Galen, *On the Teachings of Hippocrates and Plato* 7.5.
[41] Aristotle, *On the Soul* 2.1 (412a-b).
[42] Cicero, *Tusculanae disputationes* 1.10.

Aristotle's.⁴³ Here Servetus agrees with Cicero and Poliziano, saying that Aristotle would have done better to describe the soul as *endelecheia*. For the true nature of things is not static perfection, but rather energy in the form of light.

43. Here Servetus sets up a contrast between two kinds of light. Primal light is hot and dry, associated with daytime, the sun, and fire. "Secondary light," or splendour,⁴⁴ is a kind of light that is cold and moist, associated with nighttime, the moon, and water.

44. It is ironic that Servetus groups Aristotle with the sophists, since the pejorative use of the term "sophist" can be traced to the writings of Plato and Aristotle. The word "sophist" (derived from the word *sophia*, wisdom) was originally a neutral term meaning a wise person or an expert of any sort. Plato drew a distinction between the sophist and the philosopher, characterizing the sophist as acquisitive rather than productive, imitative rather than original, and insincere rather than sincere.⁴⁵ Aristotle agreed, defining sophistry as "what appears to be philosophy but is not."⁴⁶

45. In Orphic mythology, Phanes is the primordial deity, who emerged from the World Egg at the beginning of time. Phanes is often pictured as being both male and female, with golden wings and a serpent's tail. The name Phanes comes from a word meaning "to make appear" or "to bring to light."

46. Here Servetus is drawing on his knowledge of astrological medicine, a subject on which he gave public lectures while a medical student in Paris. The connection between astrology and medicine is very ancient. The earliest known reference to astrology in Greek is found in a medical book: the Hippocratic work *On Diets*, written around 400 BCE. Greek philosophy accepted the correspondence between the stars and events on earth as an aspect of the unity of the cosmos. The Christian church prohib-

---

⁴³ Angelo Poliziano, *Miscellanea* (1489) 1.1.
⁴⁴ See A.R4.16.
⁴⁵ Plato, *Sophist* (265a-e, 268a-b).
⁴⁶ Aristotle, *Metaphysics* 4.2 (1004b). Translated by W. D. Ross.

ited judicial astrology,⁴⁷ but it accepted the influence of the stars and planets on natural phenomena—which seemed undeniable, given the observed influence of the moon on tides, or the sun on the growth of plants.

Since it was commonly believed that illness and health fell within the realm of "natural" astrology, the use of astrology in medicine was relatively uncontroversial. Medical astrologers associated specific planets and signs of the zodiac with the four elements and the four bodily humours (see A.R4.48). Astrologers did not always agree as to the exact correspondences, but the examples that Servetus cites here were widely accepted. The moon was associated with water and phlegm (the "phlegmatic" temperament); Saturn with earth and black bile (the "melancholic" temperament); and Mars with fire and yellow bile (the "choleric" temperament).

47. Subject (Latin *subiectum*) is the translation of Aristotle's term *hypokeimenon*, meaning "underlying thing." When a change takes place, the subject is the underlying thing or being that persists through the change. If the properties of an individual being or thing are changed, but the individual exists both before and after the change, then the individual is the subject of the change. However, there are other kinds of change where an individual thing or being is created or destroyed. In that case, the subject—the underlying thing—is the matter, and what is changed is the form. For example, if a statue is carved from stone, the statue cannot be the subject, because it did not exist before the action. The subject is the stone, which changes from unformed stone to stone with the form of a statue.⁴⁸

---

[47] Judicial astrology is the use of astrology to make predictions that could be seen as denying human free will. Servetus was accused of practicing judicial astrology in his lectures in Paris. After being investigated by the Faculty of Medicine, the Parlement of Paris, and the Inquisition, he left Paris, apparently without completing his degree. Servetus does appear to have strayed across the line that separated permitted medical astrology from prohibited judicial astrology. In his 1538 defence of astrology, *Apologetica disceptatio pro astrologia*, he wrote that an eclipse of Mars presaged wars, plagues, and other disasters, "which God avert."

[48] Aristotle, *Physics* 1.7 (190a-b).

Annotations & Book 4

48. The ancient Greek physician Hippocrates taught that the human body contains four substances, or humours: blood, yellow bile, black bile, and phlegm. A person is healthy when the four humours are well mixed and in the correct proportions. Hippocrates classified the four humours in terms of what became known as the Hippocratic qualities: hot, cold, wet, and dry.

The four possible combinations of these qualities formed a powerful interpretive scheme that could be used to classify many different natural phenomena. In *On Generation and Corruption*, Aristotle used the Hippocratic qualities to classify the four elements: earth, air, fire, and water. The table below shows how the Hippocratic qualities could be used to categorize the four humours, the four elements, and the four seasons.

Hippocratic Qualities	Humour	Element	Season
Hot and wet	Blood (sanguine temperament)	Air	Spring
Hot and dry	Yellow bile (choleric temperament)	Fire	Summer
Cold and dry	Black bile (melancholic temperament)	Earth	Autumn
Cold and wet	Phlegm (phlegmatic temperament)	Water	Winter

Due to the great prestige of Hippocrates and Aristotle, this system continued to be used for two millennia. In time, the system of correspondences was expanded to include virtually anything associated with the number four, such as the four evangelists, the four archangels, and the four creatures in the Ezekiel's vision.

This is the only place where Servetus mentions the name of Hippocrates in connection with the Hippocratic qualities, but he refers to the qualities three times in book 4 to contrast the warming and drying light of the sun with the cooling and moistening light, or splendour, of water.[49]

49. In Aristotelian philosophy, an accident is a property of an entity or substance that is not essential to its identity. By this definition colour and the Hippocratic qualities (hot, cold, wet,

---

[49] *Restoration*, 153, 154, 161. See A.R4.43.

and dry) are accidents. But this does not mean they are unimportant. Here Servetus identifies these qualities, in particular, as those that combine with the ideal form to produce the substantial form of an object.

50. When God created the heavens and the earth, did time, space, and matter already exist? Or did God create the entire universe out of nothing? The Hebrew of Genesis 1:1-3 can be interpreted either way. Here Servetus asserts creation *ex nihilo* ("out of nothing"), which has been Christian doctrine since the time of the early Church Fathers. In particular, the Church Fathers were concerned to refute two views that they considered heretical: the Neoplatonist idea that creation is an emanation of the divine, and the Gnostic idea that the universe was created not by the supreme God, but by a lower god, the Demiurge. Augustine explained the reasoning for creation *ex nihilo*:

> In the beginning ... you [God] made heaven and earth; not from yourself, for then it would be equal to your only-begotten son, and also to you, and it would not be right for anything that is not of you to be equal to you. But there was nothing else besides yourself from which you could make things ... therefore you made heaven and earth out of nothing.[50]

51. The Hebrew word for the heavens in Genesis 1:1 is שמים (*shamayim*). The word is neither singular nor plural, but dual, as can be seen from the ending *ayim*. The dual number is used for things that naturally occur in pairs, e.g. עינים (*eynayim*, both eyes). Thus the word *shamayim* suggests not two heavens, but a double or twofold heaven.

52. Jewish sources tend to be less invested than Christian ones in the idea of creation *ex nihilo*, emphasizing instead God's creative activity in bringing order and beauty out of chaos. Rashi wrote,

> At the beginning of the creation of heaven and earth when the earth was without form and void and there was darkness, God said, "Let there be light." The text does not intend to

---

[50] Augustine, *Confessiones* 12.7.

point out the order of the acts of Creation ... The waters were created before heaven and earth, for, lo, it is written, (v. 2) "The Spirit of God was hovering on the face of the waters," and Scripture had not yet disclosed when the creation of the waters took place.[51]

Ibn Ezra admitted that most commentators interpret the word *bara* (create) to mean creation *ex nihilo*. But he noted that the same word *bara* is used in Genesis 1:27, "So God created humankind in his own image." And no one thinks that God created humans *ex nihilo* on the sixth day.[52]

53. The Hebrew word שמים (*shamayim*, the heavens) contains the word מים (*mayim*, water). The Talmud offers two explanations for the relationship between the two words. (1) *Shamayim* is an acronym for *sheshan mayim*, meaning "water is there." (2) *Shamayim* comes from *esh umayim*, "fire and water," because God made the firmament from these elements.[53] Servetus could have found this information in a Latin work such as Francesco Zorzi's *Problems in the Sacred Scriptures*.[54]

54. In Genesis 1:6, God causes the waters above to be separated from the waters below by a *raqiya*, translated in the Vulgate as *firmamentum*. The firmament—a word that is virtually unknown in English in any other context—is often imagined as a solid dome atop a flat, disc-shaped earth. However, as Servetus notes, the Hebrew word *raqiya* means "expansion" or "extension." Passages such as Psalm 104:2, Isaiah 40:22, and Jeremiah 10:12 speak of God expanding, extending, or "stretching out" the heavens. Since it is not specified exactly what God stretches out to divide the waters, we may imagine something as "firm" as a

---

[51] Rashi, commentary on Genesis 1:1. Translated by M. Rosenbaum and A. M. Silbermann, 1929-1934. https://www.sefaria.org/Rashi_on_Genesis
[52] Ibn Ezra, commentary on Genesis 1:1. Translated by H. Norman Strickman and Arthur M. Silver. Menorah Publishing Company, 1988-2004. https://www.sefaria.org/Ibn_Ezra_on_Genesis
[53] Babylonian Talmud, Chagigah 12a. https://www.sefaria.org/Chagigah.12a
[54] Zorzi, *In scripturam sacram*, 142v.

metal dome, or as simple as the layer of air between the surface of the earth and the clouds above.

55. The Hebrew word *shamayim*, like the Latin word *caelum*, means both "heaven" and "sky." Only the third heaven, the abode of the angels, is what we normally understand by the word "heaven": uncreated, ethereal, and invisible. The two lower heavens are part of the perceptible, created world. The "watery region" is the clouds; the "airy firmament" is the space between the clouds and the surface of the earth, where rain falls and birds fly.[55]

56. *Alef* (א) and *tav* (ת) are the first and last letters of the Hebrew alphabet. Together they form the grammatical particle את (pronounced *et*), which indicates a definite article in the accusative case. את is found thousands of times in the Hebrew Bible, including in Genesis 1:1, where it indicates that the verse is to be read, "God created the heavens and the earth" instead of just "God created heaven and earth."

Like the Greek "alpha and omega," or the English "A to Z," *alef tav* is sometimes thought to have a symbolic meaning, indicating "all that is." The Jewish scholar and sage Rabbi Akiva taught that את is a mark of the hand of God and an invitation to probe the text for a deeper meaning.[56] Christians (and, more recently, adherents of Messianic Judaism) have argued, as Servetus did, that since *alef tav* is the Hebrew equivalent of "alpha and omega," it is a reference to the Messiah.[57]

57. Sublimation is the transition of a substance from a solid to a gas or vapour, without passing through a liquid state. Like the

---

[55] Gen 1:20: "Let birds fly above the earth across the face of the firmament of the heavens."

[56] Babylonian Talmud, Chagigah 12a. https://www.sefaria.org/Chagigah.12a

[57] The words "I am the Alpha and the Omega" occur at least three times in the book of Revelation. The speaker is identified as the Lord God (Rev 1:8), "he who sat on the throne" (Rev 21:6), and finally as Jesus (Rev 22:13). In some version of the Bible, it also appears in Rev 1:11, where the speaker is identified as "one like the Son of Man."

more common process of distillation, it can be used to purify a substance by condensing the vapour into solid form by contact with a cold surface. In alchemy, sublimation is of symbolic importance, as it symbolizes the spiritualization of the body. However, it is of limited practical use, since most materials do not sublimate at ordinary temperatures and pressures.

58. The question of whether the forms of the four elements are preserved in a mixture was posed by Aristotle in *On Generation and Corruption* 1.10. It was much discussed by commentators on Aristotle, by the scholastics, and also in the medical literature available to Servetus. The position mentioned by Servetus — that the elements maintain their integrity when mixed — is actually more closely associated with Avicenna than with Averroes; Averroes believed that the forms of elements in a mixture are neither retained nor destroyed, but occupy an intermediate position between the two.[58]

59. The wind mentioned here, the *aquilo*, is a northeast wind that, according to Pliny, was characterized by a sudden drying up of the earth.[59] In the Bible, a similar drying effect is attributed to the *qadim*, or east wind.[60] (In contrast to the Roman system of twenty-four named winds, biblical Hebrew identifies only four; so the Bible's *qadim* corresponds to everything from *aquilo* in the northeast to *eurus* in the southeast.)

---

[58] Rega Wood and Michael Weisberg, "Interpreting Aristotle on mixture: problems about elemental composition from Philoponus to Cooper," *Studies in History and Philosophy of Science* 5 (2004), 681–706.

[59] Pliny the Elder, *Historia naturalis* 2.46, 18.77.

[60] Joseph predicts seven years of famine based on a dream of grain and cattle scorched or blighted by the *qadim* (Gen 41:6, 23, 27). The Israelites are able to cross the Red Sea when the *qadim* makes the sea into dry land (Ex 14:21). The *qadim* withers vines (Ezek 17:10; 19:12) and dries up springs and fountains (Hos 13:15).

BIBLIOGRAPHY

Abbreviations

The following abbreviations are used in the Bibliography.

Ante-Nicene Fathers	*Ante-Nicene Fathers: The Writings of the Fathers down to A.D. 325.* New York: Christian Literature Company, 1885-1896. Online edition: Christian Classics Ethereal Library, https://www.ccel.org/fathers2
Augustine Works (1528-29)	*Operum divi Aurelii Augustini.* Basel, 1528-29.
Calvini opera	*Ioannis Calvini opera quae supersunt omnia* (vol. 29-87 of *Corpus Reformatorum*, 1863-1900)
Clement Works	*Clementis Alexandrini omnia quae quidem extant opera.* Florence, 1551.
Nicene and Post-Nicene Fathers	*Nicene and Post-Nicene Fathers, Series I and II.* New York: Christian Literature Company, 1886-1900. Online edition: Christian Classics Ethereal Library, https://www.ccel.org/fathers2

Obras Completas	*Miguel Servet: Obras Completas*. Edited by Ángel Alcalá. Zaragoza: Larumbe, 2003-2006.
On the Trinity and the Bible	Michael Servetus. *On the Trinity and the Bible: An annotated translation of* The Restoration of Christianity, *books 1 and 2*. Translated by Peter Zerner and Peter Hughes. Toronto: Blackstone Editions, 2023.
Origen Works	*Origenis ... Scripturarum interpretis opera, quae quidem extant omnia*. Basel, 1536.
Servetus Writings (trans. O'Malley)	*Michael Servetus: A Translation of his Geographical, Medical and Astrological Writings*. Translated by Charles Donald O'Malley. Philadelphia: American Philosophical Society, 1953.
Tertullian Works	*Opera Q. Septimii Florentis Tertulliani*. Basel, 1521.

Bibliography

Works by Servetus

Apologetica disceptatio pro astrologia. Paris, 1538. Republished, Berlin, 1880.

[English translation] In Servetus Writings (trans. O'Malley).

Christianismi restitutio. Vienne, 1553. Republished, Nuremberg, 1790; reprint of 1790 edition, Frankfurt: Minerva, 1966.

There are three surviving copies of the 1553 edition: in the Österreichische Nationalbibliothek in Vienna, the Bibliothèque Nationale in Paris, and the University of Edinburgh Library. A facsimile of the first 576 pages of the Vienna copy is included in volumes 5 and 6 of *Obras Completas*. The Paris copy is available online on BnF Gallica, the web site of the Bibliothèque Nationale. The Edinburgh copy includes the "Edinburgh manuscript," an alternate version of the first 16 pages of *Christianismi restitutio*.

[English translation] *The Restoration of Christianity: An English Translation of Christianismi Restitutio, 1553 by Michael Servetus (1511-1553)*. Translated by Christopher A. Hoffman and Marian Hillar. Lewiston, NY: Mellen Press, 2007-2010. 4 volumes.

[English translation, books 1 and 2, annotated] *On the Trinity and the Bible*.

Christianismi restitutio [Paris manuscript]. Unpublished manuscript in the Bibliothèque Nationale, containing variant versions of book 3, 4, 5, and dialogue 1. It is available online on BnF Gallica, as Latin manuscript 18212.

De Trinitatis erroribus libri septem. Hagenau, 1531. Facsimile reprint, Frankfurt: Minerva, 1965.

[English translation] In *The Two Treatises of Servetus on the Trinity*. Translated by Earl Morse Wilbur. Cambridge, MA: Harvard University Press, 1932. Reprint, New York: Kraus Reprint Company, 1969.

In Leonardum Fuchsium apologia. Lyons, 1536.

[English translation] In Servetus Writings (trans. O'Malley).

Bibliography

Scriptures

Biblia sacra vulgata [The Vulgate].

Many editions in the late fifteenth and early sixteenth century.

Biblia sacra. Translated by Santes Pagnini.

First edition: Lyons, 1527-28.

Unauthorized second edition: *Biblia sacra iuxta germanam Hebraici.* Edited by Melchior von Neuss. Cologne, 1541.

Second edition: *Biblia sacra ex Santis Pagnini tralatione.* Edited by Servetus. Lyons, 1542.

Hebraica Biblia. Translated by Sebastian Münster. Basel, 1534.

Novum Testamentum. Translated by Erasmus.

First edition: *Novum Instrumentum.* Basel, 1516.

Second through fifth editions: *Novum Testamentu*m. Basel, 1519, 1522, 1527, 1535.

Sacra Biblia ad LXX interpretum fidem diligentissime tralata. Basel, 1526.

Latin translation of the Septuagint.

Servetus's Sources

The following list represents our best estimate of the non-Biblical sources that Servetus used in writing books 3 and 4 of *The Restoration of Christianity.* The list includes works that are explicitly mentioned in the text of *Restoration*, as well as others that have been identified, with varying degrees of certainty, as sources of quotations or information used by Servetus. All of these works were available in Servetus's day, some of them in multiple editions. The editions listed are ones that Servetus could have used, but not necessarily those that he did use.

Aristotle. *Auctoritates Aristotelis.* Paris, 1522.

A collection of excerpts from Aristotle, dating from c. 1300.

[Aristotle]. *De mundo.* In *De mundo Aristotelis lib. I. Philonis lib. I...* Basel, 1533; Paris, 1541.

Augustine. *Confessiones.* In Augustine Works (1528-29), vol. 1.
   [English translation]
   (1) In *Nicene and Post-Nicene Fathers*, series 1, vol. 1.
   (2) *Confessions.* Translated by Henry Chadwick. Oxford University Press, 1992.

———. *De civitate Dei.* In Augustine Works (1528-29), vol. 5.
   [English translation]
   (1) In *Nicene and Post-Nicene Fathers*, series 1, vol. 2.
   (2) *City of God.* Translated by Henry Bettenson. Penguin, 2003.

———. *De diversis quaestionibus LXXXIII.* In Augustine Works (1528-29), vol. 4.

   [English translation] *Eighty-three Different Questions.* Translated by David L. Mosher. Washington, DC: The Catholic University of America Press, 1982.

———. *De Trinitate.* In Augustine Works (1528-29), vol. 3.
   [English translation]
   (1) In *Nicene and Post-Nicene Fathers*, series 1, vol. 3.
   (2) *The Trinity.* Translated by Edmund Hill, O.P. Hyde Park, NY: New City Press, 1991.

Clement of Alexandria. *Adhortatorius adversus gentes paedagogi.* In Clement Works.

———. *Stromata.* In Clement Works.
   [English translation] In *Ante-Nicene Fathers*, vol. 2.

[Clement of Rome]. *Divi Clementis Recognitionum libri X.* Basel, 1526.
   [English translation]
   (1) *The Syriac Clementine Recognitions and Homilies.* Translated by Joseph Glen Gebhardt. Nashville, TN: Grave Distractions Publications, 2014.
   (2) *The Recognitions of Clement.* Translated by Douglas F. Hatten. Printed by the translator, 2007.

Cyprian. *Adversus Iudaeos.* In *Opera divi Caecilii Cypriani.* Basel, 1520.
   [English translation] In *Ante-Nicene Fathers*, vol. 5.

Bibliography

[Dionysius the Areopagite]. *De coelesti hierarchia.* In *Theologia viveficans, cibus solidus.* Paris, 1515

    [English translation] *Pseudo-Dionysius: The Complete Works.* Translated by Colm Liubheid. New York: Paulist Press, 1987.

Eck, Johann. *D. Dionysii Areopagitae De mystica theologia.* Augsburg, 1519.

Eusebius of Caesarea. *Demonstratio evangelica.* Cologne, 1539.

    [English translation] *The Proof of the Gospel.* Translated by W. J. Ferrar. Aeterna Press, 2015.

———. *Praeparatio evangelica.* Cologne, 1539.

    [English translation] *The Preparation for the Gospel.* Translated by W. J. Ferrar. Aeterna Press, 2015.

Ficino, Marsilio. *De Christiana religione.* Venice, 1518.

    [English translation] *On the Christian Religion.* Translated by Dan Attrell, Brett Bartlett and David Porreca. University of Toronto Press, 2022.

———. *Interpretatio Prisciani Lydi in Theophrastum de sensu traducta et exposita a Marsilio Ficino.* Venice, 1516.

———. *Theologia Platonica.* Venice, 1525.

    [English translation] *Platonic Theology.* Translated by Michael J. B. Allen. Harvard University Press, 2001-2006. 6 volumes.

———, trans. [Hermes Trismegistus]. *Corpus Hermeticum.* In *Mercurii Trismegesti Pymander de potestate et sapientia Dei…* Basel, 1532.

    This edition includes *Asclepius.*

    [English translation]

        (1) *Marsilio Ficino, Corpus Hermeticum.* Translated by Maxwell Lewis Latham. London: Falcon Books Publishing Ltd., 2019.

        (2) *Hermetica.* Translated by Brian P. Copenhaver. Cambridge University Press, 1992.

———, trans. Iamblichus. *De mysteriis Aegypteorum, Chaldaeorum, et Assyriorum.* In *Mercurii Trismegesti Pymander de potestate et sapientia Dei…* Basel, 1532.

    [English translation] *The Mysteries of the Egyptians, Chalaeans, and Assyrians.* Translated by Thomas Taylor, 1821.

———, trans. *Omnia divini Platonis opera tralatione Marsilii Ficini*. Basel, 1539.

> Includes Ficino's translations, commentaries, and epitomes of Plato's dialogues

> [Partial English translation] *Gardens of Philosophy: Ficino on Plato*. Translated by Arthur Farndell. London: Shepheard-Walwyn Publishers Ltd, 2006.
>> Translation of epitomes of 25 dialogues for which Ficino did not write detailed commentaries

Galatino, Pietro Colonna. *De arcanis Catholicae veritatis*. Basel, 1550.

[Hermes Trismegistus]. See under Ficino.

Hugh Ripelin of Strasbourg (Hugo Argentinensis). *Compendium theologicae veritatis*. Paris, 1543; many other editions.

> The author was unidentified in Servetus's time.

Iamblichus. See under Ficino.

Irenaeus. *Adversus haereses*. Basel, 1526.

> [English translation] In *Ante-Nicene Fathers*, vol. 1. The same translation is printed in book form as *Against Heresies*. Ex Fontibus Company, 2010.

Isidore of Seville. *Etymologiae*. Paris, 1520.

> [English translation] *Isidore of Seville's Etymologies*. Translated by Priscilla Throop. Charlotte, VT: MedievalMS, 2005. 2 volumes.

Jerome. *Epistolae*. In *Operum d. Hieronymi*, vol. 1-4. Basel, 1516, 1537.

Lactantius Firmianus. *Divinae institutiones*. Basel, 1521.

> [English translation]
> (1) In *Ante-Nicene Fathers*, vol. 7.
> (2) *Divine Institutes*. Translated by Anthony Bowen and Peter Garnsey. Liverpool University Press, 2003.

Maimonides, Moses. *Dux neutrorum seu dubiorum*. Paris, 1520.

> 13th-century Latin translation of *Guide for the Perplexed*

> [English translation] *The Guide for the Perplexed*. Translated by M. Friedländer (1903).

Bibliography

Origen. *Commentarius in Canticum canticorum*. In Origen Works, vol. 1.

> [English translation] *Origen: The Song of Songs Commentary and Homilies*. Translated by R. P. Lawson. New York: Newman Press, 1956.

———. *In Geneseos*. In Origen Works, vol. 1.

> [English translation] *Origen: Homilies on Genesis and Exodus*. Translated by Ronald E. Heine. Washington, DC: The Catholic University of America Press, 1982.

———. *In evangelium Ioannis explanationem*. Venice, 1551.

> [English translation] In *Ante-Nicene Fathers*, vol. 9.

Pagnini, Santes. *Isagoge, seu introductio in sacras literas et mysticos sacrae scripturae*. Cologne, 1540.

———. *Thesaurus linguae sanctae sive lexicon Hebraicum*. Lyons, 1529.

Paul of Burgos. *Dialogus Pauli et Sauli contra Judaeos, sive Scrutinium scripturarum*. Lyons, 1535.

Peter Lombard. *Sententiarum libri quatuor*. Paris, 1514; many other editions.

> [English translation] *The Sentences*. Translated by Giulio Silano. Toronto: Pontifical Institute of Mediaeval Studies, 2007-2010. 4 volumes.

Petrus Alfonsi. *Dialogi lectu dignissimi, in quibus impiae judaeorum opiniones ... confutantur Petri cognomento Alphonsi, ex Judaeo Christiani et Moysi Judaei*. Cologne, 1536.

[Philo of Alexandria] *De mundo*. In *De mundo Aristotelis lib. I. Philonis lib. I...* Basel, 1533; Paris, 1541.

> A collection of excerpts attributed to Philo of Alexandria. Published with a similar collection attributed to Aristotle.

Plato. See under Ficino.

[Pythagoras]. *Carmina aurea*. Included as an appendix in Constantine Lascaris, *Grammatica*. Venice, 1494-95.

> [English translation] Many available, including:
> (1) Johan C. Thom, *The Pythagorean Golden Verses* (Brill, 1994).

(2) *The Golden Verses of Pythagoras.* Adapated from translation by Nicholas Rowe (1707). https://sacred-texts.com/cla/gvp/gvp03.htm

Reuchlin, Johannes. *De arte cabalistica.* Hagenau, 1517, 1530.

[English translation] *On the Art of the Kabbalah.* Translated by Martin and Sarah Goodman. University of Nebraska Press, 1993.

———. *De verbo mirifico.* Cologne, 1532.

Simplicius. *Commentaria ... Aristotelis de Physica auditu.* Paris, 1544.

Steuco, Agostino. *De perenni philosophia.* Lyons, 1540.

———. *Enarrationes in librum Iob.* Venice, 1547.

Tertullian. *Adversus Hermogenem.* In Tertullian Works.

[English translation] In *Ante-Nicene Fathers*, vol. 3.

———. *Adversus Praxean.* In Tertullian Works.

[English translation] In *Ante-Nicene Fathers*, vol. 3.

Zorzi, Francesco. *In scripturam sacram ... problemata.* Venice, 1536.

Other Sixteenth-Century Works

Biandrata, Giorgio. *De falsa et vera unius Dei patris, filii et spiritus sancti cognitione.* Alba Iulia, 1567.

Calvin, John. *Commentarii in librum psalmorum.* Geneva, 1564.

In *Calvini opera*, vol. 32.

[English translation] *Commentary on the Book of Psalms.* Translated by James Anderson. Grand Rapids, MI: Eerdmans, 1949. Online edition in Christian Classics Ethereal Library.

———. *Commentariorum Ioannis Caluini in Acta Apostolorum.* Geneva, 1552-1554.

In *Calvini opera*, vol. 48.

[English translation] *Commentary upon the Acts of the Apostles.* Translated by Henry Beveridge, based on translation by Christopher Fethersone (1585). 1859; reprint, Grand Rapids, MI: Eerdmans, 1957. Online edition in Christian Classics Ethereal Library.

———. *Defensio orthodoxae fidei de sacra Trinitate contra prodiciosos errores Michaelis Serveti Hispani.* Geneva, 1554.

———. *Institutio Christianae religionis.* Fifth edition. Geneva, 1559.

This edition of Calvin's *Institutes* contains a number of references to Servetus and refutations of his theology.

[English translation] *Calvin: Institutes of the Christian Religion.* Translated by Ford Lewis Battles. Philadelphia: Westminster, 1960. 2 volumes.

Selected Secondary Works

Alcalá, Ángel. Introduction to *Obras Completas.*

Ciholas, Paul. "Plato: The Attic Moses? Some Patristic Reactions to Platonic Philosophy." *The Classical World* 72:4 (Dec 1978 - Jan 1979), 217-225.

Copenhaver, Brian P. *Magic in Western Culture: From Antiquity to the Enlightenment.* Cambridge University Press, 2015.

Friedman, Jerome. *Michael Servetus: A Case Study in Total Heresy.* Geneva: Droz, 1978.

———. *The Most Ancient Testimony: Sixteenth-Century Christian-Hebraica in the Age of Renasissance Nostalgia.* Athens, OH: Ohio University Press, 1983.

Greenwood, Kyle R. (ed.) *Since the Beginning: Interpreting Genesis 1 and 2 through the Ages.* Grand Rapids, MI: Baker Academic, 2018.

Heiser, James D. *Prisci Theologi and the Hermetic Reformation in the Fifteenth Century.* Malone, TX: Repristination Press, 2011.

Hughes, Peter. Introduction to *On the Trinity and the Bible.*

———. "The Christology of Michael Servetus." *Journal of Unitarian Universalist History* 40 (2016-2017), 16-53.

Schmitt, Charles B. "Perennial Philosophy: From Agostino Steuco to Leibniz." *Journal of the History of Ideas* (Oct.-Dec. 1966), 515-524.

Tester, S. J. *A History of Western Astrology.* Woodbridge, Suffolk, UK: The Boydell Press, 1987.

Williams, George Huntston. *The Radical Reformation*, 3rd edition. Kirksville, MO: Truman State University Press, 2000.

Yates, Frances A. *Giordano Bruno and the Hermetic Tradition.* University of Chicago Press, 1964.

Index

Abbreviations

The following abbreviations are used in the indexes.

A	Annotation	Reference is to book and annotation number, e.g. **A.R3.20** indicates annotation 20 for *Restoration* book 3.
Rest	*The Restoration of Christianity*	Reference is to page number in the original 1553 printing, e.g. ***Rest***: **30**
Paris	*The Restoration of Christianity - Paris manuscript*	Reference is to page number in the **printed** book, e.g. ***Paris***: **30** indicates the Paris manuscript version of text on page 30 in the 1553 printed edition. Only items that are unique to the manuscript are indexed as ***Paris***.

Index of Biblical References

Genesis

1:1	*Rest*: 156, 157; A.R4.51, A.R4.56
1:1-3	A.R4.50, A.R4.52
1:1-10	*Rest*: 155
1:2	*Rest*: 156, 160; A.R4.39
1:3	A.R3.23
1:4	*Rest*: 131
1:6	A.R4.54
1:6-8	*Rest*: 155, 156, 157, 159, 160
1:9-10	*Rest*: 155, 161
1:10	*Rest*: 131
1:11	*Rest*: 139
1:12	*Rest*: 131
1:16	*Rest*: 155
1:18	*Rest*: 131
1:20	*Rest*: 157; A.R4.55
1:21	*Rest*: 131
1:24	*Rest*: 139
1:25	*Rest*: 131
1:26	*Rest*: 102, 104; A.R3.11
1:27	A.R4.52
1:31	*Rest*: 131
2:1	*Rest*: 157; A.R4.40
2:4	*Rest*: 128, 156
2:19	A.R3.23
3:8	*Rest*: 123
3:17	*Rest*: 160
3:22	*Rest*: 105
3:24	*Rest*: 96, 99, 158
5:3	*Rest*: 104
11:7	*Rest*: 105
15:1	*Rest*: 124
16:7-13	*Rest*: 101, 136
17:1	*Rest*: 124, 126, 127
17:4	A.R4.33
18:1-15	*Rest*: 101; A.R3.7
20:13	*Rest*: 135, 136
21:17-18	*Rest*: 101
22:11-18	*Rest*: 101
22:14	*Rest*: 126
28:3	*Rest*: 126
31:13	*Rest*: 101
32:30	*Rest*: 95, 101
33:10	*Rest*: 95
35:7	*Rest*: 135, 136
35:11	*Rest*: 126
41:6	A.R4.59
41:23, 27	A.R4.59
48:3	*Rest*: 126

Exodus

Chapter 3	*Rest*: 106
3:2-4	*Rest*: 136
3:6	*Rest*: 96, 97, 101
3:14	*Rest*: 106
3:15	*Rest*: 101
4:1-17	*Rest*: 106
6:2-8	*Rest*: 126
6:3	A.R4.1, A.R4.12
13:21-22	*Rest*: 107, 120, 159
14:19	*Rest*: 107
14:21	A.R4.59
14:24	*Rest*: 119, 120
16:10	*Rest*: 100
17:15	*Rest*: 126
20:11	*Rest*: 157
20:19	*Rest*: 93, 96, 113
20:20-22	*Rest*: 93
21:6	A.R3.11
22:8-9	A.R3.11
23:20-22	*Rest*: 101, 102
24:9-11	*Rest*: 93, 99
24:16	*Rest*: 100, 119
Chapter 25	*Rest*: 99, 142
31:18	*Rest*: 134
32:15-16	*Rest*: 134

Exodus, continued

32:32	*Rest*: 139, 141
32:33	*Rest*: 141
33:9-10	*Rest*: 107
33:11	*Rest*: 94, 95, 113; A.R3.6, A.R3.8
33:14	*Rest*: 104
33:20	*Rest*: 96, 98; A.R3.6, A.R3.8
33:21-23	*Rest*: 96, 98
36:8	A.R3.14
40:34-35	*Rest*: 100

Leviticus

19:15	*Rest*: 108

Numbers

6:25	*Rest*: 95
7:89	*Rest*: 92
8:1-4	*Rest*: 142
11:24-25	*Rest*: 121, 130
12:5	*Rest*: 107
12:6-8	*Rest*: 93, 94, 143
12:8	*Rest*: 95
14:14	*Rest*: 120, 159
16:42	*Rest*: 100
21:4-9	*Rest*: 115
21:6-8	*Rest*: 99
22:31	*Rest*: 101
24:14-24	*Rest*: 143
24:17	*Rest*: 93
33:52	*Rest*: 103

Deuteronomy

1:17	*Rest*: 108
4:12	*Rest*: 93, 113, 116
4:15	*Rest*: 93
5:4	*Rest*: 93, 95
5:22	*Rest*: 93, 119
8:7	*Rest*: 141
8:15	*Rest*: 99
31:15	*Rest*: 107

31:24-26	*Rest*: 134
32:17	A.R3.11
33:2	*Rest*: 134
33:12	*Rest*: 98
33:27	*Rest*: 98, 133
33:28	*Rest*: 141
34:10	*Rest*: 95

Joshua

5:13-15	*Rest*: 101
24:19	*Rest*: 136

Judges

2:1-4	*Rest*: 136
6:11-22	*Rest*: 136
6:24	*Rest*: 126
13:22	*Rest*: 96

1 Samuel

3:10	*Rest*: 122
4:4	*Rest*: 92
9:9	*Rest*: 143
9:20	*Rest*: 143
10:2-9	*Rest*: 143
16:7	*Rest*: 108

2 Samuel

6:2	*Rest*: 101
7:23	*Rest*: 136
22:7-16	*Rest*: 135
22:8	*Rest*: 156
22:11	*Rest*: 99
22:12	*Rest*: 97

1 Kings

6:5	*Rest*: 119; A.R3.23
6:16, 19-23	*Rest*: 119; A.R3.23
6:23-28	*Rest*: 99
6:31	*Rest*: 119; A.R3.23
7:49	*Rest*: 119; A.R3.23
8:6-8	*Rest*: 119; A.R3.23
8:11	*Rest*: 100

Index of Biblical References

1 Kings, continued
8:27	*Rest*: 158
19:11-13	*Rest*: 96
22:17-20	*Rest*: 143
22:19	*Rest*: 103, 135

2 Kings
11:18	*Rest*: 103
19:15	*Rest*: 92
19:25	*Rest*: 134

1 Chronicles
13:6	*Rest*: 92, 101
28:11-19	*Rest*: 99, 142
29:11	*Rest*: 119

2 Chronicles
2:6	*Rest*: 158
3:14	A.R3.14
3:16	*Rest*: 119; A.R3.23
4:20	*Rest*: 119; A.R3.23
5:7-9	*Rest*: 119; A.R3.23
5:13-14	*Rest*: 97, 100
6:1	*Rest*: 97
6:18	*Rest*: 158
9:23	*Rest*: 95
23:17	*Rest*: 103
29:16	*Rest*: 119

Nehemiah
9:6	*Rest*: 158
9:13	*Rest*: 134
9:19	*Rest*: 159

Job
13:7	*Rest*: 108
25:3	*Rest*: 152
26:11	*Rest*: 156
26:13	*Rest*: 157
28:24	*Rest*: 137
37:18	*Rest*: 155
38:4	*Rest*: 156
42:5	*Rest*: 103

Psalms
4:6	*Rest*: 93, 98, 115
8:3	*Rest*: 155
8:5	A.R3.11
16:5	*Rest*: 130
17:15	*Rest*: 93, 116
18:11	*Rest*: 97
24:6	*Rest*: 95
27:7-9	*Rest*: 95
28:2	*Rest*: 119; A.R3.23
33:6	*Rest*: 157
34:5	*Rest*: 115
36:9	*Rest*: 128, 141, 143
42:11	*Rest*: 116
44:3	*Rest*: 93, 98, 116
50:11	*Rest*: 140
51:13	*Rest*: 156
56:8	*Rest*: 139, 141
58:11	*Rest*: 136
67:1	*Rest*: 95, 98
68:3	*Rest*: 95
68:4	*Rest*: 123; A.R3.30
68:17	*Rest*: 128
68:33	*Rest*: 158
69:28	*Rest*: 141
72:6	*Rest*: 120
73:20	*Rest*: 103
73:26	*Rest*: 130
80:1	*Rest*: 93
80:3, 7, 19	*Rest*: 93, 95
82:6	A.R4.32
87:5	*Rest*: 134
89:15	*Rest*: 93, 98
89:46	*Rest*: 99
90:8	*Rest*: 98
91:1	*Rest*: 98
93:2	*Rest*: 133, 134
99:1	*Rest*: 92
102:18	*Rest*: 123
102:25	*Rest*: 156
103:19	*Rest*: 133
103:20	*Rest*: 128

Index of Biblical References

Psalms, continued

104:2	*Rest*: 156; A.R4.54
104:5	*Rest*: 156
104:6	*Rest*: 156
104:29	*Rest*: 133; A.R4.26, A.R4.27
119:135	*Rest*: 115
136:7-9	*Rest*: 155
139:2-3	*Rest*: 148
139:6	*Rest*: 149
139:16	*Rest*: 139, 141
144:4	*Rest*: 148
148:4	*Rest*: 158

Proverbs

3:19	*Rest*: 156
7:6	*Rest*: 106
8:22-23	*Rest*: 123
8:22-31	*Rest*: 109, 137
8:27	*Rest*: 156
8:28	*Rest*: 141
8:30	*Rest*: 138; A.R4.33
10:11	*Rest*: 150
13:14	*Rest*: 141, 150
14:27	*Rest*: 150
16:22	*Rest*: 150

Ecclesiastes

1:2	*Rest*: 148
12:8	*Rest*: 148

Song of Solomon

2:9	*Rest*: 106

Isaiah

2:10, 19, 21	*Rest*: 119
4:2	*Rest*: 120; A.R3.16
6:1	*Rest*: 93, 95, 122, 133
6:2	*Rest*: 93, 95, 98, 99, 119, 135, 158; A.R3.2
6:3	*Rest*: 95, 98
6:5	*Rest*: 103
6:6	*Rest*: 135; A.R3.2
8:17	*Rest*: 95
9:2	*Rest*: 97
9:6	A.R3.1
9:19	*Rest*: 99
11:1	*Rest*: 120; A.R3.16
13:6	*Rest*: 127; A.R4.10
24:21-22	*Rest*: 158
30:33	*Rest*: 134
37:16	*Rest*: 92
37:26	*Rest*: 134
40:5	*Rest*: 98, 100
40:18	*Rest*: 103
40:22	*Rest*: 156; A.R4.54
44:3	*Rest*: 160
44:7	*Rest*: 134
45:8	*Rest*: 120
45:15	*Rest*: 97
46:3	*Rest*: 130
46:13	*Rest*: 100
48:13	*Rest*: 156
49:14-16	*Rest*: 134
51:6	*Rest*: 160
52:6	*Rest*: 98
52:8	*Rest*: 98, 114, 119
55:10	*Rest*: 120
59:2	*Rest*: 96
60:1-3	*Rest*: 95
60:19-20	*Rest*: 95, 115
61:11	*Rest*: 120
63:9	*Rest*: 130
66:18-19	*Rest*: 95, 101

Jeremiah

1:4-19	*Rest*: 143
2:13	*Rest*: 141
10:10	*Rest*: 136
10:12	*Rest*: 156; A.R4.54
17:12	*Rest*: 133
17:13	*Rest*: 141
23:5	*Rest*: 120; A.R3.16
23:6	*Rest*: 126

Index of Biblical References

Jeremiah, continued
23:36	*Rest*: 136
33:15	*Rest*: 120; A.R3.16
33:16	*Rest*: 126
51:15	*Rest*: 156

Lamentations
3:43-44	*Rest*: 96

Ezekiel
Chapter 1	*Rest*: 93
1:1	A.R4.31
1:4	*Rest*: 119, 141
1:4-28	*Rest*: 143
1:5	*Rest*: 103
1:5-11	A.R3.18
1:5-25	*Rest*: 98, 141; A.R3.2
1:7	*Rest*: 142
1:10	*Rest*: 103; A.R3.18
1:13	*Rest*: 103; *Paris*: 104
1:16	*Rest*: 103, 148
1:18	*Rest*: 135, 141
1:20-21	*Rest*: 122
1:22	*Rest*: 103
1:24	*Rest*: 135, 142
1:26	*Rest*: 100, 103
1:27	*Rest*: 100
1:28	*Rest*: 95, 98, 100, 103
3:12	*Rest*: 95, 98
3:23	*Rest*: 98
8:2	*Rest*: 103
8:3-16	*Rest*: 143
9:3	*Rest*: 100, 135
Chapter 10	*Rest*: 93, 135; A.R3.2
10:1	*Rest*: 100
10:4	*Rest*: 98, 100
10:5	*Rest*: 119
10:9-17	*Rest*: 141
10:11	*Rest*: 142
10:13	A.R4.36
10:14	A.R3.18
10:18	*Rest*: 98, 100, 141
10:19	*Rest*: 141
11:22	*Rest*: 135
11:23	*Rest*: 98
12:11-16	*Rest*: 141
12:12-14	*Rest*: 142
16:17	*Rest*: 103
17:5-6	*Rest*: 120
17:10	A.R4.59
19:12	A.R4.59
22:21, 31	*Rest*: 99
28:14	*Rest*: 99
Chapter 40	*Rest*: 142
43:1-5	*Rest*: 141
43:2	*Rest*: 98
43:4-5	*Rest*: 98
43:6-7	*Rest*: 101

Daniel
2:31-35	*Rest*: 103
3:19	*Rest*: 103
7:9	*Rest*: 135
7:10	*Rest*: 128, 135; A.R4.14
7:13	*Rest*: 94, 122
8:15-26	*Rest*: 145
9:20-27	*Rest*: 145
9:21	A.R4.15
10:4-20	*Rest*: 93
10:6	*Rest*: 135
10:13	A.R4.15
10:21	A.R4.15
12:13	A.R4.15

Hosea
6:3	*Rest*: 120
13:15	A.R4.59

Joel
1:15	*Rest*: 127; A.R4.10
2:2	*Rest*: 92

Amos
Chapter 1	*Rest*: 143
5:26	*Rest*: 103

Index of Biblical References

Habakkuk
2:3	*Rest*: 95
2:14	*Rest*: 101
3:2	*Rest*: 95
3:4	*Rest*: 95, 98

Zechariah
1:8	*Rest*: 95, 122
3:8	*Rest*: 120; A.R3.16
3:9	*Rest*: 106; A.R3.15, A.R3.16
6:12	*Rest*: 120; A.R3.16

Matthew
3:11	*Rest*: 160
3:16	*Rest*: 122
4:16	*Rest*: 97
10:30	*Rest*: 141, 149
11:13	*Rest*: 107
13:13	*Rest*: 109
13:16	*Rest*: 115
13:17	*Rest*: 95, 97, 115
16:27	*Rest*: 100
17:1-8	*Rest*: 116
17:2	*Rest*: 94, 110, 151
20:1-16	*Rest*: 134
24:31	*Rest*: 142
25:31	*Rest*: 100
25:31-46	*Rest*: 134
25:34	*Rest*: 133
27:54	*Rest*: 122
27:51	*Rest*: 97; A.R3.14

Mark
1:10	*Rest*: 122
8:38	*Rest*:100
9:2-8	*Rest*:116
12:26	*Rest*: 123
15:38	*Rest*: 97; A.R3.14

Luke
1:19, 26	A.R4.15
1:35	*Paris*: 159
1:79	*Rest*: 97
2:13-14	*Rest*: 98
3:16	*Rest*: 160
3:22	*Rest*: 122
9:26	*Rest*: 136
9:28-36	*Rest*: 116
10:18	*Rest*: 157
10:20	*Rest*: 134
10:24	*Rest*: 95, 97
12:7	*Rest*: 141, 149
12:49	*Rest*: 159
16:31	*Rest*: 123
17:21	*Rest*: 158; *Paris*: 159
23:45	*Rest*: 97; A.R3.14
24:27	*Rest*: 107
24:44	*Rest*: 107, 123
24:45	*Rest*: 123

John
1:1	*Rest*: 92, 102, 110, 114, 122
1:1-5	*Rest*: 145
1:4	*Rest*: 139, 149
1:4-9	*Rest*: 151
1:5	*Rest*: 92, 97
1:14	*Rest*: 92, 114, 122, 124
1:18	*Rest*: 95, 113, 114
1:45	*Rest*: 123
1:51	*Rest*: 157
2:19-22	*Rest*: 100
3:5-6	*Rest*: 160
3:8	*Rest*: 160
3:14-15	*Rest*: 115
3:34	*Rest*: 102, 129
4:14	*Rest*: 150
4:22	*Rest*: 118
4:24	*Rest*: 105
5:36-39	*Rest*: 95, 109, 112
5:37	*Rest*: 113, 116
5:45-47	*Rest*: 123
6:36	*Rest*: 115
6:40	*Rest*: 115
6:44	*Rest*: 114

Index of Biblical References

John, continued
6:46	*Rest*: 113, 114, 158
6:51-57	*Rest*: 102
6:65	*Rest*: 114
8:12	*Rest*: 116, 118
8:19	*Rest*: 113
8:23	*Rest*: 148
8:56	*Rest*: 96; *Paris*: 93
8:58	*Rest*: 123
10:34-36	A.R4.32
11:40	*Rest*: 115
12:41	*Rest*: 95
12:45	*Rest*: 113
12:46	*Rest*: 97
14:2-3	*Rest*: 135
14:5-11	*Rest*: 114, 118
14:6	*Rest*: 95, 112, 113, 118, 123; *Paris*: 114
14:7	*Rest*: 114
14:9	*Rest*: 93, 96, 102, 112, 113, 115, 118
15:27	*Rest*: 134
17:5	*Rest*: 92, 95, 96, 110
17:16	*Rest*: 148
17:24	*Rest*: 115
18:36	*Rest*: 148

Acts
2:3-4	*Rest*: 121, 160
4:12	*Rest*: 100
7:44	*Rest*: 99
7:53	*Rest*: 101
8:9-24	A.R3.12
9:3	*Rest*: 95
10:34	*Rest*: 108
12:7-11	*Rest*: 102
17:22-31	A.R3.20, A.R4.22
17:25	*Rest*: 132
17:27	*Rest*: 122
17:28	*Rest*: 130, 132; A.R4.22
17:29	*Rest*: 132
17:34	A.R4.14
20:28	*Rest*: 102
26:13	*Rest*: 94, 95, 109, 110

Romans
1:20	*Rest*: 111
2:11	*Rest*: 108
11:36	*Rest*: 130

1 Corinthians
2:8	*Rest*: 100
8:4-6	*Rest*: 100
8:6	*Rest*: 107; A.R3.11
10:1-4	*Rest*: 105
11:7	*Rest*: 103
12:4-11	*Rest*: 121
12:13	*Rest*: 108
12:27	*Rest*: 102
13:12	*Rest*: 93, 111

2 Corinthians
1:11	*Rest*: 108
2:10	*Rest*: 108
3:7	*Rest*: 97, 108
3:13	*Rest*: 97, 108
3:14-16	*Rest*: 97
3:18	*Rest*: 93, 111
4:3	*Rest*: 97
4:4	*Rest*: 96, 97, 117
4:5	*Rest*: 97
4:6	*Rest*: 92, 96, 97, 98, 101, 108, 112, 115, 118, 124
8:24	*Rest*: 108
10:1	*Rest*: 108
10:7	*Rest*: 108
11:14	*Rest*: 108
11:20	*Rest*: 108
12:2	*Rest*: 157, 158

Galatians
2:17	*Rest*: 102
3:19	*Rest*: 101, 106
3:28	*Rest*: 108

Ephesians

2:4-7	*Rest*: 158
3:9	A.R3.11
4:15-16	*Rest*: 162
5:13	*Rest*: 151; *Paris*: 151

Philippians

2:6	*Rest*: 149
3:21	*Rest*: 152
4:3	*Rest*: 141, 142

Colossians

1:15	*Rest*: 113, 117
1:16	*Rest*: 130, 135, 155; A.R3.11
1:17	*Rest*: 128, 130, 151
2:9	*Rest*: 97, 119, 122, 149
2:17	*Rest*: 100, 101
2:18	*Rest*: 100
3:1-4	*Rest*: 158
3:11	*Rest*: 108
3:25	*Rest*: 108

1 Timothy

3:16	*Rest*: 97, 158
6:13	*Rest*: 130
6:16	*Rest*: 95, 158

Titus

1:2-3	*Rest*: 96

Hebrews

1:1	*Rest*: 124
1:1-4	*Rest*: 100
1:2	A.R3.11
1:3	*Rest*: 95, 116, 117, 128, 151
2:2	*Rest*: 101
2:10	A.R3.11
4:12	*Rest*: 121
8:5	*Rest*: 99, 100
9:5	*Rest*: 99
9:6-15	*Rest*: 97
9:11-28	*Rest*: 100
10:20	*Rest*: 97
11:1-3	*Rest*: 95
11:3	*Rest*: 141
11:39-40	*Rest*: 97
12:9	*Rest*: 128
12:22	*Rest*: 133, 134

James

1:17	*Rest*: 128
2:1-7	*Rest*: 108

1 Peter

1:17	*Rest*: 108
1:20	*Rest*: 96

2 Peter

2:4	*Rest*: 158
3:5	*Rest*: 155, 160

1 John

1:1	*Rest*: 122
1:1-2	*Rest*: 92
1:1-3	*Rest*: 96, 114
1:5	*Rest*: 116, 117
4:12	*Rest*: 95
5:20	*Rest*: 100

Jude

1:9	A.R4.15

Revelation

1:1	*Rest*: 145
1:8, 11	*Rest*: 152; A.R4.56
1:12-20	*Rest*: 94
1:15	*Rest*: 98
3:5	*Rest*: 141, 142
4:2-4	*Rest*: 94, 100
4:6-8	*Rest*: 94, 98, 142
5:11	A.R4.14
6:9	*Rest*: 117

Revelation, continued

7:1-9	A.R4.30
10:1	*Rest*: 94
10:6	*Rest*: 155
12:7	A.R4.15
14:1-4	A.R4.30
14:2	*Rest*: 98
14:6-9	*Rest*: 145
19:6	*Rest*: 98
19:10	*Rest*: 102
20:12	*Rest*: 140, 141, 142
21:6	*Rest*: 152; A.R4.56
21:8	A.R4.30
21:24, 27	A.R4.30
22:9	*Rest*: 102
22:13	*Rest*: 152; A.R4.56

Tobit

12:11-15	A.R4.15

Wisdom of Solomon

7:22	*Rest*: 137
7:22-30	*Rest*: 123
7:25-26	*Rest*: 139

Ecclesiasticus (Sirach)

Prologue	*Rest*: 139
1:1-2	*Rest*: 139
1:1-10	*Rest*: 137
1:9	*Rest*: 139
40:11	*Rest*: 160

Baruch

3:32-37	*Rest*: 137
3:37	*Rest*: 98

Index of Authorities Cited

Abelard, Peter, A.R4.37
Albertus Magnus, A.R4.37
Ambrose
   De fide, A.R3.7
Anaxagoras, *Rest*: 130, 145, 162
Anaxamenes of Miletus, A.R4.23
Anaximander, *Rest*: 162
Anselm
   De fide trinitatis, A.R3.22
Aquinas, Thomas, A.R4.21, A.R4.37
Arama, Isaac ben Moses
   The Offering of Isaac, *Rest*: 134
Aratus
   Phenomena, *Rest*: 132-133; A.R4.22
Aristobulus of Alexandria, A.R4.35
Aristotle, *Rest*: 151-152
   Auctoritates Aristotelis, *Rest*: 111; A.R3.28
   Metaphysics, *Rest*: 112, 161-162; A.R3.28, A.R4.21, A.R4.44
   On Generation and Corruption, A.R4.48, A.R4.58
   On the Generation of Animals, A.R4.38
   On the Heavens, *Rest*: 121
   On the Soul, *Rest*: 111; A.R3.26, A.R4.21, A.R4.42
   Physics, *Rest*: 112, 162; A.R4.47
[Aristotle]
   De mundo, A.R3.10
Augustine
   Confessiones, A.R4.50
   Contra Maximinum, A.R3.7
   De civitate Dei, *Rest*: 141; A.R4.20
   De diversis quaestionibus LXXXIII, *Rest*: 141
   De Trinitate, *Rest*: 110; A.R3.1

Averroes (Ibn Rushd), A.R4.21
Bereshit Rabbah, *Rest*: 133; A.R4.28
Calvin, John
   Commentarii in librum Psalmorum, A.R4.27
   Commentariorum in Acta Apostolorum, A.R3.21
   Defensio, A.R3.21
   Institutio Christianae religionis, A.R3.21, A.R4.29
Cicero
   Tusculanae disputationes, A.R4.42
Clement of Alexandria, *Rest*: 110
   Adversus gentes, *Rest*: 140
   Stromata, *Rest*: 140, 155; A.R4.35
[Clement of Rome]
   Recognitiones, *Rest*: 110, 157
Cyprian
   Adversus Iudaeos, *Rest*: 105-106
D'Ailly, Pierre, A.R4.21
Democritus, *Rest*: 162; A.R3.24
[Dionysius the Areopagite], *Rest*: 110
   De coelesti hierarchia, *Rest*: 135; A.R4.14
   De mystica theologia, A.R4.34
Duns Scotus, John, A.R4.21, A.R4.37
Eck, Johann
   De mystica theologia, A.R4.34
Epicurus, A.R3.24
Eusebius
   Demonstratio evangelica, *Rest*: 102-103; A.R3.8
   Praeparatio evangelica, *Rest*: 103, 104, 118, 131, 139, 155, 162; A.R3.8, A.R4.20, A.R4.35
Ficino, Marsilio, A.R4.18
   De Christiana religione, A.R3.27
   Interpretatio Prisciani, *Rest*: 152

Index of Authorities Cited

Ficino, continued
   Introduction to *Corpus Hermeticum*, *Rest*: 137
   Theologia Platonica, *Rest*: 131, 132, 139, 145, 147, 148; A.R3.26, A.R3.27, A.R4.34, A.R4.35
   Translations: see under author's name
Galatino, Pietro
   De arcanis Catholicae veritatis, *Rest*: 134; A.R3.16
Galen
   On the Teachings of Hippocrates and Plato, A.R4.41
   On the Usefulness of the Parts of the Body, A.R4.38
[Hermes Trismegistus], *Paris*: 103
   Asclepius, *Rest*: 132, 133, 137, 161
   Corpus Hermeticum, *Rest*: 129, 130, 132, 133, 137, 138, 145, 152, 154, 161
Hugh of St. Victor, A.R4.37
Hugh Ripelin of Strasbourg
   Compendium theologicae veritatis, *Rest*: 110; A.R3.17
Iamblichus
   De mysteriis Aegypteorum, Chaldaeorum, et Assyriorum, *Rest*: 131
Ibn Ezra, Abraham
   Commentary on Genesis, *Rest*: 130, 155; A.R4.17, A.R4.52
Irenaeus
   Adversus haereses, *Rest*: 94, 96, 103, 104, 105, 106, 118, 140; *Paris*: 106, 108; A.R3.12
Isidore
   De summum bono, A.R4.37
   Etymologiae, *Rest*: 106; A.R3.5, A.R4.15
Jerome
   Epistolae, *Rest*: 102; A.R3.8

Julian (the Apostate)
   Hymn to King Helios, *Rest*: 152
Lactantius
   Divinae institutiones; *Rest*: 131, 153; A.R4.20
Leucippus, A.R3.24
Lucan
   Pharsalia, *Rest*: 133
Macrobius
   In somnium Scipionis, *Rest*: 131
Maimonides, *Rest*: 110
   Guide for the Perplexed; *Rest*: 105, 130, 159; A.R3.2, A.R3.26, A.R4.16
Melissus, *Rest*: 161-162
Numenius, A.R4.35
Origen
   Contra Celsum, A.R3.18
   In Canticum canticorum, *Rest*: 140-141
   In evangelium Ioannis, *Rest*: 141
   In Geneseos, *Rest*: 101
Orphic Hymns, *Rest*: 153; A.R4.34
Pagnini, Santes
   Isagoge, A.R3.16
   Thesaurus linguae sanctae, *Rest*: 141; A.R3.4
Parmenides, *Rest*: 147, 162
Paul of Burgos
   Dialogus, *Rest*: 103
Peter Lombard
   Sententiae, *Rest*: 94; A.R4.37
Petrus Alfonsi
   Dialogi, *Rest*: 103
Philo of Alexandria, *Rest*: 102, 100; A.R3.8
   On Planting, *Rest*: 104, 118
   On the Allegorical Interpretation of the Laws, *Rest*: 139
   Questions on Genesis, *Rest*: 104, 131, 139
   Special Laws, A.R3.9

Index of Authorities Cited

[Philo]
    De mundo, *Rest*: 104; A.R3.10
Pico della Mirandola, Gianfrancesco, A.R4.21
Pico della Mirandola, Giovanni, A.R3.27
Plato, *Rest*: 137, 139, 140, 145; A.R3.27, A.R4.18, , A.R4.27, A.R4.35
    Cratylus, *Rest*: 130-131; A.R4.19
    Parmenides, *Rest*: 130-131
    Phaedo, *Rest*: 130-131
    Republic, *Rest*: 148
    Second Platonic epistle, *Rest*: 140
    Sophist, A.R4.44
    Timaeus, *Rest*: 131, 133, 146, 148; A.R4.41
Pliny the Elder
    Historia naturalis, A.R4.59
Plotinus, *Rest*: 110, 145
    Enneads, *Rest*: 131-132
Plutarch
    Moralia, *Rest*: 131
[Plutarch]
    Stromateis, *Rest*: 162
Poliziano, Angelo
    Miscellanea, A.R4.42
Porphyry
    On Philosophy from the Oracles, *Rest*: 131; A.R4.20
Proclus, *Rest*: 110, 145
    Platonic Theology, *Rest*: 131
Pythagoras, *Rest*: 130; A.R3.27, A.R4.41
[Pythagoras]
    The Golden Verses, *Rest*: 132; A.R4.22
Rashi (Rabbi Shlomo Yitzhaqi)
    Commentary on Genesis, *Rest*: 155; A.R4.52
Reuchlin, Johannes
    De arte cabalistica, *Rest*: 162; A.R4.15, A.R4.35
    De verbo mirifico, A.R3.13, A.R4.22
Sa'adia Gaon, A.R4.33
Seneca
    De beneficiis, *Rest*: 131
    Letter to Lucilius, *Rest*: 138-139
    Quaestiones naturales, *Rest*: 131
Servetus, Michael
    Apologetica disceptatio pro astrologia, A.R4.46
Simplicius
    De physica, *Rest*: 155, 162
Steuco, Agostino
    De perenni philosophia, *Rest*: 131, 132, 133, 137, 138, 139, 140, 144, 145, 153, 155, 161-162; A.R3.9, A.R3.26, A.R4.22, A.R4.35
    Enarrationes in Iob, *Rest*: 132-133
Talmud, A.R4.28, A.R4.53, A.R4.56
Targum Jonathan, *Rest*: 107; A.R3.16
Targum Onkelos, *Rest*: 105
Tertullian, A.R3.25
    Adversus Hermogenem, *Rest*: 140
    Adversus Marcionem, A.R3.12
    Adversus Praxean, *Rest*: 96, 103, 104, 140; *Paris*: 108
    Apologeticus adversus gentes, A.R4.35
    De carne Christi, A.R3.1
    De praescriptionibus adversus haereses omneis, A.R4.35
Thales of Miletus, *Rest*: 155
Xenophanes, *Rest*: 162
Zoroaster, A.R3.27
[Zoroaster], *Rest*: 130; *Paris*: 103
    Oracles of Wisdom, *Rest*: 131
Zorzi, Francesco
    In scripturam sacram ... problemata, A.R4.53

www.ingramcontent.com/pod-product-compliance
Lightning Source LLC
Chambersburg PA
CBHW071954070526
44583CB00015B/1192